Law and State

Central and Eastern European Forum for Legal, Political, and Social Theory Yearbook

Edited by Jürgen Busch / Péter Cserne / Michael Hein /
Miklós Könczöl / Miodrag Jovanović / Marta Soniewicka

Volume 5

PL ACADEMIC RESEARCH

Luka Burazin / Đorđe Gardašević / Alessio Sardo (eds.)

Law and State

Classical Paradigms and Novel Proposals

PL ACADEMIC RESEARCH

Bibliographic Information published by the Deutsche Nationalbibliothek
The Deutsche Nationalbibliothek lists this publication
in the Deutsche Nationalbibliografie; detailed bibliographic
data is available in the internet at http://dnb.d-nb.de.

Library of Congress Cataloging-in-Publication Data
Central and Eastern European Forum for Legal, Political and Social Theory (6th : 2014 :
Zagreb, Croatia)
Law and state : classical paradigms and novel proposals / Luka Burazin, Đorđe Gar-
dašević, Alessio Sardo (eds.).
pages cm. — (Central and Eastern European Forum for Legal, Political, and Social Theo-
ry Yearbook, ISSN 2191-8317 ; volume 5)
ISBN 978-3-631-66692-0
1. State, The—Congresses. 2. Sovereignty—Congresses. 3. Law—Philosophy—
Congresses. I. Burazin, Luka, 1979- editor. II. Gardašević, Đorđe, 1974- editor. III.
Sardo, Alessio, 1983- editor. IV. Title.
K3169.A6C46 2014
340'.11—dc23

2015035386

The Yearbook was published with the financial support
of the Zagreb Faculty of Law (Croatia).

ISSN 2191-8317
ISBN 978-3-631-66692-0 (Print)
E-ISBN 978-3-653-06184-0 (E-Book)
DOI 10.3726/978-3-653-06184-0

PL Academic Research is an Imprint of Peter Lang GmbH.

Peter Lang – Frankfurt am Main · Bern · Bruxelles · New York ·
Oxford · Warszawa · Wien

This publication has been peer reviewed.

www.peterlang.com

Contents

Contributors

Martin Belov, assistant professor, University of Sofia "St. Kliment Ohridski", Faculty of Law, Bulgaria

Marco Stefano Birtolo, Adjunct Professor, University of Molise, Department of Humanities, Education and Social Sciences, Italy

Robin Caballero, PhD student, University Panthéon-Sorbonne Paris 1, France, Humboldt University of Berlin, Germany

Domenica Dreyer, PhD student, University of Bonn, Institute of Political Sciences and Sociology, Germany

Fruzsina Gárdos-Orosz, research fellow, Hungarian Academy of Sciences Centre for Social Sciences, Institute for Legal Studies, Hungary

Giovanni Battista Ratti, associate professor, Tarello Institute for the Philosophy of Law, Department of Law, University of Genoa, Italy

Axelle Reiter, adjunct professor, University of Verona, Department of Economics, Italy

Silvia Salardi, senior researcher, University of Milano-Bicocca, Department of Legal Systems, Italy

Alessio Sardo, postdoctoral researcher, Bocconi University, Department of Law, Italy

Michel Troper, professor emeritus, University of Paris Ouest Nanterre La Défense, France

Monika Zalewska, postdoctoral researcher, University of Lodz, Faculty of Law and Administration, Poland

Silvia Zorzetto, assistant professor, University of Milan, Department of Legal Sciences Cesare Beccaria, Italy

Introduction

This volume is the fifth in the series of the Central and Eastern European Forum for Legal, Political, and Social Theory Yearbooks.

The twelve papers in the volume, selected by the volume's editors and peer-reviewed by international experts in the field, were presented and discussed at the 6th CEE Forum, held at the Faculty of Law, Zagreb, Croatia, on 9–10 May 2014. The Zagreb Forum put special emphasis on two major general topics: (1) Important features of law and (2) Contemporary state: Functions, position and crisis management.

The first topic was dedicated to one of the most fundamental questions in legal theory: What features should or must something have in order to be or be regarded as "law"? We especially welcomed contributions addressing the following questions: Is the essentialist approach to "law" possible at all? Would it be better to analyse law by giving an account of its important features instead of only dealing with its essential or necessary features? How do various theoretical/philosophical approaches to law (e.g., positivism, jusnaturalism, realism) differ with respect to their treatment of the features of law? What are the most important features of law? Has contemporary legal theory achieved at least a certain degree of consensus about some of the purported (important) features of law, such as normativity, coerciveness, institutional character, law's claim to being a legitimate authority, law's claim to correctness, law being a union of primary and secondary rules, law being a hierarchical system of norms and law having conventional foundations? What would be the most appropriate methodology (e.g. conceptual analysis, naturalised jurisprudence, normative jurisprudence) for approaching the important features of law?

The second topic was meant to attract papers dealing with the contemporary notion of the state, in particular the (modern) functions of the state, its position with respect to other international and domestic subjects and its "crisis management". The participants were invited to address the following issues: What are the main functions of the contemporary state? Are the notions of "liberal", "social" or "welfare" state still applicable? Is the state's primary role still that of "guardian" of private (e.g. citizens') interests or have some other levels of domestic and international protection become more significant? Is public law still the crucial context for providing guarantees or are we witnessing a kind of overall "privatisation" of the social services? What are, in this respect, the consequences of the ongoing tendency towards state regionalisation? What is the influence of the rather significant (constitutional?) development of supranational organisations (e.g. the EU) and their institutions? Has a qualitatively new type of direct relationship between individuals and supranational organisations been established? Are modern types of crises genuine in the sense that they cannot be predicted (e.g. contemporary terrorism; economic crisis)? Does the concept of the state's "legitimate defense" thus take on a new meaning? What is the relationship between the state and law in modern states of emergency?

The contributors to this volume addressed in one way or another some of the abovementioned issues. Their papers discuss a wide range of subjects, each of which is more related either to the first topic (law) or to the second topic (the state). Since one of our tasks as editors was to arrange the papers in a meaningful order, we divided them into six thematic parts, following the dividing line between the two central topics of the Zagreb Forum. The Yearbook thus starts with two keynote papers addressing issues relating to law and state respectively (Part I – Law and State), constituting a sort of an interlude to the following five parts, three of which are more related to the first topic (Part II – Methodological Approaches, Part III – Language and Law, Part IV – Constitutional and EU Law) and two of which to the second topic (Part V – Contemporary State, Part VI – State and Crisis).

The first part contains the two Zagreb CEE Forum's keynote papers which are devoted to two main topics in legal philosophy: Law and State. In his paper entitled 'Law from a Logical Point of View: Three Basic Questions', Giovanni Battista Ratti examines the puzzling connections between Law and Logic. He rejects the idea that legal systems have an inner logical structure and inquires into the role of logic within legal theory. In order to answer this question he analyses three basic problems: the logical form of legal conditionals, the concept of defeasibility, and the notion of logical consequences. The main thesis defended throughout his paper is the following: logic can be used as a tool that enables us to evaluate the formal correctness of legal argumentations and to reveal how legal reasoning is not logically stringent. Michel Troper's paper, entitled 'The Emergence and Survival of the Modern State', deals with two central historical and theoretical issues: the date of the emergence of modern states and the problem of establishing how, and when, normative hierarchies appeared in legal systems. Troper shows the connection between these two problems and performs an analysis which sheds lights upon both of them. He adopts a truly Kelsenian approach, implemented by means of a deep historical analysis: Law and State are pretty much the same thing; if we discover when the normative hierarchies came into existence in legal systems, then we also know the time of emergence of the concepts of sovereignty and modern state for there is a deep connection between them.

The second part of this volume is entirely devoted to methodological issues. In her paper 'Two Approaches to the Methodology of Legal Theory: Hans Kelsen and Jerzy Wróblewski', Monica Zalewska compares the methodological assumptions and postulates adopted by Hans Kelsen with those endorsed by Jerzy Wróblewski. She evaluates the explicative power of Kelsen's Pure Theory and compares it with Wróblewski's syncretism. The basic intuition put forward by Zalewska is that, in order to grasp the concept of law, we should not stick to a narrow approach but use altogether different methods. In her paper 'The Concept of 'Human Nature': An Attempt to Approach Law from an Essentialist Perspective?' Silvia Salardi examines the very possibility of approaching law from an essentialist perspective based on the notion of human nature. This notion has been implied many times in non-positivistic approaches, which is precisely the reason why the topic is extremely important. She argues that Human Nature is an obscure concept and therefore cannot be used in order to ground, or justify, the legal order. Moreover, she inquires into the practical consequences and the cultural effects of employing this concept, with special regard to the topic of discrimination.

The third part deals with linguistic analysis and law. Alessio Sardo's paper, entitled 'Legal Philosophers, Meaning, and Force', provides an essential analysis of the difficult relationship between meaning and force: the quandary is whether illocutionary force should also be considered a part of the semantic meaning of a certain utterance or whether it should be claimed that these two features of the speech act are neatly separated. Starting with Alf Ross and Ota Weinberger, Sardo develops several arguments in favor of the first view. The second paper of this section, entitled 'On Impossibility in Law', written by Silvia Zorzetto, highlights the different uses of "impossibility" in legal discourse and outlines a typology of its different applications. Zorzetto outlines the linguistic relationships between impossibility, and other central legal and philosophical notions, such as reasonableness, uncertainty, and necessity. The method used by Zorzetto in her analysis is the one first developed in the 1960's by the founders of the Italian Analytical School (Bobbio and Scarpelli).

The fourth part consists of two papers on constitutional and EU law. In 'Judicial Review of Constitutional Amendments: A Theoretical Approach' Fruzsina Gárdos-Orosz argues that it might become possible to respect the constituent power and at the same time empower constitutional courts to review unconstitutional constitutional amendments. She further argues that it might be possible to justify the acts of the constituent, including its acts amending the constitution, as part of the state's functioning and thus bound to a certain extent by the rule on the checks and balances. Gárdos-Orosz finds that certain acts of the constituent power might also be checked and balanced and claims that this is not human rights fundamentalism but rather a lively normativist approach to the discussion. In the paper entitled 'The Substance and Effects of EU Law and Jurisprudence under the Social Constructivist Research Agenda' Dominica Dreyer claims that legislation and jurisprudence are seemingly self-evident phenomena which enjoy the authority of legitimacy by the rule of law but which also contribute deeply to the shaping of European societies. She argues that the positivist approach to law does not suffice if one is striving to uncover the underlying norms and the process of creation of social reality and that this can arguably be best addressed by means of the social constructivist research agenda, which is briefly presented in the paper with respect to its objectives, core aim, methods and added value.

The fifth part brings together two papers generally discussing the notion of contemporary state as an institution in which the classical paradigms face new challenges. In his article 'Can We Still Drive the State Machine the 'Old School' Way? Structural and Functional Deficits of the Modern State' Martin Belov tackles three important types of constitutional crisis related to the phenomenon of constitutional geometry: the representation crisis, the territoriality crisis and the temporality crisis. Belov suggests that the broken lines of representation, trust and responsibility, the broken pyramids of the vertical distribution of public power, and the broken spiral of time winding up political cycles and distorting the political rhythm of the system are the main causes for the malfunctioning of contemporary constitutional systems. In 'Privatising Law in Western Multi-Faith and Multicultural Democracies' Marco Stefano Birtolo questions whether the Western neutralist idea of secularism, characterised by the belief in the necessity of exclusion of religious elements from the political sphere and law, guarantees equality in the context of the religious pluralism spread. He focuses on the proposal for religious diversity inclusion, introducing systems based on legal pluralism, based on an experiment conducted in England. Birtolo attempts to emphasise the need to reconsider the role of the government in responding to problems of multicultural democracies, moving from the idea that neutral political and legal spheres are not theoretically possible.

The final sixth part includes two papers addressing the relationship between state and crisis. In 'States of Crisis and Crises of the State: Redefining the Limits of National Sovereignty and State Powers in Times of Emergency' Axelle Reiter claims that the contemporary evolution of the notions of state and legitimate state powers is the result of a double process of internationalisation of sovereignty and normalisation of exceptional situations. Reiter stresses that the contradictory premises of these two conflicting phenomena cannot be reconciled in a coherent legal or theoretical framework and that there is no place for balancing between legal rights and consequentialist considerations; law itself is the balance. And finally, in 'Peacebuilding and Recognition of States: Failures of the International Territorial Administrations in Bosnia and Herzegovina and Kosovo' Robin Caballero argues that the peacebuilding missions in both countries have failed to resolve the conflicts between the different communities and to establish efficient institutions. He stresses that the absence of a coherent policy of recognition by the international community during the dissolution of Yugoslavia prevented the missions from implementing efficient institutions and, furthermore, that the lack of democracy and legitimacy in the provisional institutions prevented the implementation of the policies led by the international missions, thus implying the rejection of these authorities by a large majority of the population, in particular the Serbian minority. Caballero argues that the failures of these missions are a direct challenge to the concept of peacebuilding under international law.

Taken as a whole and just as its title suggests this volume considers and sheds new light on some of the classical paradigms in the treatment of two highly prominent topics, those of law and state, but also offers novel proposals on how best to approach them. We therefore hope that the readers will find the volume illuminating and inciting and a source of inspiration for their own research in these fields.

Finally, we would like to express our gratitude to the Zagreb Faculty of Law for its generous financial and organisational support without which the Zagreb CEE Forum would not have been possible. We also thank the reviewers for ensuring the quality of the Yearbook's content and to Ana Burazin for her language advice throughout the editting process.

Zagreb – Milan, July 2015 The Editors

Part I
Law and State (Keynote Papers)

Giovanni Battista Ratti

Law from a Logical Point of View. Three Basic Questions

1. The received view(s) on law and logic

Most jurists and legal theorists think that law has an inner logical structure, which can be discovered and accounted for by means of logical tools.

On the first view, many of them have the pernicious tendency to think that law is a logically unified whole: i.e. a set of sentences which is necessarily consistent and complete. When they argue in favour of such a view, they often refer to logic (broadly and sometimes loosely understood) as their source of justification. So – we are frequently told – antinomies between legal norms are only apparent (consistency) and the law always provides a solution for any question whatsoever (completeness). For law – as any other discourse – is regarded as based on a certain set of rational, and indeed logical, principles (see, paradigmatically, Kelsen 1945, 347ff, 402ff).

Traditionally, the 'holy trinity' of logical principles applied to law is composed of the principle of identity, the principle of non-contradiction, and the principle of the excluded middle.

As is known, in propositional logic, they amount (or are reducible) to one and the same proposition. As a matter of course, the following sentences – respectively formulating identity, excluded middle, and non-contradiction – are just three different ways of representing the same relation:[1]

[1]	$p \supset p$	[identity]
[2]	$p \vee \sim p$	[excluded middle]
[3]	$\sim(p \,\&\, \sim p)$	[non-contradiction]

Still, the propositions expressed by such sentences convey a full array of information. The first one states that every sentence implies itself. The second one states that, given a certain proposition *p*, it must be either true or false. The third one

1 Following standard notation, '⊃' stands for the material conditional, 'v' stands for disjunction, '&' for conjunction, and '~' for negation. The variable 'p' stands for any proposition whatsoever, and 'O' is for the deontic character 'Obligatory'.

states that it is not the case that a certain proposition *p* is, at the same time, true and false.

Analogously, in the normative domain, the three following sentences (the 'normative transposition' of the above-mentioned principles) are considered as logically equivalent:

[i]	Op ⊃ Op	[N-identity]
[ii]	Op v ~Op	[N-excluded middle]
[iii]	~(Op & ~Op)	[N-non-contradiction]

These three principles state, for the normative domain, that: (i) every norm entails itself, (ii) that a certain norm or its norm-negation are valid (completeness), and (iii) that it is not the case that a certain norm and its contradictory norm are both valid (consistency). These tenets have sometimes been used to hold the view that law, as any other normative system, is necessarily (i.e. for logical reasons) consistent and complete.

Indeed, the famous principle of closure 'Everything that is not (legally) prohibited is (legally) permitted' is just a reformulation of (ii). Let's substitute 'Op' with 'O~p' (i.e. prohibited that *p*), and what we obtain is: (ii') O~p v ~O~p. This sentence exactly states that any conduct whatsoever *p* is either prohibited or permitted. By disjunctive syllogism, we can easily derive that, if *p* is not prohibited, then it is indeed permitted.

But all these kinds of equivalences and inferences are of course question-begging when applied to some formal aspects of *actual* legal systems. Logic has nothing to say about the content of *actual* legal systems. It only states that, if we have certain normative systems that are such-and-such, we can safely derive certain conclusions.

In particular, sentences (ii) and (iii), when jointly considered, may be regarded as definitions of consistent and complete normative systems (as it were, of *ideal* normative systems). However, they do not rule out the circumstance that we can have – as our experience suggests – normative (and especially legal) systems which contain incompatible norms or contain no norm at all regarding a certain case. In other words, definitions of completeness and consistency within the normative domain *do not* rule out incompleteness and inconsistency as matters of fact, in the same way as the principles of excluded middle and non-contradiction do not rule out 'cognitive gaps' and contradictions in actual conversation.

Due to these limitations, another view on the relations between law and logic has recently been propounded. Law is normally characterised by linguistic and logical shortcomings: consequently, its explanation calls for the creation of 'deviant' or, more cautiously, 'new' logics. On this view, logic constitutes a sort of cognitive method for accounting for law's structure and functioning.[2] So far, so good. The problem with this second view, however, is that, according to it, logic should be moulded in accordance with law's contingent features. So, if law is gappy, logic should also be 'gappy'; if law is fuzzy, so must be logic; if law is inconsistent, we should search for some sort of paraconsistent logic; and so on. Thus, such a second view is roughly characterised by the tenet that logic should *mimic its object of inquiry*. This view is questionable for the simple fact that logic is fundamental in discovering several aspects, and particularly deficiencies, of the language to which is applied, but this task can be carried out only if logic does not always mimic its object-language. This feature will become manifest when we deal with the defeasibility of legal norms and see that no defeasible logic is needed to account for this supposed phenomenon of legal norms.

Observe that the thesis defended here is not that legal norms, or legal systems, necessarily have no logical relations or properties. On the contrary, the thesis which will be argued for is rather that logic is fundamental in detecting the problems which stem from the logical reconstruction and treatment of legal norms, especially of conditional legal norms. This view is clearly at odds with the traditional tenet according to which law is globally determined because of logic, or with the more recent tenet that logic should mimic law's logical 'peculiar' structure.

2. The logical form of legal conditionals

Very few things may be said to be more agreed upon amongst jurists than the thesis that legal norms are, by and large, to be regarded as conditionals connecting some key operative facts to legal consequences. When it comes to applying logic to such an intuition, jurists usually refer to very common schemata of reasoning (such as *modus ponens*) to support the view that legal conditionals, in many ways, have the same logical behaviour as material conditionals have in propositional logic. The antecedent of a norm is thus regarded as a sufficient condition of the consequent, and (more dubiously so) the consequent is regarded as a necessary condition of the antecedent. This has the upshot, among many others, of making the so-called 'enrichment' (or 'strengthening of the antecedent') applicable to legal

2 For this view, see paradigmatically Haack (2007). This view is also present in Kelsen's thesis that logic is indirectly applicable to law through the logic of normative propositions. See Guastini (1996, 101–113).

norms: given a certain legal conditional, any atomic sentence whatsoever added to the antecedent does not alter the original relation between it and the consequent.[3]

Agreement dissolves, though, when it comes to reconstructing the exact logical (*viz.* symbolised) form of such conditionals norms. Norms such as 'If it rains, you ought to slow down your vehicle', or 'Any act whatever of man, which causes damage to another, obliges the one by whose fault it occurred, to compensate it'[4] are usually liable to be reconstructed in at least two diverging ways.[5]

In formalizing conditional norms, some authors – like Ross (1968) and, more questionably, von Wright[6] – have favoured the so called 'insular conception', which reconstructs conditions as a part of the scope of deontic operators. Consequently, the logical form of hypothetical norms is represented as follows: '$O(p \supset q)$'.

By contrast, other writers – such as Alchourrón and Bulygin (1971) and Kelsen (1945) – prefer the so called 'bridge conception', which conceives of conditions as external to the scope of deontic operators. Consequently, the logical form of hypothetical norms is represented in the following way: '$p \supset Oq$'.

Both representations present several shortcomings. Here we shall dwell only on few of them.

According to the standard definition of the material conditional, the sentence '$O(p \supset q)$' is equivalent to the sentence '$O(\sim p \vee q)$'.[7] On the insular conception, this feature makes any conditional norm equivalent to a disjunctive obligation, one which puts the norm-addressees in a situation where they can choose freely between two states of affairs in order to comply with the norm. This, in turn, is quite

---

3 In propositional logic, enrichment (or strengthening of the antecedent) is symbolised as follows: $(p \supset q) \supset ((p \ \& \ r) \supset q)$. In the case of norms, it can be symbolised in the following manner (depending on which conception of normative conditionals one favours):
Bridge Conception: $(p \supset Oq) \supset ((p \ \& \ r) \supset Oq)$
Insular Conception: $O(p \supset q) \supset O((p \ \& \ r) \supset q)$.

4 This is the widespread English translation of section 1382 of the French Civil Code.

5 The dichotomy 'insular conception'/'bridge conception' is borrowed from Alchourrón (1996).

6 As Moreso (1996, 94, note 4) observes: 'The position of von Wright [...] has, on this point so central to the logical representation of norms, been one of vacillation'. In 1980, von Wright admitted 'mixed' formulas (such as '$p \supset Oq$') formed of propositional variables, sentential connectives, and deontic expressions. However, later on, von Wright (1983, 151) stated 'that if the standard connective in question is a truth-connective, then this "linguistic hybrid" is a monster with no place in meaningful discourse'.

7 In propositional logic, '$p \supset q$' is equivalent to '$\sim p \vee q$', which in turn is equivalent to '$\sim(p \ \& \sim q)$'.

unsatisfactory if we want to reconstruct those cases when the norm-addresses cannot control the conditions of application of the norm. Take for instance the previously mentioned norm 'If it rains, you ought to slow down your vehicle'. Representing it by means of the sentence 'O(~p v q)' suggests the idea that the person receiving the norm is able to choose freely between the states of affairs 'not raining' (~*p*) and 'slowing down the vehicle' (*q*), but this is clearly not the case, since he or she cannot create or control the states of affairs consisting, respectively, in 'raining' or 'not raining'. In the event of raining, there is an obligation to *q*. But the norm does not provide anything regarding the case when it does not rain (~*p*). So, the proposed formalization is unsuitable for situations of this sort. By contrast, the insular conception is useful in reconstructing the norms' antecedents which are under the control of the norm-addressees, as happens in such norms as 'If you go and visit your granny, you ought to bring her flowers' or 'If you are to comply with a contract, you ought to do it in good faith'.[8]

The bridge conception fares better in representing the above-mentioned situations where norm-addressees cannot control the state of affairs on which the antecedent bears upon. However, it is characterised by at least one main logical difficulty. Indeed, under Hume's principle, it does not allow *modus tollens* as a valid schema of reasoning, since from two norms it would allow one to derive a factual proposition. In fact, from the hypothetical norm 'p ⊃ Oq' and the categorical norm '~Oq', one would be entitled to derive '~p': what manifestly constitutes the inverse of the naturalistic fallacy.

At any rate, contemporary literature suggests that a complete reduction to just one logical form of all conditional (duty-imposing) norms is not viable (see Moreso and Rodríguez 2010). Both logical forms are necessary to reconstruct different kinds of norms. However, what is of the utmost importance here is that, whatever form one assigns to such conditional norms, there are problems concerning their logical behaviour, and in particular their negation. Indeed, if one applies to such norms the *classical* properties of conditional negation, one obtains remarkable, and indeed counterintuitive, results.

On the bridge conception, by analogy with propositional logic, the negation of a conditional rule like 'p ⊃ Oq' would apparently be expressed by the negated conditional sentence '~(p ⊃ Oq)'. By contrast, the conditional sentences 'p ⊃ Oq' and 'p ⊃ ~Oq' (the latter being the so-called 'conditional denial') would not bring about any inconsistency. If this were the case, some remarkable consequences

8 This is a norm one may derive from combining articles 1372 and 1375 of the Italian Civil Code.

would follow: (1) There would be a contradiction between conditional norms whenever the same set of rules allowed one to derive, at the same time, 'p ⊃ Oq' and '~(p ⊃ Oq)'. From such a set *any norm* would follow. (2) Again analogously to what happens in propositional logic, the conjunction of the conditional norms 'p ⊃ Oq' and 'p ⊃ ~Oq' would be equivalent to the negation of the common antecedent: that is '~p' (see Ross 1968, §36 for a very interesting critical discussion). A set containing such two rules would *not* be inconsistent or trivialised. Indeed, this twofold view is generally, though not universally, rejected as untenable.

In fact, nobody interprets '~(p ⊃ Oq)' as the genuine negation of a conditional norm: such a formula is rather construed as a proposition stating that such a conditional norm does not belong to a certain normative system (Bulygin 1982; Wróblewski 1984, 466ff). So, sentences 'p ⊃ Oq' and '~(p ⊃ Oq)' does not collide, since they belong to different levels of discourse. In turn, the conjunction of the conditional norms 'p ⊃ Oq' and 'p ⊃ ~q' is regarded as the paradigm of a conflict between conditional norms, and not as a way of affirming '~p'. And this for an intuitive reason: if, say, the case of 'raining' is connected to inconsistent normative consequences (say, 'it is obligatory to slow down' and 'it is not obligatory to slow down'), nobody would derive from that that the normative authority has asserted that it is not raining (for a discussion from the point of view of the insular conception, see Ross 1968).

On the insular conception, the norm-negation of 'O(p ⊃ q)' – that is, '~O(p ⊃ q)', amounting in turn to 'P(p & ~q)' – is well-formed, but seems to lose any feature of conditionality. Indeed, it amounts to a categorical norm permitting to bring about simultaneously (atomic) states of affairs *p* and *~q*.

This leads to the view that normative conditionals show a partially different behaviour from material conditionals. In particular, in juristic reasoning, the antecedent of a norm is taken, as it were, as a 'case-identifier' condition, rather than a sufficient condition of the consequent. The normative consequences provided by hypothetical norms generally apply only when the key operative factors singled out by the antecedent obtain. When the norm antecedent does not materialise, the consequence does not follow, since the norm is simply not applicable: but, unlike propositional logic (where the conditional is true when both the antecedent and the consequent are false),[9] this does not render the normative conditional, as it were, 'true' or 'satisfied'. Consequently, an inconsistency between conditional

9 One should bear in mind that, in propositional logic, a conditional is always true when the antecedent is false.

norms materialises whenever a certain case *p* is connected to two categorical norms which are contrary or contradictory.

Summing up: (1) unlike in propositional logic, then, the simultaneous membership in a certain sentential set of '(p ⊃ Oq)' and '~(p ⊃ Oq)' brings about no inconsistency, since, as we have seen, the second sentence is better regarded as a meta-linguistic sentence bearing on some possible attributes of a normative system.[10] By contrast, (2) the simultaneous membership of 'O(p ⊃ q)' and '~O(p ⊃ q)' in a certain normative system brings about normative inconsistency, but this does not seem a correct reconstruction of actual antinomies between *conditional norms* which are found in normative documents and the way they are read by jurists. (3) As mentioned before, ordinary antinomies between conditional norms consist in the connection of two incompatible normative solutions (*viz.* categorical norms) to the same set of key operative factors. In other words, a certain case *p* is inconsistently qualified by different norms. The current reconstruction of this phenomenon is correctly provided by the bridge conception, by stating that we have an antinomy whenever a normative system contain norms like 'p ⊃ Oq' and 'p ⊃ ~Oq', or norms which can be logically derived from them. More precisely, it is usual to distinguish between different kinds of inconsistency, taking into account the possible relations of complete overlapping, inclusion, or intersection, between the antecedents of the conflicting norms (see Ross 1958, 128ff; cf. also Guastini 2011, 108ff). Here, we shall briefly recall such a classification with an eye to the expressed or implicit character of the conditional norms involved in the conflict. We have an antinomy between *two expressed norms* whenever a certain normative system α contains two norms of the sort we have just mentioned ('p ⊃ Oq' and 'p ⊃ ~Oq'), since their antecedents *completely overlap*. We have an antinomy between *an implicit norm* (derived by enrichment from the more general norm) *and a more specific expressed norm*, whenever the normative system α contains norms like 'p ⊃ Oq' and 'p & r ⊃ ~Oq', since α is inconsistent only regarding the whole antecedent of the more specific norm (which is totally included in the antecedent of the more generic norm), so that α is partially free from contradictions regarding case *p*, in the partition *p & ~r*. Finally, we have an inconsistency regarding *only implicit norms* (both derived by using enrichment) whenever the normative system α contains two norms like 'p ⊃ Oq' and 'r ⊃ ~Oq', since α is inconsistent only regarding the *intersecting case p & r*, and is free from contradictions when the

10 Of course, if the first sentence is also taken as expressing a normative propositions, then we would face a contradiction between normative propositions, the former stating that the conditional norm at hand belongs to a certain normative system, while the latter denies such a state of affairs.

antecedents of both norms do not intersect (i.e. in cases *p & ~r*, *~p & r*, and of course *~p & ~r*). Observe that this classification *presupposes* the application of *enrichment*. But, in turn, enrichment presupposes the logical behaviour of material conditionals.

By way of conclusion of this discussion, we may say that jurists and legal theorists usually call a *normative inconsistency (or antinomy)* a sentence of the kind '(p ⊃ Oq) & (p ⊃ ~Oq)' – or '(p ⊃ Oq) & (p ⊃ O~q)' – which is no conflict in propositional logic, but rather the conjunction of a material conditional and the corresponding conditional denial. Moreover, on this reconstruction, the *ex contradictione quodlibet* principle does not affect normative systems in their whole, since a normative contradiction trivialises only the case referred to by the antecedent to which two incompatible consequences are connected (see Atienza 1992). There are reasons to think that this view is too positive, and that the effects of a normative conflict exceed the trivialization of the case referred to in the antecedent of the conflicting norms, but the articulation of these reasons is far beyond the scope of this paper (for the first articulation of these reasons, see Ratti 2013a, 81–93). Here, it suffices to notice that, according to lawyers, only relevant norms must be taken into account in order to solve a certain legal question and this seems to allow one to limit the destructive effects of conflicts between norms.[11]

This juristic 'logical package', despite appearances to the contrary, is inconsistent from the logical point of view. In particular, the bridge conception affirms, at the same time, that the normative conditionals *do have* the same logical behaviour as material conditionals (what is presupposed in current juristic taxonomy of different kinds of antinomies) and that the normative conditionals *do not have* the same logical behaviour as material conditionals (what is presupposed in current juristic definition of inconsistency between conditional norms and the rational reconstruction of its effects). In fact, we may only identify and classify antinomies as we have done (and as is commonly done) if we embrace enrichment as a valid form of inference: i.e., only if *we do treat* normative conditionals as material implications. By contrast, we may rule out the traditional effects of inconsistency between conditionals and the conjunction of a normative conditional with its conditional denial only if we *do not treat* normative conditionals as material implications. The same holds, *mutatis mutandis*, for the insular conception.

---

11 This idea is perfectly epitomised by Alchourrón & Makinson (1981, 134): 'Now imagine the situation of a judge or administrative officer who is called upon to apply an inconsistent code and reach a verdict on a specific question. What ways are open to him to mitigate or transcend the contradiction? One idea is to distinguish between those parts of the code that are directly *relevant* to the case in hand, and those which are not'.

The result of the analysis carried out so far is at least twofold: (a) the traditional view, which takes law's (supposed) 'systematic nature' as based on an analogy with propositional logic, is put into question by the very circumstance that the concepts of conditional negation and consistency usually employed in juristic discourses are very different from those of propositional logic; (b) the recent view, according to which logic should mimic law's logical behaviour, need provide the tools liable to represent the peculiarities we have referred to, without losing much of the inferential power associated to propositional logic.

3. The defeasibility of legal norms

A recent trend in legal philosophy has consisted in explaining law through one of its presumed attributes: defeasibility (see Ferrer and Ratti 2012). In particular, legal norms are said to be defeasible in that all legal standards are *potentially overridable* in certain cases where they bring about results which are regarded, for some reasons, as unsatisfactory (see, for instance, Schauer 1991, 73ff).

This, in turn, presupposes that there are *material sources* of defeasibility. Here at least two contrary options are normally available: (1) we have a set of objective axiological resources, imposing ordering hierarchies which determine the defeat of a certain legal standard in some given circumstances; (2) such a set does not exist or is not completely knowable, and for this reason the applicators have to make a discretional decision as for the defeasibility of the legal standard at hand.

When needed, I shall assume here, contrary to the prevailing literature, the second perspective and, when dealing with the material source of implicit exceptions to legal norms, I shall analyse defeasibility as a factor regarding the legislator's tacit intentions or goals underlying expressed rules.

Of course, so conceived, defeasibility has a bearing on the logical form of norms. On the one hand, conditional norms the logical form thereof is, *prima facie*, '$p \supset Oq$' are rendered defeasible by substituting the material conditional with the defeasible conditional (symbolised by the corner '>', which in turn renders the 'deviant' connective 'If, then *presumably*').

Some conceptions clearly state that conditional norms are defeasible for they do not allow *modus ponens* or enrichment. The corner would thus be a way to represent these kinds of logical failure. This leads to the questionable view that there may be normative systems which contain normative conflicts but, in spite of that, do not need to be revised in order to overcome such a difficulty, since such systems, by not allowing *modus ponens* and enrichment, would not be liable to be trivialised under the *ex contradictione quodlibet* principle. This argument seems to conflate different aspects of the problem of normative conflicts (for criticism, see Alchourrón 1991, 424–425). Here it suffices to say that, without the application of *modus ponens* and enrichment, it is clear that no antinomy may be spotted within normative systems. On the one hand, it is impossible to derive incompatible solutions for a concrete case, if *modus ponens* is not admitted. On the other hand, it is also impossible to determine whether two antecedents, which are connected to incompatible solutions, completely or partially overlap, if we do not admit enrichment (for a detailed discussion, see Ratti 2013b).

However, we may understand formal defeasibility in a more charitable and interesting way. From this perspective, the corner may be seen as a compendious way for concealing the role of traditional negation. In a seminal paper, Alchourrón (2012 [1996]) holds the view that legal defeasibility may be fruitfully approached from a pragmatic standpoint about the counterfactual intentions of the lawgiver: that is, what the lawgiver would have done if it had considered some circumstances which it could not (or would not) have taken into account. Such considerations on the counterfactual intentions of the lawgiver bring about the defeasibility of legal standards and allow one to logically reconstruct defeasibility as a problem of application of the principle of enrichment.

More precisely, at least three dispositions or attitudes of the lawgiver about the defeat of a certain conditional normative standard 'If p then Oq', on the grounds of a certain implicit circumstance *r*, can be envisaged (ibid., 47–48): 1) the lawgiver may have a disposition to accept both 'If p then Oq' and 'If p and r then Oq': in this case *r* counts as an implicit non-exception (thus, enrichment is applied); 2) the lawgiver may have a disposition to accept 'If p then Oq' whilst rejecting 'If p and r then Oq': circumstance *r* is thus to be regarded as an implicit exception (so, enrichment is not applied); 3) the lawgiver may have no disposition at all about whether to consider *r* as an exception (like in case 2) or a non-exception (like in case 1). Accordingly, *r* is undetermined as an exception (so the application of enrichment is not univocally determined).

The symbolic counterpart of this pragmatic stance is that defeasible conditionals such as 'p > Oq' may be fully reconstructed by introducing negation into the sentence. Let *r* stay for any defeater whatsoever. So, a fully developed defeasible conditional rule – provided that there is only one defeater – would amount to the conjunction of the following two sentences: 'p & r ⊃ ~Oq' and 'p & ~r ⊃ Oq'.

This reconstruction makes it possible to regard defeasibility as a phenomenon of *tacit inconsistency* within the normative system at hand. In particular, there is a conflict between a logical consequence of an expressed rule and a norm which can be derived (in a strictly logical manner or, more frequently, by means of unsound reasoning) from some of the lawgivers' goals or counterfactual intentions. Let us again assume that 'p ⊃ Oq' is the lawgiver's expressed norm N1 and *r* is the defeater (the implicit exception, as Alchourrón would have it) which can be 'derived' by (or justified on the basis of) the lawgiver's goals or unspoken intentions. From thus envisaged goals or intentions, one can construe that the lawgiver intended another norm N2 which provides that 'p & r ⊃ ~Oq'. This implicit norm is clearly at odds with the implicit norm N3, logically derived from N1, according to which 'p & r ⊃ Oq'. On this reading, defeasibility consists in *giving priority* to the norm derived from the implicit norm over the one derived from the expressed norm (Mendonca 2012).

As a matter of course, such a priority can be more or less frequently at play depending on the institutional design of a certain legal order. As Schauer (2012, 87) has recently shown, the resistance of expressed rules to implicit exceptions (or, more broadly, to underlying justifications) depends on 'how some decision-making system will choose to treat its rules'. In this sense, it all depends on a meta-rule (or a set of meta-rules) imposing a certain defeasible or indefeasible treatment of (some or all of) the other rules of the system.

From our previous analysis it follows that (a) if defeasibility is understood as a kind of logical failure of conditional norms, we may save juristic intuition that antinomies are apparent, but norms lose all their inferential power; (b) if defeasibility is, by contrast, regarded as a kind of implicit ordering between different kinds of derived norms, we have saved enrichment and the inferential power of norms, but we fall back within the logical compass we have analysed in section 1 and the conceptual problems related to it. Consequently, no logically sound explanation of jurists' intuitions regarding legal conditionals and their behaviour seems currently available.

4. The notion of logical consequence in the legal domain

The twofold problem we have sketched so far may be approached by discussing the notion of logical consequence in the legal domain. According to a widespread approach, propositional logic investigates exactly the notion of logical consequence (or entailment among sentences) within truth-functional discourses. In propositional logic, the notion of logical consequence is related to that of 'truth preservation': a sentence is a logical consequence of another sentence whenever the former is derived from the latter by means of a strictly truth-preserving reasoning (Agazzi 2011). Norms being neither true nor false, we encounter great difficulties in shaping a corresponding notion of logical consequence within the normative domain.

Leaving this fundamental problem aside, we must notice that, obviously, the concept of implication is strictly related to that of consistency, since a consistent system is characterised as a set of sentences which does not entail any sentence. The problem we have analysed in section 1, regarding the logical form of normative conditionals and what follows from them especially in case of inconsistency, is obviously related to the notion of logical consequence within the legal domain. In particular, the so-called 'criterion of deducibility', according to which a norm which is a logical consequence of an expressed norm is valid within the legal system at hand, is vacuous in so far as the concept of consistency is not clearly determined. In particular, when the concept of consistency is not determined, the criterion of deducibility cannot be *recursive*, for it is not possible, in a finite number of passages, to determine exactly which norms belong to the system at hand. This problem is eventually worsened by the fact that the set of norms which belong to a legal system does not constitute the only relevant set for legal application. If, for instance, we consider the set of so called 'norms in force' – the norms the judicial application whereof is widely predictable – we may indeed ponder whether they are subsumed under the notion of logical consequence or not. There are very strong reasons to think that they are not so subsumed, since a certain norm may be in force, while some or most of its logical consequences might not be regarded as such. For instance, in applying the general norm 'All thieves ought to be punished' (or, what is the same, 'If someone is a thief, then s/he must be punished') to a blue-eyed man, probably we would not say that the judge is applying the norm 'All blue-eyed thieves ought to be punished'. However, the second norm is logically entailed by the first one.

Someone could also object that law is composed only of expressed norms and that derived norms are not valid, but, as it were, 'applicable', in that there are legally valid norms which impose their application. This move, of course, does not solve the problem at hand. It just changes its level, for what we now have is uncertainty about the derived rules, which are or are not applicable. We may have, *ex hypothesi*, complete certainty about valid norms, but we do not exactly know what the derived norms are: hence, we do not know a substantial part of the norms which form the set of applicable laws.

Be this as it may, let us assume, for the sake of the argument, that enrichment is the *main criterion* to determine which norms are 'relevant' logical consequences of other legal norms. We can now wonder about whether all derived norms (i.e. the logical consequences of norms) are legally valid.

A first answer defends the view that, indeed, all 'relevant' derived norms are valid, by pointing to the idea that unless we accept the rules of inference of classical deductive logic, law, as a normative set, would be a completely idle thing: we could not qualify reality by means of classifications (i.e. subsume individual entities under generic categories) and, consequently, law could not be applied by judges. Moreover, many legal orders seem to justify this thesis since some of their rules on the solution of antinomies and the filling-up of gaps seem to be grounded on a classical deductive logic of norms, without the acceptance of which it would make no sense to take care of the logical defects of legal systems.

However, there are several other conceptions which defend the view that not all logical consequences following from legal norms are valid but only some of them.

In recent jurisprudential literature one can find at least three theses regarding the validity of norms that are logical consequences of expressly formulated rules (for a more detailed analysis, see Ferrer and Ratti 2010).

The first thesis (which can be dubbed 'teleological thesis') suggests that we accept as valid logical consequences of expressed rules only those consequences that comply with rules' underlying reasons. On this view, the law contains the logical consequences of expressed legal rules that are *not in conflict* with the set of their underlying reasons, *plus* the logical consequences of such reasons. Expressed rules, thus, are to be considered as defeasible in that they are liable to be defeated by reasons, in the specific sense that underlying reasons can 'delete' those logical consequences of the rules that are incompatible with the former.

A second conception of logically derived rules (which can be called the 'authoritative thesis') is contrary to the teleological thesis in that it relies on the idea that legal norms cannot be defeated by their underlying reasons, since, if that were the case, they would lose any capability of guiding human conduct: they would be unable to make any 'practical difference'. Legally valid logically derived norms are those norms which are derived in accordance with the lawgiver's actual intentions. This is possible due to the fact that, according to this thesis, any property, which has not been expressly considered by the lawgiver, has to be regarded *ipso facto* as irrelevant in the intention of the lawgiver.

A third conception of derived norms – relying on the notion of a *counterfactual* intention (rather than that of a real intention) and a pragmatic approach to the notion of logical consequence – has been called 'dispositional thesis'. What is relevant here in order to determine the valid consequences of a legal norm is neither its alleged objective ratio (like in the case of the teleological thesis) nor law's claim to work as an exclusionary reason (like in the case of the authoritative thesis). It is rather the lawgiver's subjective disposition (i.e. attitude) regarding the application of a certain norm to those cases that are characterised by the presence of an element which is not contemplated by such a norm, but is regarded as potentially relevant for some other reasons.

From the sketch on the conceptions of derived norms we have just proposed it follows that the notion of logical consequence within the legal domain is uncertain and is liable to render the whole system indeterminate. Again, logic is used here neither to justify the thesis that law is a coherent and unified whole, provided with an inner logic, nor to assert that law has an inner 'peculiar' structure which can be captured by means of a 'deviant' logic. It is used, rather, to state that the notion of logical consequence in the legal domain is unclear and does not allow one to identify a legal system in a recursive fashion (as one would prima facie expect by applying logic to the legal domain).

5. Conclusions

In the previous pages we have pointed to three logical problems which affect law or its rational reconstruction.

In particular, by means of logical analysis we have shown that the notion of the conditional norm, as it is usually understood by jurists as well as legislators, leads to logical inconsistency which affects the rational reconstruction of law as a structured set of sentences. We have also shown that introducing defeasibility of legal conditionals is no way out for we either lose all of the inferential power we want the norms to have or we fall back into the predicaments stemming from the rational reconstruction of legal conditionals.

These problems lead to investigate the notion of logical consequence within the legal domain. Several alternative conceptions of logical consequence are available within such a domain, and there is no univocal way of determining which one is the most appropriate. Unluckily, in so far as we do not have a univocal notion of logical consequence, we cannot determine the full scope of a legal order or of the set of the norms which are applicable within such a legal order.

One of the main results of our discussion is that, contrary to the received views we commented upon, logical analysis is fundamental in discovering that law has serious logical flaws:[12] briefly put, in order to say that law is 'illogical' we need logic.

References

Agazzi, Evandro. 2011. Consistency, Truth and Ontology. *Studia Logica* 97: 7–29.

Alchourrón, Carlos Eduardo. 1991. Conflicts of Norms and the Revision of Normative Systems. *Law and Philosophy* 10: 413–425.

12 This way of conceiving logic, so to speak, as an 'ally' of legal realism in spotting legal indeterminacy, was clearly advocated by Ross (1969).

Alchourrón, Carlos Eduardo. 1996. Detachment and Defeasibility in Deontic Logic. *Studia Logica* 57: 5–18.

Alchourrón, Carlos Eduardo. 2012 [1996]. On Law and Logic. In *The Logic of Legal Requirements. Essays on Defeasibility*, edited by Jordi Ferrer Beltrán and Giovanni Battista Ratti, 39–52. Oxford: Oxford University Press.

Alchourrón, Carlos Eduardo, and Bulygin, Eugenio. 1971. *Normative Systems.* Wien: Springer.

Alchourrón, Carlos Eduardo, and Makinson, David. 1981. Hierarchies of Regulations and their Logic. In *New Studies in Deontic Logic*, edited by Risto Hilpinen, 125–148. Dordrecht: Reidel.

Atienza, Manuel. 1992. Sobre los límites de la lógica en el derecho. *Theoria – Segunda época* VII: 1007–1018.

Bulygin, Eugenio. 1982. Time and validity. In *Deontic logic, computational linguistics and legal information systems*, edited by Antonio A. Martino, 65–81. Amsterdam: North Holland.

Dworkin, Ronald. 1986. *Law's Empire*. London: Fontana.

Ferrer Beltrán, Jordi, and Ratti, Giovanni Battista. 2010. Validity and Defeasibility in the Legal Domain. *Law and Philosophy* 29: 601–626.

Ferrer Beltrán, Jordi, and Ratti, Giovanni Battista (eds.) 2012. *The Logic of Legal Requirements. Essays on Defeasibility*. Oxford, Oxford University Press.

Guastini, Riccardo. 1996. *Distinguendo. Studi di teoria e metateoria del diritto.* Torino: Giappichelli.

Guastini, Riccardo. 2010. *Le fonti del diritto. Fondamenti teorici*. Milano: Giuffrè.

Guastini, Riccardo. 2011. *Interpretare e argomentare*. Milano: Giuffrè.

Haack, Susan. 2007. On Logic in the Law: 'Something but not All'. *Ratio Juris* 20: 1–31.

Hart, Herbert L. A. 1983. Self-Referring Laws. In Id., *Essays in Jurisprudence and Philosophy*, 145–158. Oxford: Oxford University Press.

Kelsen, Hans. 1945. *General Theory of Law and State*. Cambridge (Mass.): Harvard University Press.

Mendonca, Daniel. 2012. Exceptions. In *The Logic of Legal Requirements. Essays on Defeasibility*, edited by Jordi Ferrer Beltrán and Giovanni Battista Ratti, 202–208. Oxford: Oxford University Press.

Moreso, José Juan. 1996. On Relevance and Justification of Legal Decisions. *Erkenntnis* 44: 73–100.

Moreso, José Juan, and Rodríguez, José Luís. 2010. Estudio introductorio: Carlos E. Alchourrón y la máxima de la mutilación mínima. In Carlos E. Alchourrón,

Fundamentos para una teoría general de los deberes, 11–38. Madrid: Marcial Pons.

Ratti, Giovanni Battista. 2013a. *Studi sulla logica del diritto e della scienza giuridica*. Madrid: Marcial Pons.

Ratti, Giovanni Battista. 2013b. Normative Inconsistency and Logical Theories: A First Critique of Defeasibilism. In *Coherence: Insights from Philosophy, Jurisprudence and Artificial Intelligence*, edited by Michał Araszkiewicz and Jaromir Šavelka, 123–135. Dordrecht: Springer.

Rodríguez, Jorge Luís. 2006. La tensión entre dos concepciones de los sistemas jurídicos. *Análisis filosófico* 26: 242–276.

Ross, Alf. 1958. *On Law and Justice*. London: Stevens & Sons.

Ross, Alf. 1968. *Directives and Norms*. Routledge & Kegan Paul.

Ross, Alf. 1969. On Self-Reference and a Puzzle in Constitutional Law. *Mind* 78: 1–24.

Schauer, Frederick. 1991. *Playing by the Rules. A Philosophical Examination of Rule-based Decision-making in Law and in Life*. Oxford: Clarendon Press.

von Wright, Georg H. 1983. Norms, Truth and Logic. In Id., *Practical Reason. Philosophical Papers*, Vol I., 130–209. Oxford: Basil Blackwell.

Wróblewski, Jerzy. 1984. Negation in Law. In *Theorie der Normen*, edited by Werner Krawietz, Helmut Schelsky, Günther Winkler and Alfred Schramm, 457–471. Berlin: Duncker & Humblot.

Yablo, Stephen. 1993. Paradox Without Self-Reference. *Analysis* 53: 251–252.

Michel Troper

The Emergence and Survival of the Modern State

1. Introduction

For the most part, legal theory, at least in the European tradition, is ahistorical. It aims at giving a general description of the structure of the legal system, the function of the law or the particularities of legal reasoning in general terms, a description that should be valid not for one particular legal system, but for all legal systems of all countries and all times. According to Kelsen it should even be valid not only for existing but also for every possible legal system. Legal theorists have therefore little curiosity in historical analysis.

On the other hand, unlike other disciplines, legal theory does not create all of the concepts that it uses, but extrapolates them from its object, i.e. from the law itself. This is the case with, e.g., 'constitution', 'contract', 'interpretation', etc., which, since they are rooted in particular historical circumstances, are often ill-suited for a general analysis or for the analysis of systems that are different, so historians, even legal historians (or anthropologists), can make little use of them.

Thirdly, a large and important part of legal theory is kept pure from the social sciences, including history, for several reasons, but in particular on the assumption that the law is not a system of facts and thus cannot be analysed through the principle of causality.

This essay is an attempt to bridge the disciplines, not by adopting a multidisciplinary approach, but by using some of the concepts of legal theory to examine one historical puzzle which for the purposes of this paper is mainly two-fold: the emergence of the State in the political and legal language of the 16th and 17th centuries, it's survival in our contemporary world and the possibility of a legal causality.

Starting from Kelsen's theory of the unity of law and State, which is closer than one might think to Weber's conception of the state, I will try to show how, in spite or maybe because of its weaknesses, it can shed some light on the problem of the emergence and survival of the State.

2. Kelsen's theory of the unity of law and State

Kelsen's theory of the unity of law and the State is well known and it is sufficient to summarise his main arguments. His is first and foremost a negative theory directed against the traditional theory and aiming at dissolving some of its aporias. According to the traditional theory, the Law and the State are two distinct entities and it is therefore necessary to analyse their relation. In particular the theory examines which is superior and Kelsen easily shows that it leads to a logical difficulty: if one views the State as the sole source of law, then it cannot be bound by law; but, on the other hand, the State can only be a source of law if it has been empowered by some legal rules and in that case it is limited by those rules. The traditional view is therefore constrained to make a bizarre construction and view the State as being at the same time bound and unbound by law or as being bound by its own law.

The traditional view also views the state as a social reality, but Kelsen argues that it is impossible to find a definition of the State as a fact separate from the law, which would be independent from legal concepts. He thus analyses several attempts at defining the State in sociological or psychological terms and shows that every such definition presupposes a legal concept (Kelsen 1928). The most important of such analyses is a comment on Max Weber's famous definition of the State as 'an entity that successfully claims a monopoly on the *legitimate* use of violence'. He stresses that this monopoly is obviously not a *de facto* monopoly, because there are many acts of violence that are not committed by the State; it is only a monopoly of the legitimate use of violence. 'Legitimate' here does not mean that the use of violence by the State is just or in accordance with certain fundamental values. It means that acts of violence are performed according to legal rules. This corresponds to what Weber called 'rational legitimacy'. On the other hand, the State is an abstraction and thus incapable of exercising violence. Only human beings can exercise violence, but the acts accomplished by some individuals are imputed to the State and this is only made possible by way of legal rules that prescribe which acts by which individuals will be imputed to the State.

Yet, while it is impossible to give a purely sociological definition of the State, it is also impossible to define it in purely legal terms. If we look at the traditional definition which incorporates three elements (a people, a territory, a public government), we can see that it is impossible to define these elements taken one by one without a tautology: a people is not an objective entity that could be defined independently of the State; the people of France cannot be defined by some common psychological, religious or ethnic characteristic, but only as the class of human beings who are subject to the French State or, in other words to the same legal order; similarly, the territory of the State can only be defined as that portion of space that is subject to a particular State or, in other words, to the legal order of that State; moreover, it is the State that decides on the content of the class of subjects that constitute the people or on the limits of the portion of space that constitutes its territory; finally, the public government is the government of the State or the highest power in the legal order and what constitutes the government of a State is also decided by the State. Thus, these three elements cannot define the State because they are themselves defined by the State and since in each case we can substitute in the *definiens* the words 'Legal order' or 'Law' for 'the State', these words are just two names for one and the same reality. 'State' is only a name given to the legal order when we want to personify it.

Finally, the traditional dualist theory is closely linked to the idea that law is a product of the will. While every rule is posited by an act of the will, every act of the will does not produce a rule. Only those acts of the will that have been accomplished according to a rule, which has also been posited by a higher act of the will and so on, produce a rule. If the highest rule has been produced by the State, one is compelled to interpret it as the expression of the will of the State, but the will is a psychological phenomenon that only exists in human beings. Thus either we construe a myth of the State as a sort of superman endowed with a capacity to will, or we only consider the wills of certain human beings as the will of the State. However, these wills form a unity not because of some common psychological feature, but only because they are all imputed to the State by some legal rules. It is the legal rules that make the State.

Understanding the State and the legal order as one and the same thing presents at least two series of enormous advantages. Kelsen stressed two of them. The first and most obvious is that it eliminates the problem of their mutual relation. The second advantage is that, by unmasking the ideology inherent in the dualist theory, it reveals that the Law and the State is nothing but an organisation of force.

The State or the law is nothing but a specific form of political power. As Kelsen famously wrote on several occasions:

> Whoever looks for an answer to the eternal question of what stands behind the positive law will never find, I fear, either an absolute metaphysical truth nor the absolute justice of natural law. Who lifts the veil and does not shut his eyes will find staring at him the hideous Gorgon head of power. (as quoted by Metall 1969, 30)[1]

The image of the Gorgon and the phrase that the law is the veil of power can be interpreted in two different ways. First it can simply mean that law is the form of which the real substance is not justice but power. But it can also be understood in the light of Weber's famous definition of the State. If the State is the entity that successfully claims a monopoly on the *legitimate* use of violence and if violence is legitimate when it is exercised as prescribed by rules, then the State is the entity

1 Kelsen had already used the image of the Gorgona in Kelsen 1927.

that exercises power by means of rules, laid down in conformity to other rules. In other words, the State only exists when there is a hierarchy of norms and the description of the structure of the law is a political analysis, because it unveils the mode in which the State operates.

This analysis shows the profound mistake in the argument made against Kelsen's monist theory according to which this theory tends to obscure the hard fact that the State is made up not only of law but also of bureaucrats, the police, guns and prisons. On the contrary, he clearly shows that the bureaucrats and the police can be understood as part of the State precisely because rules have created them, given them powers and prescribed that their actions be imputed to the State.

However, it seems that this analysis can be carried a few steps further when we realise some of the shortcomings of Kelsen's theory.

The most obvious comes from the fact that we can certainly replace the words 'the French State' with 'the French legal order', but we cannot replace 'the international legal order' by the 'international State', or 'the medieval legal order' by 'the medieval State' because there is no such thing as an international State and the feudal system of the Middle Ages was different from the government that we call the State. Kelsen is thus constrained to introduce in his definition a new element: centralisation. Some legal orders are centralised, i.e. specialised organs, such as a parliament, an executive, have a monopoly over the production of the most general norms, that are valid for the entire population, on the entire territory, and whose addressees are the subjects, whereas others, like the international legal order, are decentralised because the norms are produced, interpreted and applied by the addressees themselves. Thus, the French or the German legal order is a State but the international legal order is not.

Unfortunately, this distinction does not really help because the central organs of legal orders constitute precisely what the classic dualist theory called the 'State'. Kelsen is forced to admit that there are two different concepts of the State: the State *lato sensu*, which is identical with the legal order, and the State *stricto sensu*, which is the system of organs that have the power to produce the highest and more general norms. But then we are left with the same puzzle. If Law and State are really one and the same thing, then the question of their mutual relation is obviously nonsensical. As the State *stricto sensu* is not the same thing as the Law, we are confronted with the initial questions: is this State the source of law or is the law the basis of the State? Can the law that the State itself has created limit the State?

Thus, Kelsen seems to have failed. However this failure is a *felix culpa*. It provides what seems to be a fruitful opportunity to analyse the relation between the State *lato sensu* and the State *stricto sensu*. In a brief introduction to the second edition of his *Der soziologische und der juristische Staatsbegriff*, Kelsen remarks that the latter concept presupposes the former (Kelsen 1928).

He probably understood this as a purely logical or conceptual connection because you cannot think of the State *stricto sensu* without conceiving it as the set of those organs that produce the norms that are at the top of the entire legal order, i.e. at the top of the State *lato sensu.* Nevertheless, we can also view it as a real historical and possibly also causal connection.

3. The unity of law and State as an explanation for the historic emergence of the State

For the most part, Kelsen's general theory is clearly ahistorical in the sense that he is not interested in the development and change in the structure of the legal system and writes as if the description he gives were valid for all systems that qualify as legal systems, defined as immanent orders of constraint. This is particularly problematic as far as the State is concerned. While the very general definition of the law as an immanent order of constraint fits very different systems: national legal systems, international law, feudal law or the law of primitive societies, it does not work so well when applied to the State as identical to the law. Even if we consider only centralised legal systems, we must conclude that such centralised legal systems did not exist at all times because the power to produce the highest norms in the system can only exist when and where there is a hierarchy of norms and the existence of a hierarchy is not universal.

This is much more obvious when we consider not the State *lato sensu*, but the State *stricto sensu.* Although historians may differ as to the precise date when the process of the formation of the State *stricto sensu,* the modern State, started, most of them agree that the State *stricto sensu* did not exist in every period of History and that this process was not completed until the 17th or 18th century.

I will consider the following hypothesis: if we define the legal system and thus the State *lato sensu* not merely as an immanent order of constraint but by the formal characters identified by Kelsen, as a hierarchy that is both static and dynamic, then the emergence of the State *lato sensu,* the hierarchy of norms, can explain the emergence of the State *stricto sensu.*

We can start from the observation that in western Europe, particularly in France, the hierarchy of norms appeared gradually in the 16th and 17th centuries and that the modern State *stricto sensu* also appeared during that period. This is not enough to allow us to speak of a causal connection, but the connection becomes clearer when we view the State as a specific mode of exercising power through law, i.e. by means of a hierarchy of norms. This is already apparent in

Weber's conception of rational legitimacy, but also reflects the distribution of power that results from the hierarchy of norms.

The hierarchy of norms allows a central authority to produce general norms empowering lower authorities to produce more detailed or more local norms. Thus, the central authority can exercise power through these authorities. Power is being delegated without being lost, because the lower authorities are bound by the general rules they apply and they can also be subject to controls. At the same time, the lower authorities benefit from the hierarchy in two ways: their decisions are rationally justified because they can always claim that they only apply higher norms, yet the power they exercise is real because the higher norm may have given them some discretion in the application of the rule and because the norms that they apply has been expressed in a document that can always be subject to interpretation.

On the other hand, power is exercised by means of some intellectual constructs. Kelsen often stressed the ideological character of several legal doctrines, for instance the distinction between public and private law, that serves as an argument against a socialist economy, or the Rechtstaat that presents the State as both creator of law and bound by law. They are ideologies in the Marxist sense: they are false theories but they serve a political function, because they help justify certain political situations or actions.

However, this view of ideology overlooks an important point: these theories, as descriptions of positive law, even if they serve some political or economic interest and even if they are based on false premises or lack consistency, cannot be considered false if they reflect the actual practice of legal actors, such as lawmakers or courts. Kelsen recognised that law is not governed by logic, because a legal system is mainly dynamic. The validity of a court decision does not depend on the validity of an inference of its content from the content of a higher norm, but only on the fact that the court has been empowered to make that decision (Kelsen 1991 [1979]; Gianformaggio 1987). Therefore, a correct description of the law should be a description of the actual reasoning of the courts, something that cannot be done without mentioning the use of such concepts as the division between public and private law or the Rechtstaat.

The law thus appears to be an instrument of power to the extent that it is a system not only of norms but also of concepts that are the material for legal argumentation. The State *stricto sensu* is an instrument of power not only because it is an organisation that uses soldiers and prisons – something which many other political systems also do – but also because the violence that it exercises is claimed to be legitimate in two different ways: on the one hand, as Weber clearly showed, its decisions are logically deduced from higher norms; on the other hand, these decisions are justified by a set of arguments based on a small number of specific concepts, such as sovereignty, personality of the state, continuity of the state, or representation. Kelsen's critique of these arguments as ideological overlooks the point that they are actually necessary for the exercise of power in the political system that we call 'the state' and that we cannot describe the state without describing and analysing them.

They are truly 'constitutive' of the State. 'Constitutive' generally means 'essential' and most lawyers would agree that all states are sovereign and no entity that is not a State is fully sovereign. However, the term can also be understood in Searle's sense of a constitutive rule, one that defines the game that is being played (Searle 1969, 33). In the present case, we can see that in the modern State authorities use arguments resting on the theory of sovereignty in order to justify their decisions. This is one of the principles that define the game of the State.

The hypothesis can therefore be reformulated in the following way: the emergence of the hierarchy of norms in the 16th century has given rise to the emergence of the constitutive principles of the State *stricto sensu*, particularly the modern concept of sovereignty. This implies that this development will not be considered from the point of view of the history of political thought or from that of a history of institutions, but from the point of view of legal argumentation on the assumption that the hierarchy of norms is a specific style of legal argumentation that requires the use of a concept of sovereignty.

The word 'sovereign' has been understood in many ways. Carré de Malberg distinguishes between three concepts:

> In the original sense, the word 'sovereignty' refers to the supreme character of the State's power. In a second sense, it refers to the whole range of the powers included in the State's authority and it is therefore synonymous with that authority. Thirdly, it is used to characterise the position occupied within the State by the highest organ of the State's authority and in that sense, sovereignty is the same thing as the power of that organ. (Carre de Malberg 2003 [1967], 79)

Carré de Malberg rightly stresses that the French language is poor and contains only one word for these three concepts of sovereignty, while the German language has three words, one for each of these senses. *Souveranität* corresponds to sovereignty in the first sense, i.e. the supreme character of the State on the international as well as on the domestic level. *Staatsgewalt* is the power of the State in the second sense. *Herrschaft* is the power of domination by an organ.

However, Carré de Malberg's distinction does not give sufficient account of some sentences that we find in constitutional and political discourse. Take for example, 'the sovereign is the French people' or 'sovereignty belongs to the people' (Constitution of 1958, art. 3). Such a sentence obviously does not mean that the French people *is* the State and effectively acts on an international level, nor that it exercises a power of domination and certainly not that the people alone can really exercise a range of powers. These propositions do not refer to any reality and they are only used to justify other sentences: e.g. in French legal discourse 'sovereignty belongs to the people' was used during the Third Republic to justify 'Parliament is sovereign' or 'the law is sovereign'. It meant that Parliament exercised a sovereignty that was not its own, but that belonged to the people and was exercised *in the name of* the people, or that the law expressed the will of the sovereign people. In this context, when imputed to the people, the word 'sovereignty' is thus used in a fourth sense: it refers to the quality of a being in whose name some power, in any one of the first three senses, is exercised. Indeed, the theory of sovereignty generally implies a distinction between the essence and the exercise of sovereignty. Because of the hierarchy of norms, what is imputed to a sovereign is not only legislation or decisions in international affairs, but also every single act, presumed to have been performed in virtue of a delegation. This is why e.g. justice is rendered in European countries 'in the name of' the French, Italian or German people as it was before 'in the name of the king'. To Carré de Malberg's three concepts we must therefore add a fourth sense: the doctrine of sovereignty is a principle of imputation and a sovereign in that sense is the entity presumed to possess the essence of a sovereignty exercised by others in its name and thus to be the author, direct or indirect, of every single norm in the system.

By distinguishing between four different concepts of sovereignty, we can see that, whereas sovereignty in the Middle Ages is discernible only in its two senses, namely independence from the pope or the emperor and the quality of being an authority whose decisions cannot be legally challenged, it is only in the 16th century that it exists in all four senses.

Thus, in the Middle Ages, the adjective 'sovereign' applied not only to the king but to any supreme authority who could make a decision in the last instance, like barons or courts and had no superior.

In the late Middle Ages the word 'sovereign' had also a stronger meaning; the sovereign exercised *Herrschaft* or domination. However, nobody claimed at that time that this implied *Staatsgewalt* or the unlimited power to decide by legislation or otherwise on all human affairs and to be the sole source of law.[2]

2 Helmut Quaristsch rightly speaks of the 'Unmögligkeit "mittelalterlicher" Souveränität' (Quaritsch 1986, esp. 34).

As we have already seen, legislation was not entirely an expression of the king's will and human affairs were regulated for the most part not by the king, but by custom, the courts or canon law.

Most importantly, since there was not one single legal order, all decisions are not imputed in the last instance to the king's will. Indeed, most, as in the case of customary rules, cannot be imputed to anyone's will. As Yan Thomas wrote about the roman Republic 'there could be no sovereignty – imputation of all decisions to one single centre – in a system where the powers of every organ rested on an autonomous foundation' (Thomas 1991, 385). Thus sovereignty in the full sense of the word did not exist until the 16th century.

But from the 16th century onwards, sovereignty became much closer to Carré de Malberg's analysis and corresponded to the four concepts. First, as was already the case in the Middle Ages, the king claimed to possess a power that was supreme in the sense that there was no other power above his own, so that neither the pope nor the emperor could produce legislation on temporal matters that would be binding in the realm.

Secondly, also as in the Middle Ages, he was the highest authority within the realm. Thus, it is not surprising that the Latin expressions used for sovereignty were the same as in the medieval period, *summa potestas* by Grotius or *majestas* by Bodin. But these terms had once only conveyed the idea of a relative superiority not of an absolute supremacy and did not imply that the bearer of that *potestas* or *majestas* had the power to do anything they pleased.

What was different from the Middle Ages then was the type and the range of powers that the king could exercise. Now, the terms acquired new meanings and the king's power could extend to all human affairs.

Finally, the fourth concept of sovereignty, imputation, also appeared in the 16th century. Previously, such an idea had been inconceivable because of the plurality of legal orders, but now institutions did not rest on separate basis and all possible legal norms were finally either laid down by the king, by an authority explicitly or implicitly delegated by him or tacitly authorised. Imputation was thus simply an expression of the hierarchy of norms.

How is sovereignty related to the hierarchy of norms? In a system thus structured, every norm is produced on the basis of another norm laid down by a higher authority, who, in turn has been empowered by a norm produced by an even higher authority and so on until one reaches an ultimate authority that has not been empowered. That authority, whether the individual who produced the highest norm or an abstract entity, such as the people, the nation or the state, in whose name the highest norm is supposed to have been produced, must be presumed to possess its power in virtue of its own nature. That authority becomes the ultimate point of imputation, the sovereign in the fourth sense of the word. From the fact that it has not been empowered, it follows that this power has no limits.

Sovereignty thus appears to be a concept that one is bound to encounter whenever there is a hierarchy of norms that are thought of as produced by the will.

It can best be understood by analogy with Kelsen's theory of the *Grundnorm*. It is well known that for Kelsen the validity of every norm is based on a higher norm, which in turn is based on an even higher one and so on until one reaches the highest norm in the system. Since it is the highest there is no higher norm on which it could be based and yet if it is not valid, it cannot serve as the basis for the validity of the lower norms. This is the reason why we have to assume that the highest norm is valid on the basis of a *Grundnorm*, which states: 'the highest norm is valid'. Everybody is of course perfectly aware of the fact that there is no such norm and Kelsen does not pretend that there is. On the contrary, he calls it a fiction. But this fiction is necessary because without it we could not treat any norm as valid.

However, Kelsen's theory rests on the ontology of norms, conceived as ideal entities that are not and cannot be produced by the will, because they belong to the sphere of 'ought', whereas the will is a fact and belongs to the sphere of 'is'. The validity of a norm can only be based on another norm, not on a fact. When an authority wills a rule, that rule is not valid because of the will, but only because the higher norm that empowered that authority has prescribed that if the authority expresses the will to create a rule, then the rule is valid and binding. Thus Kelsen was able to avoid imputing the *Grundnorm* to a will.

But, the legal system in 16th-century France presupposed a very different ontology, inherited from Roman law, namely that law is an expression of the will.[3] In that case, every decision or norm in the system is valid because an authority delegated or authorised by a legislative rule has willed it, but this rule must also express the will of some entity, a will that has not been authorised by any earthly authority (Martin 2009). Just as with the Grundnorm, we must therefore assume that this entity (whether the people, the king or an aristocracy) possesses an inherent quality that enables it to produce law without having been authorised. This quality is sovereignty.

It is therefore not surprising that lawyers easily made that assumption. Sovereignty has not been invented by Bodin or by anybody else, just as Kelsen did not

3 Alchourrón and Bulygin call it the *expressive* as opposed to the *hyletic* ontology (Alchourrón and Bulygin 1979; Alchourrón and Bulygin 1981).

invent the Grundnorm, no more than he could have discovered it in positive law. He only claimed that it was an assumption or presupposition of any lawyer who purports to treat something as valid law and that he, Kelsen, just brought this hidden assumption to consciousness.

That there is a necessity because of the hierarchy of norms to use the argument of sovereignty as a principle of imputation is shown clearly in the 18th century struggles between the king and the *Parlements*. The *Parlements* claimed the right to refuse the registration of the King's ordinances when they conflicted with their interpretation of the 'fundamental laws of the realm'. The Parlements claimed to 'discover' these fundamental laws in ancient customs and practices. This was clearly an attempt to extend the hierarchy by creating a new level above the king. Since they exercised wide discretion in the interpretation of fundamental laws, this was a means to participate in the exercise of legislative power, without admitting it. However, even if this interference in the legislative power was disguised as judicial review, the idea that the king's power could be checked was difficult to reconcile with the doctrine that the king was sovereign. The most efficient way to attempt such reconciliation was to claim that since the *Parlements* were delegated by the sovereign, when they exercised a check on the king, they still acted in the name of the sovereign (Di Donato 2010).

4. The survival of the State

We can now see why this concept is central to the modern State. We do not find it in some older political systems like the feudal system and we can use it in the same way as political theory to characterise what is specific about the modern State. But it is more than that: political authorities use it as an instrument of government and they are constrained to use it because of the hierarchy of norms.

The modern State (the State *stricto sensu)* is a set of institutions exercising political power in the form of the law, i.e. by means of commands, prohibitions and authorizations rationally justified because they have been issued according to higher rules and are therefore considered to be binding. But political power in the State is also justified substantially by using specific theories, such as sovereignty, separation between office and holder or personality and continuity of the State. These two forms of justification are closely linked because of the hierarchy of norms, whereby every single legal norm in the system is directly or indirectly imputed to a unique entity, a king, the nation or the people. Since there is no higher legal norm that empowers this entity, one is constrained to assume that it acts *suo jure*, because of a special quality called sovereignty. Thus, if sovereignty is a constitutive character of the concept of a State, then it can safely be said that the State emerges from the hierarchy of norms.

This theory can be tested against modern developments. If the legal system can still be described as structured by a hierarchy of norms, then we should observe that theories of sovereignty are still alive and well.

There are, however, many contemporary theories that describe a crisis or a decline of the State. Authors who defend these theories agree on the symptoms of the crisis, which are both internal and external. They include the development within the State of powerful economic or social forces, the decline of the public services and the increasing privatisation of public corporations, the loss of control of the economy by the State and the domination of the market, the fact that, in several countries, many very important activities are regulated not by the State but by independent agencies, the developing role of minorities or the dramatic changes that they see in the legal system because of such phenomena as the growing importance of international organisations or legal pluralism. Even the rule of law is seen as a symptom of the crisis of the State, because it means that the power of the State is limited (Ferrajoli 1997). External symptoms are various manifestations of the development of international law, for example the development of international organisations, the international criminal court, WTO, the EU etc. All stress that the symptoms affect not mere peripheral characters of the State, but its very essence: sovereignty. Because of all these developments the State, it is argued, has lost its sovereignty.

Many of these theories are clearly normative, some authors regret the decline of the sovereign state, while others see it as a happy development. We should, however, evaluate them as descriptions. Is it true that such a decline has taken place? It is certainly true if sovereignty is a character and a measure of the actual might of the State (Troper 2010).

But theories of sovereignty from the 16th to the 20th century ds not pretend to describe the actual or effective organisation of power, but only the type of argumentation that characterises the State. This answer should come as no surprise. When we speak of States in international law and when we describe them as sovereign, we call 'State' any entity, China or the United States as well as Monaco or Andorra, that fits the definition, regardless of their size, strength or actual capacity to act independently.

The same is true of the hierarchy of norms in the 16th and 17th centuries. The King may face resistance from other institutions. He might even fail completely to impose his will. The fact remains that he claims that courts have been empowered by him, that they are his courts, that they should apply his laws, that he can overrule their decisions or that marriages are to be celebrated according to his rules. The hierarchy of norms is a type of argument that one makes about the reason why a rule is valid or binding and these arguments are being used by various authorities. They can be more or less successful but the simple fact that they are being used is evidence for the existence of a legal system. Similarly, the existence of a hierarchy of norms leads to the argument that there is a sovereign, whether the claim is made by the sovereign himself or by another authority. The argument may be thought persuasive or not. The fact remains that it is actually being made, unlike what happened in previous political systems, where different kind of arguments drawn from canon law, custom or feudal relations were used by those who wished to impose their authority. The power that is being exercised by means of arguments that there is a hierarchy of norms and a sovereign can thus be identified as a State.

And the argument is still being made today. States claim to be sovereign in international relations. Indeed, even submitting to international law is regarded as a sign of sovereignty. They will not accept any other authority within and they claim to have absolute power to regulate every single domain of human affairs, even if they do not exercise that right. Every authority justifies its actions as the direct or indirect expression of the will of the sovereign people.

We can thus conclude that the argument from sovereignty in the four different meanings of the term is still the only argument that can be used in a world which from other points of view has undergone such dramatic changes.

References

Alchourrón, Carlos E., and Bulygin, Eugenio. 1979. *Sobre la Existencia de las Normas Juridicas*. Valencia-Venezuela: Universidad de Carabobo.

Alchourrón, Carlos E., and Bulygin, Eugenio. 1981. The Expressive Conception of Norms. In *New Studies in Deontic Logic*, edited by Risto Hilpinen. Dordrecht: Reidel.

Carré de Malberg, Raymond. 2003 [1920]. *Contribution à la théorie générale de l'Etat; spécialement d'après les données fournies par le droit constitutionnel français*. Paris: Dalloz.

Di Donato, Francesco. 2010. *La rinascita dello Stato – Dal conflitto magistratura-politica alla civilizzazione istituzionale europea*. Bologne: Il Mulino.

Ferrajoli, Luigi. 1997. *La sovranità nel mondo moderno*. Roma-Bari: Laterza.

Gianformaggio, Letizia. *In difesa del sillogismo pratico ovvero alcuni argomenti kelseniani alla prova*. Milano: Giuffrè.

Kelsen, Hans. 1927. Diskussionsbeitrag. *Veröffentlichungen der Vereinigung der Deutschen Staatsrechtslehrer* 3: 53–55.

Kelsen, Hans. 1928. *Der soziologische und der juristische Staatsbegriff. Kritische Untersuchungen des Verhältnisses von Staat und Recht*. 2nd edition. Tübingen: Scientia Verlag.

Kelsen Hans. 1991 [1979]. *General theory of norms*. Translated by Michael Hartney. Oxford: Clarendon.

Martin, Frédéric F. 2009. Jean Bodin et les formes. In *Normes et normativité Études d›histoire du droit rassemblées en l›honneur d›Albert Rigaudière*, edited by Pierre Bonin, Florent Garnier, Corinne Leveleux-Teixeira and Anne Rousselet-Pimont. Paris: Economica.

Metall, Rudolf. 1969. *Hans Kelsen. Sein Leben und Werk*. Vienna: Verlag Franz Deuticke.

Searle, John R. 1969. *Speech Acts: An Essay in the Philosophy of Language*. Cambridge: Cambridge University Press.

Quaritsch, Helmut. 1986 *Souveränität: Entstehung und Entwickung des Begriffs in Frankreich und Deutschland von 13 Jh. bis 1806*. Berlin: Duncker & Humblot.

Thomas, Yan. 1991. L'institution de la majesté. *Revue de Synthèse* 3–4: 331–386.

Troper, Michel. 2010. The survival of sovereignty. In *Sovereignty in Fragments. The Past, Present, and Future of a Contested Concept*, edited by Hent Kalmo and Quentin Skinner, 132–150. Cambridge: Cambridge University Press.

Part II
Methodological Approaches

Monika Zalewska

Two Approaches to the Methodology of Legal Theory: Hans Kelsen and Jerzy Wróblewski

1. Introduction

For decades in every discipline which can be called scientific the problem of demarcation, i.e. distinguishing Science from pseudoscience, has been considered as one of the most important in governing the shape of future theory. Not only does it determine the correctness of a theory with regard to both its theoretical aspect and its meritorical content, it also provides the answer to some practical issues (for example, in medicine, concerning expert testimonies or in science education). For centuries, great thinkers have built the criteria first for *episteme* and then for a theory of Science itself. In the 19th century, methodology was regarded as the most important factor for solving the demarcation problem. Hence, it is no surprise that discussions about methodology are very well developed and engage most participants of the scientific world at one point or another. After Larry Laudan published *The Demise of the Demarcation Problem* in 1983 in which he denies that it is possible to find a solution to the problem of demarcation, interest in the topic declined for many years. Recently, it seems that, thanks to such thinkers as Mahner (2013) and Pigliucci (2013), interest in the demarcation problem has been revitalised (Hansson 2014). These remarks also concern jurisprudence. The demarcation problem in jurisprudence has been reformulated as that which refers to the question of how to distinguish law from morality (Leiter 2010, 161). Although it was perceived as one of the most essential issues in jurisprudence for many years, discussed by such important thinkers as Hans Kelsen, Herbert L.A. Hart and Joseph Raz, its present day necessity is strongly questioned, especially by Leiter (2010), who takes inspiration directly from Laudan. It is not the aim of this paper to discuss the correctness of Leiter's argument. At this point, considering the new trend in Philosophy mentioned above, it appears too soon to determine whether his point of view will remain dominant. Since jurisprudence takes inspiration from Philosophy, albeit with a slight delay, it seems rational to hold a traditional position and consider the demarcation problem in jurisprudence as central, from both the theoretical and the practical points of view.

Undoubtedly, it is much easier to define the status of empirical science, in which objects are observable. However, even in empirical science, the demarcation problem was found to be not an obvious one, particularly since Laudan's critique of the efficiency of such criteria (Laudan 1983). The situation is much more complicated with the Humanities and some parts of Social Science, which are often not regarded as scientific disciplines as they deal with abstract, non-observable objects. This problem also exists with legal theory. In this paper, I will focus on some necessary assumptions for my further arguments. For the sake of argument, Science will be treated in the broad sense, which will allow the Humanities and Social Science to be regarded, under certain methodological conditions, as two scientific disciplines. The aim of the article is to present Kelsen's and Wróblewski's approaches to the methodology of legal science and then to analyse which methodological conditions serve this purpose best.

As Wróblewski's theory, when compared with the Kelsenian approach, seems to be in some parts a meta-theory and appears to act as a suitable framework for the pure theory of law, the two theories will be analysed in the conceptual rather than chronological order. The first section will discuss Wróblewski's concept of methodology: the one-level and multilevel models of legal science. Next, Hans Kelsen's methodology in his Pure Theory of Law will be described with an emphasis on the 'Is' and 'Ought' dimensions in the context of legal science. The final paragraph will contrast those theories and describe their advantages and disadvantages.

With such an approach, the main aim is to determine what conditions should be fulfilled in order to regard legal theory as scientific, according to these two thinkers. In order to address this critically important point, it is necessary to first determine how legal science should be understood and for the purposes of this article it is most appropriate to base this analysis on Wróblewski's understanding of Science.

2. Jerzy Wróblewski's view on legal methodology

Wróblewski was one of the most important and influential figures in Polish legal theory and he took part in the most important discussions in this field with the most prominent thinkers of his time. His concepts are well known to everyone who studied law in Poland. He was also one of the noblest commentators on Kelsen in Poland and even Kelsen himself referred to his writings: in *Allgemeine Theorie der Normen,* he analyses Wróblewski's concept of the meaning of the legal norm (see Kelsen 1979, 221). The interpretation of legal theory was not the only interest which Wróblewski and Kelsen shared. One very important issue can be distinguished from the many other topics they addressed, such as legal norms: the conditions for the legal science. Wróblewski begins by stating four questions which should be answered concerning the problem of 'legal science'. 1) What do we mean by the 'scientific character' of some statements? 2) What do we mean by 'jurisprudence'? 3) What is the relationship between Science and jurisprudence? 4) How should jurisprudence be constructed if it is to be called scientific? (1965, 102) These questions clearly presuppose a tight connection between appropriate methodology and Science. Concerning the first question, Wróblewski writes that two main approaches to legal science are possible: a normative one and a descriptive one. While the normative approach recommends how legal science should be constructed, the descriptive one shows how legal science is constructed (ibid., 102–103). Wróblewski notes that the normative approach frequently prevails over the descriptive one, resulting in the elimination of any other methodological concepts, as well as any theories based on them. According to this approach, an author who constructs a legal theory, first constructs some methodological assumptions, and then denies the correctness of any theories that do not conform with these criteria. This observation conforms to Laudan's point of view that demarcation criteria serve as '*machines du guerre*' in scientific discourse (Laudan 1983, 119). It can be noted here that this is how Kelsen builds his Pure Theory of Law. In contrast, Wróblewski takes both normative and descriptive approaches, but does so in a different order: he first describes possible approaches to methodology before presenting the one he believes to be most appropriate.

In another article, Wróblewski deals very precisely with the problem of verification in legal science (1980, 7–25). First he distinguishes between verification and justification, explaining that verification is a part of justification *sensu largo.* While justification *sensu largo* explains the reasons behind a particular form of behaviour or statement, or provides arguments which justify such statements or behaviour (see ibid., 8), verification is the procedure, or the result of such, gained from determining whether proposition A in language P is true or false (see ibid.). Hence, for a statement to be verified, the following must be established: 1) the meaning of 'true' and 'false' and 2) the procedures allowing statement A to be determined as true or false. 'True' and 'false' qualities depend on the ontology and epistemology accepted in language P and, in the context of verification in legal science, will depend on a specific kind of existence. Wróblewski mentions three types of such existence: a) materialistic, where the proposition in language P is true when it conforms with materialistic ontology; b) idealistic, where proposition in language P is true when it conforms with the non-materialistic ideal world of values and obligations; c) cultural, where the proposition is valid in language P, when it conforms with the cultural reality defined by Wróblewski as a world of artefacts with ascribed specific meaning or value (ibid., 9).

The procedures mentioned in point 2) are dependent on these factors, and three types of such procedure can be distinguished: empirical procedures, non-empirical procedures based on accepted epistemology and cultural procedures based on interpretation (see ibid., 10). Based on this criterion, Kelsen's Pure Theory of Law appears to fall within the category of non-empirical verification: the Is/Ought dichotomy, as Kelsen's basic methodological assumption which requires law to be examined only in the 'Ought world', rules out the possibility of empirical and cultural verification.[1] What is more, Kelsen subsidies his theory with a Neokantian epistemology and transcendental argument, which clarifies why legal science is possible only on his own terms. This transcendental argument has been reconstructed by Stanley L. Paulson. First, Kelsen treats legal science as a given fact, and he posits that the category of basic norm, the category of imputation (the equivalent of causality in the Ought world), or the category of Ought are presupposed as necessary components of legal cognition. Hence, he concludes that such categories are constitutive aspects of legal science (see Paulson 2000, 1775–1779). Regarding the second question on the nature of jurisprudence, Wróblewski discusses the term 'jurisprudence'[2] (*prawoznawstwo*) both in terms of legal theory (*teoria prawa,* in German: *Rechtstheorie)* and what Wróblewski terms *legal dogmatics* (*dogmatyki prawnicze,* in German: *Rechtsdogmatik*) (1965, 102). As Kelsen's Pure Theory of Law only refers to the theory of law itself, I will also limit my analysis of Wróblewski's thoughts to this extent.

The next step, which also answers questions three and four regarding the relationship of jurisprudence with science and its scientific construction, concerns the most famous element of Wróblewski's methodological theory. He divides theories of law into one-level and multilevel models of legal science (see ibid., 107). While the starting point of the one-level model is the assumption that law is a phenomenon of a certain type, and that methods should conform with that type of phenomenon, multidimensional theories assume several points of view on law and that methods can vary depending on which aspect of law is examined. The 'Scientific' approach is bound with the correct application of a method rather than with the application of a certain method itself (see ibid., 108). Wróblewski emphasises

1 Wróblewski attributed Kelsen's theory to the cultural verification arguing that language is a cultural phenomenon (see Wróblewski 1980, 16). However, such an argument seems to be against Kelsen's implicit statement (see Kelsen 1911, 8).

2 Wróblewski uses term '*prawoznawstwo*' which does not have corresponding translation in English. As it is treated as synonym of '*jurysprudencja*' it seems that the most appropriate term in English is Jurisprudence, however the meaning of this term is not the same as commonly used.

three key disadvantages of multilevel models of legal science (1981, 75–76): firstly, it is against the positivistic, and also the normative, paradigm which attempts to limit methodology to only one method, that is the examination of a legal text. Although Wróblewski adds that this method is against the reduction of the legal phenomenon to the norm, he does not deny that this method is a fundamental part of legal science. A second disadvantage concerns its reduction to social or psychological facts, or both, and the empirical methods of Science. Wróblewski observes that such phenomena are very important since they are bound with the origin of law, but he also emphasises that it is impossible to establish what law lacks, considering its normative character. A final disadvantage is that it also rules out concepts attributed to emotive concepts of axiological irrationalism, since according to Wróblewski, absolute values may not be the subject of legal science. However, the rational justification of values, and hence the evaluation of law, is possible.

Wróblewski argues that the multilevel group of theories is heterogeneous and provides several examples of how such a combination might appear. Some theories could be attributed to the cultural concept of law if they combine facts and values altogether, while others might just consider the normative, factual, axiological or logical aspects of law, among others. Finally, this group also includes theories which treat law as a phenomenon composed of norms, and facts bound with norms, or ones which treat norms as social facts (see Wróblewski 1980, 17)

Both models, one-level and multilevel, can be analysed from ontological and methodological points of view (see Wróblewski 1965, 109) From a descriptive aspect, in one-level models, law can be regarded ontologically as a norm, as a social fact, as a legal experience, or in some cases, as a value. From the methodological point of view, law can be regarded, and examined, in terms of its logical-semiotic, sociological, psychological, and sometimes axiological, dimensions. Wróblewski additionally points out that although these are the main dimensions, and thus the most obvious ones, others are not excluded[3]. According to Wróblewski, only the multilevel approach may facilitate a profound understanding of the complexity of legal phenomena, provided that the autonomy of jurisprudence, understood as remaining distinct from other disciplines of Science, is not compromised (see Opałek and Wróblewski 1969, 329). This approach he terms the *integration of*

---

3 Wróblewski points out that law might be also examined from the cybernetic point of view, but he does not develop his thought, what he means by it, and what kind of phenomenon a norm would be (see 1965, 110). Nowadays it is argued that we could also speak about economical, and evolutionary level (see Stelmach and Brożek 2006, 126–158).

legal sciences, within which can be defined 'internal' and 'external' characters (see Wróblewski 1965, 112): Internal integration postulates to break with the isolation of legal disciplines from others and interdisciplinary research, while external integration postulates the use of various methodological tools in legal science which are also characteristic of disciplines of a non-legal character (see Wróblewski 1981, 75). As legal science is placed somewhere between other scientific disciplines, such as Psychology, Sociology, Politology, Economy and Semiotics, to name the most important, it is impossible to speak about law in scientific terms without using the tools of these other disciplines (see Nowaka and Wronkowska 1968, 107)

An interesting reconstruction of the importance of integrating legal science is suggested by Jakub Łakomy (2011, 61–62), who uses the metaphor of a hotel where all apartments are strictly separated and the windows are oriented in the same direction. It is difficult for the guests to communicate since they speak different languages, the walls are thick and all doors are closed. The only means of communication is to go to their balconies, which due to being on different floors afford different perspectives on the surrounding area, and use tools such as binoculars. The guests try to observe a very interesting, far-away object, which they are unable to identify due to its lack of detail and the fact it can only be seen in two dimensions. What is more, some elements of the object are hidden behind other elements of the surroundings. Such a metaphorical hotel does not conform with the concept of integrating legal science. To integrate, all doors must be removed and the walls knocked down, a common language should be established followed by a plan of studies involving all participants. Łakomy claims that only this form of cooperation would allow for full identification of the examined object (ibid., 62).

Unfortunately, this metaphor concerns the empirical rather than the ideal or cultural world. This example might work in empirical disciplines, it might well describe the examination of empirical objects, but law, as an object of legal science, whose character is primarily normative, not empirical, might not suit this metaphor for reasons which will be further discussed in section three. At this point it is worth pointing out that while a metaphor highlights some aspects of phenomena, it also hides what is inconvenient for argumentation (see Johnson and Lakoff 1980, 9). For example, regarding this metaphor, it could be asked who should be invited to the hotel. As it will be demonstrated below, the answer with the multilevel approach is not obvious.

3. Hans Kelsen's view on the methodology of legal theory

The Pure Theory of Law can be interpreted in many different ways. The most obvious and popular interpretation comes down to the vision of the structure of law. Although this part of Kelsen's theory is very important, without a doubt, it is merely a result of his epistemological and methodological assumptions, implying that the key interpretations of the Pure Theory of Law are epistemological and methodological. However, while the epistemological interpretation has its roots in Neokantian doctrine and is strictly bound to Philosophy, specifically Epistemology, the methodological interpretation is a query for legal science. Kelsen was convinced that not only is reflection on methodology crucial for legal science, but also that methodological syncretism is an unsuitable method of creating something of value from the scientific point of view (1911, 3–4).

The methodological dimension is arguably one of the most important in the Pure Theory of Law, since it works as a filter for further interpretations. Kelsen's main goal was to build a legal science, and he believed the starting point of this project to be the construction of an appropriate methodology (ibid., 3). This insight affords the reader a more profound understanding of his vision of law, and highlights which elements of this vision are crucial and which are not. It also facilitates a better understanding of why Kelsen made a dramatic shift in his last phase of publishing, his so-called sceptical phase, (see Paulson 1999, 351) and why, in his last book, he chose to neglect his famous Pure Theory of Law to a great extent. However, if his work is regarded as a single project intended to understand the condition of legal science, then some of Kelsen's shifts are no longer a mystery: it could be argued that he was not afraid to end a very successful project after realising this project failed to fulfil his scientific expectations.

Before we move forward to the issue of legal science, we should ask the essential question: what are the basic methodological assumptions of Kelsen's Pure Theory of Law? As Paulson points out (1992, 313–319) Kelsen works with two main theses[4]: the separability thesis, concerning the separation of law and morality, and the normative thesis, concerning the separation of Is and Ought. When Kelsen presented this idea, it was a new quality. Previously, legal philosophy was believed to contain a strict unconquerable dichotomy between natural law doctrines and legal positivism. Natural law doctrines stated that a necessary connection is present between law and morality, while legal positivists believed that no such necessary connection exists. Kelsen postulated that there are not two, but four theses, which creates one more option, normativism, for legal theories: the two additional theses being normative and reductive. While the reductive thesis states that law is a fact

4 Although Kelsen did not use this parlance (separability and normative thesis), as S.L. Paulson in 1992 demonstrated, they serve very well to reconstruct Kelsen's version of normativism.

and as such should be examined, the normative thesis posits a separation of the Is and Ought spheres, and that law belongs to the Ought sphere. To sum up, in the same way as legal positivists, Kelsen claimed that no necessary connection exists between law and morality, but he neglected the positivistic thesis that law is a fact.

The two theses mentioned above are his most important methodological assumptions and are fundamental for his whole theory. Kelsen believed that they are the keys to the construction of an autonomous legal science, distinct from other scientific disciplines. How is that possible? When Kelsen rejected the necessary connection between law and morality, he did so for the sake of objectivity, claiming that otherwise it would not be a science but an ideology, understood in a narrow sense as the 'nonobjective presentation of the subject influenced by subjective value judgments and glorifying or disfiguring the subject of cognition' (1960, 105). Kelsen creates a clear dichotomy of Science versus ideology (*sensu stricto*), with Science being a desirable property of a legal theory and ideology being worthless. According to him, the necessary link between law and morality must lead to ideology, because the content of morality is undefined, and law is thus glorified or disfigured from the point of view of such subjective values (see ibid., 105–106). There is no single specific criterion which can be used to clearly distinguish the moral from the immoral. Kelsen is a relativist, and as such, believes that no single universal morality exists. If this is the case, every moral doctrine has an ideological character and cannot be scientific. Hence, from a scientific point of view, law can have any content, as long as this content is of a normative character or rather, is considered in the Ought sphere. This is the second methodological assumption: the Is/Ought dichotomy.

What distinguishes Kelsen's Pure Theory of Law from other positivistic theories of that time is the normative thesis. In recalling Hume's guillotine and Moore's naturalistic fallacy, Kelsen claims that an abyss is present between Is and Ought: they are two worlds with no points in common (1911, VI). He concludes that law, which obviously belongs to the Ought sphere, cannot be scientifically described by recalling facts (1960, 76). Obviously law is dependent on facts, as it is created and applied by concrete people. What Kelsen meant is that the normative sphere can be compared with the reflection from a mirror. All categories are supposed to have their specific, normative meaning in the Ought sphere, even though in the Is sphere they would be understood otherwise (such as category of person). Another example is *desuetudo*, which Kelsen defines as a 'negative legal effect of custom' (1945, 119). Clearly *desuetudo* is a result of facts strictly bound with efficiency. Although the Is/Ought dichotomy appears to be broken in this case, it must be remembered that the will of an organ which will not impose a sanction is a necessary condition for *desuetude*. Thus, this factual will of organs in the world of Ought has a normative character and can be identified by central imputation with the will of the state. At this point, there is an 'abyss' mentioned by Kelsen between factual and normative will. To conclude, Kelsen does not deny that facts influence law. He rather makes an effort to describe law only in normative terms (in the world of Ought) and claims that only such a description has a scientific character. *Desuetudo* is not necessarily an argument against the Is/Ought dichotomy, but rather it provokes questions about the place of custom, also in *desuetudo* form, in a legal system.[5]

Does the use of the normative thesis help Kelsen construct a legal science? Apart from gaining a deep philosophical foundation rooted in the claim of naturalistic fallacy, which is followed by an extensive metaethical discussion, Kelsen's approach has two key benefits. First, he avoids the danger of his theory becoming an ideology. Secondly, he provides very strict criteria for the object of legal science. There is no doubt that in examining law, it is necessary to focus only on strictly normative phenomena, which are basically norms. By making a few further epistemological steps, Kelsen elaborates a method to distinguish legal norms from others based on the use of basic norms and imputation (1960, 104). This is a huge advantage of his theory: the object of legal science, the legal norm, is made explicitly clear (ibid., 70). In empirical science, the question of the object of examination is very often trivial: be it a human being, an animal or a particle, it is not necessary to spend too much time deliberating what a human or animal or particle is. As the definition of law presents a considerable problem for legal science, an obvious starting point for an empirical science is in fact the first obstacle to forming a legal science. Fortunately, Kelsen provides a very clear and elegant answer to that question, by equating law with legal norms. I will deal further with this argument in the Conclusion.

The pure theory of law is not the only dimension which Kelsen addressed. He also showed great interest in, among others, the theory of democracy, constitutionalism and even ethnology. Does it mean that this thought, either ideological or referring to facts, is not scientific in Kelsen's terms? Although the theory of democracy and constitutionalism entail many elements of pure theory of law, they also refer to the content of law. 'Society and nature' is a book which discusses evolution from retribution to causality principle. It is not bound strictly with law, but the context of this book allows a better understanding of the principle of imputation in law, which corresponds with that of retribution. It seems that all the topics mentioned above are either bound with some kind of ideology, particularly the texts concerning democracy, or they refer to facts. It may be the case for Kelsen that while 'Society

5 Insightful analysis of this problem can be found in Amado 2005, 96–105.

and Nature' is just a scientific book, albeit one that does not belong to the sphere of legal science, his texts about democracy and constitution lie within the scope of legal science, as long as they conform to the methodological rules of normativism (Jestaed and Lepsius 2006, XVIII). Fortunately it is easy to distinguish texts which fulfil this condition, such as *Staatsform und Weltanschauung*, from the others with a more ideological character. Kelsen is quite clear about that.

The other question is whether such disciplines as the legal sociology of Psychology can be accounted as Science. According to Kelsen although they clearly do not have a legal-scientific character, they can have a scientific character (Kelsen 1960, 1). By distinguishing the explicative (based on causality) and normative (based on imputation) disciplines of Science (ibid., 76), he did not forbid other methods of examining law, he just denied such theories the status of a 'legal science'. This type of science would be explicative and concern reality, while legal science concerns the ideal world of Ought (see Kelsen 1911, VIII–IX). In addition, Kelsen explains the meaning of 'normative science', as the term might be misleading and confused with practical philosophy as opposed to theoretical philosophy. He distinguishes between the will and the form of thought (*Denkform*). While practical theory is based on the will of the subject (e.g. 'you shall not steal!'), normative science concerns forms of thought, which are of normative character. Such science is obviously theoretical (see ibid.). To summarise, Kelsen's strict criteria concern legal science, whose task is to describe law itself without any other, sociological or psychological, context. However, this does not mean that law cannot be examined by any other method; Such an examination would just not have the status of legal science (1960, 1).

4. Comparison

As it was mentioned before, from a methodological point of view, Hans Kelsen's Pure Theory of Law is normative. Kelsen argues at great length (for example in *Hauptprobleme der Staatsrechtslehre*) why other theories are incorrect and are clearly a wrong methodological choice. Although someone could argue that his method is more complex than just a simple division between Is and Ought, such argumentation clearly places Kelsen's Pure Theory of Law in the group of one-level theories. Even if Kelsen used more than one method in his research, it is obvious that, by using Wróblewski's terminology in a logical-semiotic sense, he treated the norm as a normative phenomenon, in the world of Ought, separated from facts. His theory is one-level not because he bases it only one method, but because he refuses to treat a norm in any other way than as a normative phenomenon, making the central, most important, method normative. Hence, Kelsen's theory must be one-dimensional, as according to Kelsen, a norm is not a social fact, nor a social experience, nor a value, at least not when it is regarded in the context of legal science.

It can be concluded that Kelsen and Wróblewski disagree on which approach should be applied. Wróblewski clearly disagrees when Kelsen rules out all non-normative methods as being not scientific when applied to law: Wróblewski argues that all propositions of jurisprudence are justified and as such cannot be excluded as unscientific (1980, 13). Wróblewski, noticed that logico-semiotic approach and thus normativity of law must be prior to the others and perceived Kelsen's theory (from the methodological point of view) rather as incomplete than false. This incongruity highlights a key difference between the two authors. Which methodological approach is better suited for scientific purposes? In both cases, something is gained and something lost. As mentioned earlier, the Pure Theory of Law presents a very clear definition of the nature of law. If something has a normative character and certain special properties, such as basic norm imputation and a system of empowerments, then it is the law. For science, the primary step, and an essential one, is to define the object of examination: for our investigation of flies to be worth anything, we must examine flies rather than spiders.

But Kelsen's approach also has disadvantages. If such strict boundaries are imposed, it might happen that some very important elements of law might lie outside them: for example, in Kelsen's case, the problem of efficiency of law, which is strictly bound with facts and the sphere of Is.[6] No such risk exists in Wróblewski's approach, provided that the method is applied in an appropriate way. However, while his multidimensional approach guarantees that every aspect of law will be considered and examined, the problem arises of the choice of relevant criteria and the formulation of an acceptable justification of what would or would not be considered a legal phenomenon. With this approach, there are no strict boundaries, only individual elements, each of which demands a single and broad justification for why it was either accepted or rejected; with regard to the hotel analogy, we can say that we don't know which scientists should be invited or which tool should be applied to examine the object – if we invite everyone and apply every tool then we won't create a science of law, but a chaotic account of law. Every such justification will be disputable and called into question, which would prevent such a theory from ever becoming stable. Of course, although we acknowledge the existence of a common sense premise, and that according to Quine, Science is contiguous to common sense, we still need to accommodate the fact that firstly Science needs

6 My thesis is strongly supported by Polish doctrine where the argument of arbitrary criteria in integration of legal science is presented (see e.g. Bator 2004, 8–9).

to explain common sense, which is sometimes misleading, for example the belief that the sun orbits the Earth, and secondly, it is sometimes difficult to distinguish between common sense and a deeply-held belief (Sankey 2010, 11–12).

Although the methodological aspect is very important here, this hypothetical discussion between Kelsen and Wróblewski has one more important issue: the definition of *legal science*, and whether it should be interpreted in a broad sense, as Wróblewski intends, or in a narrow one, as Kelsen does. The accepted methodology will specify the definition which will be chosen, and as it was mentioned before, both approaches have advantages and disadvantages.

5. Conclusion

To sum up, Kelsen claims that although it is possible to examine law in psychological or sociological terms, for example, it cannot be termed legal science. Legal science concerns law itself: pure law, without any additions. Additions can make a very interesting combination but say nothing about the substance of law. In this context, Kelsen's theory appears to be deeply philosophical, strictly bound with ontological traditions. It seems that the main difference between Kelsen and Wróblewski is that what Kelsen would see as a group of theories about law, such as legal science, sociology of law or psychology of law, Wróblewski saw as one integrated theory.

An important dilemma lies at the heart of the construction of any legal theory which tends to be scientific. It can be built in a very narrow framework, which will allow a certain aspect of law to be examined in a highly detailed and consistent way but will preclude the analysis of some important features of law. Alternatively, a battery of methods can be applied to generate a complete and comprehensive picture of law, but one whose consistency is put at risk when the legal character of some examined elements may be questioned and others may be considered as not having this character. Ultimately, the choice of method may well depend on the aim of each individual study, and it is impossible to clearly nominate the best one for all occasions.

References

Amado, Juan A. G. 2005. Grundnorm und Gewohnheitnorm bei Kelsen. In *Hans Kelsen als Staatrechtslehrer und Rechtsphilosoph*, edited by S. L. Paulson and M. Stolleis, 96–105. Tübingen: Mohr Siebeck.

Bator, Andrzej. 2004. *Kompetencja w prawie i prawoznawstwie* [*Competence in Law and Jurisprudence*]. Wroclaw: Wydawnictwo Uniwersytetu Wrocławskiego.

Brożek, Bartosz, and Stelmach, Jerzy. 2006. *Metody prawnicze* [*Legal Methods*]. Krakow: Wolters Kluwer Polska.

Hansson, Sven Ove. 2014. *Science and Pseudo-Science*. In *The Stanford Encyclopedia of Philosophy* (Spring 2014 Edition), URL = http://plato.stanford.edu/archives/spr2014/entries/pseudo-science/, edited by Edward N. Zalta.

Jaestaed, Matthias, Lepsius, Otto. 2006. Der Rechts- und Demokratietheoretiker Hans Kelsen – Eine Einführung. In *Verteidigung der Demokratie Abgandlungen zur Demokratietheorie*, edited by Matthias Jaestaed and Otto Lepsius. Tübingen: Mohr Siebeck.

Johnson, Mark, and Lakoff, George. 1980. *Metaphors we live by*. London: The University Of Chicago press.

Kelsen, Hans. 1979. *Allgemeine Theorie der Normen*. Vienna: Manzsche Verlags- und Universitätsbuchhandlung.

Kelsen, Hans 1945. *General Theory of Law and State*. New Jersey: The Lawbook Exchange Ltd Union.

Kelsen, Hans. [1911] 1960. *Hauptprobleme der Staatsrechtslehre*. Darmstadt: Scientia Aalen.

Kelsen, Hans. [1960] 2002. *Pure Theory of Law*. New Jersey: The Lawbook Exchange Ltd Union.

Laudan, Larry. 1983. The Demise of the Demarcation Problem. In *Physics, Philosophy and Psychoanalysis. Essays in Honor of Adolf Grünbau*, edited by Robert S. Cohen and Larry Laudan, 111–127. Dordrecht: Reidel.

Leiter, Brian 2013. The Demarcation Problem in Jurisprudence. In *Neutrality and Theory of Law*, edited by Jordi F. Beltran, Jose J. Moreso and Diego M. Papayannis, 161–174. Dordrecht: Springer.

Łakomy, Jakub. 2011. Pojęcie integracji zewnętrznej nauk prawnych [The meaning of external integration of legal science]. In *Wpływ teorii Jerzego Wróblewskiego na współczesne prawoznawstwo*, edited by Tomasz Bekrycht and Marek Zirk-Sadowski. Warsaw: C. H. Beck.

Mahner, Martin 2007. Demarcating Science from Non-Science. In *Handbook of the Philosophy of Science: General Philosophy of Science – Focal Issues*, edited by Theo Kuipers, 515–575. Amsterdam: Elsevier.

Nowak, Leszek, and Wronkowska, Sławomira. 1968. Zagadnienia integracji nauk prawnych w polskiej literaturze teoretyczno-prawnej [Problem of Integration of Legal Science in Polish Legal-Theoretical Literature]. *Studia Metodologiczne* 5: 107–113.

Opałek, Kazimierz, Wróblewski, Jerzy. 1969. *Zagadnienia z teorii prawa* [*Problems of Legal Theory*]. Warszawa: Państwowe Wydawn. Naukowe.

Paulson, Stanley, L. 2000. On Transcendental Arguments, Their Recasting in Terms of Belief and the Ensuing Transformation of Kelsen's Pure Theory of Law. *Notre Dame Law Review* 75: 1775–1795.

Paulson, Stanley L. 1999. Arriving at a Defensible Periodisation of Hans Kelsen's Legal Theory. *Oxford Journal of Legal Studies* 19: 351–364.

Paulson, Stanley L. 1992. The Neokantian Dimension of Kelsen's Pure Theory of Law. *Oxford Journal of Legal Studies* 12: 311–332.

Pigliucci, Massimo. 2013. The demarcation problem. A (belated) response to Laudan. In *Philosophy of Pseudoscience. Reconsidering the demarcation problem*, edited by Massimo Pigliucci and Maarten Boudry, 9–28. Chicago: Chicago University Press.

Sankey, Howard. 2010. Science, Common Sense and Reality. *Discusiones Filosóficas* 11: 41–58.

Wróblewski, Jerzy. 1981. Badania prawnoempiryczne a metodologia prawoznawstwa [The Empirical Examination and Methodology of Jurisprudence]. *Problemy Rad Narodowych* 50: 73–90.

Wróblewski, Jerzy. 1965. O naukowości prawoznawstwa [On the Scientific Character of Jurisprudence]. *Państwo i Prawo* 8/9: 102–203.

Wróblewski, Jerzy. 1980. Weryfikacja i uzasadnienie w naukach prawnych [Verification and Justification in Legal Science]. *Studia Prawno-Ekonomiczne* XXIV: 7–26.

Silvia Salardi

The Concept of 'Human Nature': An Attempt to Approach Law from an Essentialist Perspective?

1. Introduction

Human Nature is a fascinating concept with a long history. Since ancient times, important philosophical attempts have been made to identify all of the determinants, features, and components of a biological, emotional, psychological, social, and cultural kind that potentially make up a holistic identity: *The Human Nature* (H.N.) The majority of these approaches to H.N. had their roots in the essentialist tradition. To put it succinctly, according to this perspective things are what they are because that is their nature, essence, or definition (see Fuchs 2001). To deal with H.N. from this essentialist point of view means to search for an all-embracing, holistic definition of the concept. But essentialist efforts to cover an all-embracing definition of H.N. are not just a thing of the past.

In current times, general interest in the topic of H.N. has increased because of peculiar challenges facing European societies. In this paper, I will take into account two main challenges. The first one is deeply connected with advances in science, particularly in genetics. Indeed, since it has become possible to 'read the book of life' (see Kay 2000), new strategies have been developed to ground, once and for all, H.N. on our genome, in particular considering genes as the essential determinants of human identity. As a matter of fact, developments in genetics, especially in their early stages (see Rutter et al. 2006), were interpreted according to a reductionist approach, termed genetic essentialism, or genetic determinism (see Salardi 2010). This represents a revised version of *strict* determinism. Nelkin and Lindee put the definition of genetic essentialism in a very effective way: 'Genetic essentialism reduces the self to a molecular entity, equating human beings, in all their social, historical, and moral complexity, with their genes' (see Nelkin and Lendee 1995, 2). This conception has made its way into the public and the institutional perception of genetic advances has contributed to influencing the way genetics is generally perceived (see Dar-Nimrod, Ilan, Heine, Steven J. 2011; Salardi 2014). Although it is widely accepted among experts that genetic essentialism – and the corresponding genetic deterministic views – of our destiny have long been scientifically disavowed (see Margenau 1967; Lewontin 2005), the deterministic view has nonetheless taken roots in public opinion, and has reinforced the conviction that genetics can answer ultimate questions regarding precisely our identity, that is The Human Nature.

The second challenge is represented by mass migration. Since Europe has been facing this phenomenon, there have been constant institutional and social tensions regarding the way to handle it. On the one hand, there are stances based on human rights philosophy (see Ferrajoli 2007; Touraine 2013) – of which Europe is the cradle.[1] Supporters of these positions point at the necessity of overcoming exclusive interpretations of categories like citizenship. The main reason for this request – they argued – is that such interpretation of citizenship collides with the main legal features of fundamental rights in the current constitutional framework, i.e. universality of fundamental rights and their unavailability on the part of the political power (see Ferrajoli 2001). On the other hand, political trends and consequently legal rules at the intermediate level of legal production (in particular legislative level) are anchored to a particular use of citizenship, that is as warrantor of fundamental rights (only) of a selected group of individuals, i.e. citizens. Citizenship may indeed alternatively play a role of inclusion in or exclusion from enjoinment of fundamental rights. Behind uses of this category with the intention of excluding individuals, there is a precise way of dealing with sociocultural differences. In other words, from this perspective sociocultural differences are used to discriminate among individuals and to decide who is a member of a selected community and can consequently enjoy fundamental rights, or conversely who is to be considered out of it.

Although the two mentioned challenges refer to two different phenomena, which do *de facto* give rise to different legal questions and demand specific solutions, they nonetheless share one common element, relevant to my discussion, that is they both correlate to attempts which ferment an essentialist perspective of H.N. as briefly mentioned above. In line with this approach, at the very heart of H.N. there is the acknowledgement that human beings share features and determinants of identity, which, once established, could unveil *Who* we really are, or in other words, explain our deep essence. And consequently, ethical, social, political, cultural, and legal solutions concerning how life, both individual and social, should be are derived from these elements as though these solutions were a kind of logical inference.

---

1 At the European institutional level, this is the approach of the Council of Europe. See, for instance, *1st Quarterly Activity Report*, 2012 and 2013, of the Commissioner for Human Rights, available at https://wcd.coe.int/ViewDoc.jsp?id=1918625&Site=&BackColorInternet=B9BDEE&BackColorIntranet=FFCD4F&BackColorLogged=FFC679.

H.N., intended according to this holistic approach, does not only arise philosophical concerns, but it produces legal, important implications when it is used to base a legal order.

The paper critically argues against a Human Nature based Law and the renewed attempts to ground Law on this concept. Indeed, it is assumed that H.N. is a critical and unstable concept, and consequently not adequate to build a legal order on, especially if it claims to prevent discrimination among human beings.

In order to develop my arguments I focus on the following three main questions, which include, of course, other related questions: why is H.N. a critical concept? Is H.N. an adequate concept to build a legal order on? And what are the social and cultural impacts of a Human Nature based Law, especially on the topic of discrimination?

In this work, these questions are taken as fundamental. This because, if these essential aspects were not cleared up, all the other questions would be redundant.

Before answering these questions, we need to put them into a context. This is the reason why the next paragraph deals briefly with general considerations on essentialism.

2. Important features of Law: is an essentialist approach desirable at all?

Although it cannot be denied that it is currently difficult to find experts who do not agree that language is the result of a convention among individuals who use it, it must however be admitted that the conventional approach to language has not always been a constant and shared element of human history (see Formigari 2001).

Indeed, for quite a long time, essentialism has been the 'normal' way to explain both reality (ontological level) and language, especially concepts (conceptual essentialism.) Roots of this perspective, which historically presents various variations and different formulations, are to be found in Plato's idealism, and they can be summed up as follows: things do possess given properties, for which there is no empirical control, and these properties determine how things are; these properties, which are different from any other accidental property a thing may or may not possess, do necessarily reflect on the meaning of concepts used to designate real entities (see Nino 1996).

Thus, concepts and their meanings are a representation of *essential* elements. Therefore, according to this conception, to ask for the meaning of an entity means to search for its essential elements, for concepts mirror these essences. Hence, the meaning of a concept is determined by reality, and this is why many supporters of conceptual essentialism do indeed use etymological analysis to determine the meaning of terms.

Indeed, from an essentialist perspective, concepts stand for signs, and are not symbols of something, as it is assumed from a conventionalist viewpoint (see Barberis 2008). This means that there is a *natural* relationship between concepts and things they refer to, that is irrespective of human will. This way of conceiving relationships between concepts and things does impact the way human beings approach, represent, and understand reality (see Carnap 1966; Kantorowicz 1958).[2]

Moreover, the definitions and explanations of concepts do present peculiar features. In particular, according to the philosophical essentialist tradition, concepts do have a *univocal* and *true* meaning, which can be grasped by means of investigating a non-empirical reality.

Consequently, definitions of concepts are only true or false, and refer to *res* (see Scarpelli 1976). To follow the essentialist approach means to remain anchored in a reductionist view of language and definition, and more in general of our worldview. The brief overview of the features and implications of this reductionist viewpoint is relevant to the legal world. It is indeed possible to find traces of the abovementioned perspective in the history of Law.

Consider, for instance, the concept of 'person'. According to the Natural Law tradition, this concept coincides with the human being considered as a biological entity. And for quite a long time, this identification has deeply influenced the legal interpretation of the concept of 'person'. The traditional conception has also caused heated debates about the possibility of attributing criminal liability to corporations.[3] For a long time, the concept of legal person has in fact been defined *per relationem* with regard to the physical one (see Kelsen 1952). However, the concept of 'person' is not an assertion of fact, it is a normative concept, which is used – as Scarpelli clarifies – when specific facts are qualified by specific legal or moral norms (see Scarpelli 1985). And the only acceptable definition for such concepts is the nominalist one, which describes and proposes a rule to use the term, that is its meaning (see Pintore 1982).

With regard to the legal sphere, the nominalist definition is more appropriate than the realistic one – *definitio quid rei* – because the latter appears to be too narrow (see Scarpelli 1976, 191; Ross 1976). Indeed, human beings are not always concerned with the essence of things. In many cases, and in particular in the legal context, definition is used neither to grasp the essence of an entity (essentialist approach) nor to control the truth or falsity of an assertion (logical empiricism).

---

2 Carnap has well summed up the essentialist idea in the expression 'the magical view of language'.

3 On this topic with regard to the Italian legal system see, for instance: De Nitto 1982/83, De Maglie 1999 and De Maglie 2002.

Rather, it is used to limit what is Law from what is not, and to achieve this goal, it is necessary to broaden the idea of definition in such a way that it is possible to understand the values which underlie and inspire choices (of a political, ethical, social, and cultural kind) in favour of a specific definition of a concept to the detriment of another.

If this is true, it follows that an essentialist approach to Law risks limiting the worldview and therefore losing sight of the fact that many apparently unsolvable problems may very often be, if not completely solved, at least got into perspective by means of re-definitions of terms (see Calderoni 1924; Borsellino 1979, 333). Moreover, the essentialist perspective does not permit to highlight that concepts like H.N., but also freedom, responsibility, equality, and so on, which do not have a semantic referent in the empirical world, do not have a fixed meaning, but they change it as their use implies ethical and legal choices for balancing specific interests in any given historical period and for a particular model of society.

Despite the fact that essentialism has been brought into question,[4] traces of this tradition show up in common language as well as in political and legal language. This is the reason why this paper wants to throw some light on the essentialist roots in the public and institutional debates on H.N. Thus, an examination of this concept will be useful to this purpose.

3. Human Nature: why is it an unstable and critical concept?

As highlighted in the introduction to this paper, there is a new interest in the concept of H.N. mainly due to contingent factors that have contributed to its *revival*, i.e. the two aforementioned challenges facing European society.

The concept of H.N. has a long history and there is a considerable body of literature on it.[5] It is a fascinating concept as its use gives the illusion that it is possible to definitively satisfy the constant craving of humans to find, once and for all, the features and determinants that constitute human identity. However, despite the fascination it may exercise over human minds, H.N. is an insidious concept for many reasons. The first aspect to be mentioned is that definitions of H.N. have often been grounded on an essentialist approach as referred to earlier.

And it has long been treated as though it were a descriptive factual concept. Indeed, efforts to define H.N. focused historically on the identification of any

---

4 Since the advent of the scientific Revolution many enduring mysteries like the functioning of the natural world according to the principle of causality have been cleared up.

5 There is a widespread literature on the evolution of the concept of *Human Nature* in different scientific fields (see Harré 1999; Harré 2002; Wallace 1996).

factual feature that potentially makes up an allegedly common shared identity and have their roots in the works of ancient Greek and Roman philosophers like Aristotle and Seneca (see Aristotle 1993).

Historically, the majority of these attempts to define H.N. have made the mistake to mix two different levels: descriptive and normative.[6]

On the one hand, the search focused indeed on empirical features of a biological, psychological, emotive, and behavioural nature to define the concept, and, on the other hand, these descriptive elements were used to provide prescriptions of a social, political, and legal kind. Consider, for instance, Thomas Hobbes who grounded his political philosophy on an image of H.N. based on the smallest axioms of the Nature of human beings as organisms. Hobbes' idea that everything – society, nature, and so on – ought to be explained according to such a perspective has inspired the modern biological theory of H.N.

But there are other examples worthy of consideration here. In the 19th century, following the unprecedented boost in different scientific fields, the Italian School of Criminology tried to apply the 'scientific method' to penal law in order to explain criminal attitudes and conducts of individuals from a strictly biological viewpoint. According to the main thinkers of this School, Cesare Lombroso and Enrico Ferri, evidence of a deviated H.N. can be found in peculiar somatic traits of individuals (see Lombroso 1995), or it can be traced back to the social and environmental contexts in which individuals grow up (see Ferri 1929).

The biological explanation of H.N. as a deviated H.N. was used to support criminal law policies that focused criminal liability on concepts like *social defence*, *social dangerousness*, rather than on *freewill*. This biological explanation and definition of H.N. is not just a thing of the past. Since advances in genetics have boomed, especially after completion of the Human Genome Project in 2003, some have began to identify H.N. with the human genome or genetic make-up. This operation that reduces individuals to their genes has been supported by the revival of the old, though scientifically disavowed, theory of genetic essentialism.

Despite all the abovementioned efforts made to define and treat H.N. as an all-embracing term covering the whole terrain of descriptive factual elements referring to human beings, none of these attempts could successfully explain H.N. Indeed, over time, H.N. has not become a clearer concept. The reason for the

---

6 John Stuart Mill clearly clarifies that the two main meanings of the word 'nature' and of its derivatives, that is, the descriptive sense and the normative sense, have long been intertwined with each other in philosophy and ethics, and this entanglement is the main cause of 'copious sources of false taste, false philosophy, false morality, and even bad law' (see Mill 1998, 3).

persisting obscurity of the concept is not – as some believe – the fact that it refers or pertains to experience we cannot access (kind of metaphysical dimension) and that it therefore offers different unverifiable solutions. Rather, it is because H.N. and all the questions related to it are not linked with a univocal idea or concept since they varied historically and changed their intellectual, emotive, social, etc. implications. And all the different associations developed over time have with the leading concept a simple relationship of contiguity and not of logical interdependence (see Calderoni 1924). To deal with a concept like H.N. means indeed to address a 'question of word' (see ibid.). This means that the use of a term like H.N., which brings with itself a multitude of correlated meanings and representations, requires a definition of its content on the part of the speaker. Put differently, the concept of H.N. needs to be contextualised and the meaning clarified by the speaker using it in order to avoid misunderstandings.

A second reason for H.N. to be a critical concept is that, despite its instability due to the contingent representations it carries, it has long been considered and worked as a 'scientific' concept. This occurred especially from the second half of the 19th century onwards when advances in science boomed and the abovementioned Italian School of Criminology arrived on the institutional scene.

Despite the fact that H.N. is an unstable concept, it has been used – under the guise of a scientific concept – to identify both biological referents of identity and cultural referents of identity (see Barker 1981) for the purpose of arranging individuals or groups into classes. To classify individuals into categories is not a negative operation *per se*. Indeed, classifications facilitate the understanding of complex phenomena as they allow identification of the main features involved in any phenomenon and permit to build general and abstract models.

However, classifications may hide different and opposite purposes. With particular regard to the concept of H.N., classification under the determinants of a biological or a cultural kind may have an inclusive or an exclusive purpose.

And human history has often witnessed the latter one, that is H.N. being used as a strategy for excluding selected categories of individuals from sharing some kind of benefits and deciding who is and who is not a member of a community by making specific human beings biologically and culturally inferior.

This historically widespread trend in using the concept of H.N. was reinforced by its allegedly scientific nature. As a matter of fact, despite the impossibility to find a common scientific definition, this concept has often been referred to as though it has a scientific foundation. However, Foucault, for instance, displays a rather critical attitude towards this way of qualifying H.N. In his famous book *The Chomsky-Foucault Debate: on Human Nature*, Foucault observes that the concept of H.N. has served as an epistemological indicator but that it is not a scientific concept. As Foucault highlights, H.N. has been used to distinguish among different discourses and disciplines dealing with some aspects of human identity. If we can agree with this qualification of the concept, we can further broaden the definition of this term and suggest that H.N. is more like an 'umbrella term', including a wide universe of topics, features, and determinants that were historically used to differentiate among groups or individuals. But in this universe, it is impossible to find any kind of reasonable ethical, cultural, legal, logical, or scientific connection among the different elements inhabiting it. Nonetheless, these attempts to use H.N. as a scientific and all-embracing concept have often ended up – at the institutional and social level – in the supremacy of specific groups to the detriment of others.

Before dealing with the specific impacts of a Human Nature based Law, we can draw some intermediate conclusions on the concept of H.N. In short, if it is undoubtedly true that H.N. could be used to give factual differences among individuals an adequate consideration, it is however arguable that it would be used in Law for such purpose and not, on the contrary, to translate factual differences in legal inequalities. The legal use of H.N. defined according to factual features may cause discriminatory practices to increase and not to diminish because of its semantic instability and the correlated impossibility of establishing significant correlations and interconnections of an ethical, scientific, or logical kind among the determinants of identity allegedly embraced by the concept. After these considerations, the question we should try to answer is that of whether we are willing to use the concept of H.N. to ground Law, or more precisely a legal order. I will give my reasons for answering this question negatively.

4. What are the impacts of a Human Nature based Law on society?

The question to be answered is that of whether the concept of H.N. as defined above is adequate to ground a legal order or, more precisely, of whether the different determinants of a biological and sociocultural kind would be acceptable within a constitutional rule of law that protects fundamental rights as 'universal' and 'unavailable' rights (see Ferrajoli 2001).

Efforts to ground Law on the 'nature of human being' have a long history, and there is a widespread literature[7] on it.

7 There is a persistent legal-philosophical debate on *Human Nature* (see Descola 2013; Ingold 2006; Ingold 1987; MacIntyre 1981; Sahlins 2008; Sahlins 2013).

These attempts go back to the Natural Law tradition. According to this tradition, there are universal, immutable features of H.N that Law ought just to recognise and regulate. From this viewpoint, conducts ruled by Natural Law are *per se* good or bad (*mala in se*), and consequently Natural Law states *a priori* what is good or bad. To follow this approach means to search for innate referents or determinants of human identity. Such innate determinants have an *a priori* 'natural' qualification that Law ought just to take into account and regulate. Inclinations, instincts, impulses, reason, feelings, and, in the modern view, genetic-based features are *a priori* defined as good or bad and are intended to fill the essence of H.N. It is well-known that the Natural Law tradition has come under radical criticism on the part of the thinkers of Legal Positivism. The criticism focused on the assumption that there are no *a priori* good or bad conducts that Law has to recognise and regulate. On the contrary, following the principle of utility, conducts receive a specific legal qualification just because (and after) they have been qualified by legal norms in a specific way (see Kelsen 1952; Bobbio 1996).

With regard to the allegedly *natural*, immutable features that ground H.N. in the Natural Law perspective, Kelsen (see Kelsen 1957) convincingly underlined that such different referents of identity used to define H.N., for instance, inclinations, instincts, impulses, reason, feelings do coexist with their opposites. And who decides which are good or bad? According to which values?[8]

Today, there are attempts to ground H.N. on genetic characteristics following an essentialist, reductionist conception of what humans are.[9] But also with regard to this *modern* approach to H.N., questions similar to those identified by Kelsen concerning the Natural Law tradition are still at stake: which genes should be selected for a genetic foundation of H.N.? Those relating to an emphatic, mild, intelligent H.N. or those giving rise to an aggressive, anxious, crafty etc. human being? And who is in charge of such a selection? According to *Whose* values? (see Salardi 2014).

---

8 In his essay on 'Nature', already quoted in footnote 5 of this paper, John Stuart Mill anticipated the perplexities which Kelsen would later note with regard to the identification of the authority in charge of the selection of natural features relevant to a moral judgment (see Mill 1998, 35).

9 Some current examples of this trend can be found both in legislation and in court cases. See, for instance, European Court of Human Rights, S. and Marper v. The United Kingdom (2008); decision September 18, 2009 of the Italian Corte D'Assise of Trieste; French Immigration Law Article 13, Loi n. 2007–1631 du 20 novembre 2007 relative à la maîtrise de l'immigration, à l'intégration et à l'asile; UK Border Act 2005 Article 5.

While proceeding with this selective operation, we should at least explicitly admit that we are deriving the 'ought to be' from the 'is'. However, even if we were so intellectually honest and disclosed the operation of transition from the descriptive to the normative level, we would not avoid the negative impacts of this action on three key aspects of Law, namely legal language, typology of legal norms, and legal order.

A first negative impact of the use of H.N. on Law concerns indeed the risk of contaminating legal language with *infiltration* of terms, which not only discriminate on the basis of status, personal, and sociocultural conditions, but which are also connoted in an emotive way. An example is the expression 'illegal immigrant', which has been used in many European legal rules to qualify the conduct of migrants crossing the boarders of any European country without legal permission to do so. These semantic infiltrations are not legitimate if we take *seriously* the fact that legal language is an *administered* language (see Jori 1995, 1995a, 2014) that needs authorities to administer it, that is to exercise power. Such authoritative control finds a limitation in the substantial framework of fundamental rights anchored in rigid Constitutions. To respect this framework commits us to controlling the contents of legal norms and the language through which such contents are expressed. This framework poses both formal and substantial limits to what can be expressed through legal language, and to respect it means to take *seriously* the formal and substantial consistency of Law.

The second impact of a Human Nature based Law concerns the typology of legal norms. In a Human Nature based Law 'constitutive norms' (that produce the effect, which is their aim and content, by achieving it) (see Carcaterra 1974; Conte 1983; Guastini 1983) tend to prevail on or even replace 'regulative norms' (that produce an event by exercising pressure on someone's behaviour). The term *constitutive norms* refers to norms whose effects are immediately constituted or produced by the norm itself, irrespective of the fact that a given conduct actually takes place. These norms belong to the category of *performative* utterances through which we do things with words (see Austin 1962). For the purpose of my discussion, it is necessary to specify the precise meaning of constitutive norms I refer to in this work. Indeed, all norms are constitutive 'of provisions which constitute their meaning' (see Ferrajoli 2007, 224). However, it is possible to highlight a stricter sense of what is termed *constitutive*, namely the meaning referred to norms that 'immediately constitute status and issues they qualify' (see ibid.). In penal law, constitutive norms, in this stricter sense, punish directly and immediately the 'status' of the offender and not the illegal act committed (see Ferrajoli 1994). And human history has witnessed a quite wide set of such norms: punishment of witches in the Middle Ages, penal sanctions against heretics, persecution of Jews, to mention just a few. And in modern penal codes and legislation, traces are visible in rules pertaining to vagabonds, recidivists, not to mention the more recent rule on illegal immigration.[10] Unless we want to face the accusation of axiological inconsistency, these norms are, despite their persistence, no longer legally endurable in legal orders based on the principles of individual responsibility and equality before the Law. Indeed, constitutive norms as above defined do contradict the philosophy inspiring protection of fundamental rights in the current European legal framework. This protection is based on a normative conception of equality in rights and not on a descriptive, factual idea of equality grounded on biological, sociocultural, and personal differences.

The last impact I want to briefly discuss refers to Law intended as a legal order. A H.N. based Law would contradict a meta-principle of the current constitutional model of law, that is the principle of *laïcité*, or secularism. Indeed, to take this principle *seriously* means to avoid Law being grounded on one moral vision. From this perspective Law ought not to be shaped by ideological (ethical or scientific) interpretations of H.N. If this happens, there follows the subordination of the judgment on the validity of legal norms and, more generally, of the legal order to a moral judgment.

5. Does a Human Nature based Law contribute to combating discrimination? Some conclusive remarks

The current legal framework in Europe promotes the protection of fundamental rights and is inspired by principles like freedom, equity, dignity, and responsibility. Protection of individuals against abuses on the part of groups of interests and of power is guaranteed by 'equal freedom in rights' (see Ferrajoli 2007).

---

10 In Italy this kind of qualification was introduced by the Immigration Act n. 189/2002, termed *Legge Bossi-Fini*. And later other Acts stipulated specific aggravating circumstances for the condition of 'illegal immigrant', for instance Act n. 125/2008 concerning public security, and introduced the crime of immigration, see Act n. 94/2009 concerning public security. In 2014 the new government has repealed the crime of illegal immigration. The qualification or discriminatory treatments connected with this qualification or with the position of 'migrant' are also present in European and international Acts: Article 79 of the Treaty on the Functioning of the European Union concerning development of a common immigration policy; Art. 96 of the Convention implementing the Schengen Agreement; German Act, Gesetz zur Begrenzung der Zuwanderung und zur Regelung des Aufenthalts und der Integration von Unionsbürgern und Ausländern 2005 etc.

However, there are insidious revivals of the essentialist tradition that follow, mainly surreptitiously, the direction of a foundation of Law on factual determinants of identity. But these trends do contradict the axiological legal framework inspiring protection of fundamental rights in current times, and they are doomed to increase and not to diminish discrimination among individuals.

What kind of discrimination? I propose discrimination be defined as illegitimate treatment of individuals or groups based on ideological claims which serve to maintain the privileges of specific groups or individuals' which could either be a majority or a minority in any given historical period. The ideological claims may be of a different kind. However, when we deal with discrimination perpetrated at the institutional level, the historical evidence shows that it is mainly centred on biological features (for instance the genetic make-up), on status differences (citizens v. aliens or the stateless), and on sociocultural differences (political, religious, moral convictions etc.).

Discrimination in this sense can be successfully overcome only if we adopt the stance of equal freedom in rights. Only equal freedom in rights represents indeed the condition to protect all individuals by unequal treatments. In particular, equal freedom in rights is useful to combat *multiple discrimination* affecting primarily *vulnerable* categories of individuals. Current legal trends in the European Union towards this phenomenon are contradictory. If, on the one hand, the European Union presents itself as the main promoter of the human rights idealism, on the other hand, these rights seem to be reduced to a mere rhetoric by all the slippery slopes concerning legal production in some selected topics, for instance migration.

However, if we want to seriously face the challenge of discrimination, axiological consistency between legal rules at the intermediate level of legal orders and constitutional guarantees appears to be an unavoidable value and a principle that ought to continue to inspire legal regulation.

Axiological consistency is granted if we take seriously into account that in its linguistic dimension Law is an *administered* language (Jori 1995; 1995a). This means not only that Law is in an intermediate position between instrumental-artificial languages and the natural language, but it also means that legal language needs authorities that administer it. But these authorities are themselves limited by the authoritative control as it restricts the power to say everything and the opposite of everything through legal norms. Indeed, in modern legal orders of countries with rigid constitutions, legal norms cannot have whatever content, because these legal systems are not completely dynamic. Indeed, the possibility of changing the system ought to take into account the substantial framework of fundamental rights anchored in constitutions (see Borsellino 2003). Respect for this framework, which poses both formal and substantial limits to what can be expressed through legal language at intermediate levels of production, is relevant to the formal and substantial consistency of Law.

If we agree with these considerations, it follows that, should axiological consistency be preserved, constitutive norms, which may transpose into Law discrimination grounded on ideological claims centred on biological and status differences, are no longer valid in legal orders based on equal freedom with respect to rights. And axiological consistency should be preserved if we want the system to satisfy the requirement of legal certainty.

To sum up, a Human Nature based Law is often a risky solution as it is doomed to fail in achieving the aim of accounting for differences among individuals without transforming them into legal inequalities. And this occurs for many reasons. But the main one is the instability of the notion of H.N. and the correlated impossibility to determine significant connections from any ethical, scientific or logic viewpoint among the determinants of identity embraced by the concept.

References

Aristotle. 1993. *Politica*. Edited by Renato Laurenti. Roma: Laterza.

Austin, John, L. 1962. *How to do Things with Words*. Oxford: Clarendon Press.

Barberis, Mauro. 2008. *Filosofia del diritto: un'introduzione teorica*. Torino: Giappichelli.

Barker, Martin. 1981. *New Racism*. London: Function Books.

Bobbio, Norberto. 1996. *Il positivismo giuridico*. Torino: Giappichelli.

Borsellino, Patrizia. 1979. Libertà, giustificazione della pena e metodo delle discipline penali in Calderoni. *Rivista critica di storia della filosofia* 3: 317–349.

Borsellino, Patrizia. 2003. I diritti fondamentali oltre lo Stato. Le implicazioni metateoriche di un recente dibattito. In *Ordinamento giuridico, sovranità, diritti*, edited by Enrico Diciotti and Vito Velluzzi. Torino: Giappichelli.

Calderoni, Mario. 1924. I postulati della scienza positiva ed il diritto penale. In *Scritti di Mario Calderoni*, vol. 1. Firenze: Società Anon. Editrice 'La Voce'.

Carcaterra, Giovanni. 1974. *Le norme costitutive*. Milano: Giuffrè.

Carnap, Rudolph. 1966. *The Philosophical Foundation of Physics. An introduction to the philosophy of science*. New York: Basic Books, inc.

Chomsky, Noam, Foucault, Michel. 2006. *The Chomsky-Foucault Debate: on Human Nature*. New York: New Press.

Conte, Amedeo, G. 1983. Regola costitutiva, condizione autonomia. In *La teoria generale del diritto*, edited by Scarpelli, Uberto. Milano: Edizioni Comunità.

Dar-Nimrod, Ilan; Heine, Steven J. 2011. Genetic essentialism: On the deceptive determinism of DNA. *Psychological Bulletin* 137: 800–818.

De Maglie, Cristina. 1999. Corporate Crime and Sentencing: The Italian Solution. In *Criminal Responsibility of Legal and Collective Entities*. International Colloquium: Berlin, May 4–6 1998, edited by Eser Albin, Heine Günther and Huber Barbara. Freiburg im Breisgau: Iuscrim.

De Maglie, Cristina. 2002. *L'etica e il mercato*. Milano: Giuffrè.

De Nitto, Achille. 1982/1983. Dottrina e realtà delle persone giuridiche pubbliche tra fine '800 e inizi del '900 in Italia. In *Quaderni fiorentini per la storia del pensiero giuridico moderno*. Milano: Giuffrè.

Descola, Philippe. 2013. *Beyond Nature and Culture*. Translated by Janet Lloyd. London: The University of Chicago Press.

Ferrajoli, Luigi. 1994. Modelli del linguaggio legislativo penale. In *Il linguaggio del diritto*, edited by Uberto Scarpelli and Paolo Di Lucia. Milano: Edizioni Universitarie di Lettere Economia Diritto.

Ferrajoli, Luigi. 2001. *Diritti fondamentali*. Roma–Napoli: Laterza Edizioni.

Ferrajoli, Luigi. 2007. *Principia Juris. Teoria del diritto e della democrazia*, 2. Roma–Napoli: Laterza Edizioni.

Ferri, Enrico. 1929. *Sociologia criminale*. Torino: UTET.

Formigari, Lia. 2001. *Il linguaggio:storia delle teorie*. Roma-Napoli: Laterza Edizioni.

Frigessi, Delia, Giacanelli, Ferruccio, and Mangoni, Luisa (eds.) 1995. *Cesare Lombroso, Delitto, genio follia, scritti scelti*. Torino: Bollati-Boringhieri.

Fuchs, Stephan. 2001. *Against Essentialism. A Theory of Culture and Society*. Cambridge: Harvard University Press.

Guastini, Riccardo. 1983. Teoria delle regole costitutive. *Rivista internazionale di filosofia del diritto* 4: 548–564.

Harré, Rom. 1999. The Rediscovery of the Human Mind: The Discursive Approach. *Asian Journal of Social Psychology* 2(1): 43–62.

Harré, Rom. 2002. *Great scientific experiments: twenty experiments that changed our view of the world*. Mineola (NY): Dover.

Ingold, Tim. 2006. Against human nature. In *Evolutionary Epistemology, Language and Culture. Theory and Decision Library A*. 39: 259–281.

Ingold, Tim. 1987. *The appropriation of nature: essays on human ecology and social relations*. Iowa City: University of Iowa Press.

Jori, Mario, and Pintore, Anna. 1995. *Manuale di Teoria Generale del Diritto*. Torino: Giappichelli.

Jori, Mario. 1995a. Definizioni giuridiche e pragmatiche. In *Analisi e diritto. Ricerche di giurisprudenza analitica*, edited by Paolo Comanducci and Riccardo Guastini. Torino: Giappichelli.

Jori, Mario, Pintore, Anna. 2014. *Introduzione alla filosofia del diritto*. Torino: Giappichelli.

Kay, Lily E. 2000. *Who wrote the Book of Life? A History of the Genetic Code*. Stanford: Stanford University Press.

Kantorowicz, Hermann. 1958. *The Definition of Law*. Edited by A.H. Campbell. Cambridge: University Press.

Kelsen, Hans. 1952. *Lineamenti di dottrina pura del diritto*. Torino: Einaudi.

Kelsen, Hans. 1957. *What is Justice? Justice, Law, and Politics in the Mirror of Science*. Berkeley: University of California Press.

Lewontin, Richard. 2005. *Biology as ideology. The doctrine of DNA*. UK: Penguin Books.

MacIntyre, Alasdair. 1981. *After Virtue*, Italian Translation *Dopo la virtù*. 1988. Milano: Feltrinelli.

Margenau, Henry. 1967. Quantum Mechanics, Free Will and Determinism. *The Journal of Philosophy* 21: 714–725.

Mill, J. Stuart. 1998. *Three Essays on Religion. Nature, The Utility of Religion, Theism*. New York: Prometheus Books.

Nelkin, Dorothy, and Lindee Susan M. 1995. The *DNA Mystique*: The *Gene* as *Cultural Icon*. New York: W. H. Freeman.

Nino, Carlos S. 1996. *Introduzione all'analisi del diritto*. Torino: Giappichelli.

Pintore, Anna. 1982/1983. Il concetto di persona giuridica nell'indirizzo filosofico analitico. In *Quaderni fiorentini per la storia del pensiero giuridico moderno*, 736–747. Milano: Giuffrè.

Ross, Alf. 1976. Tûtû. In *Diritto e Analisi del Linguaggio*, edited by Uberto Scarpelli. Milano: Edizioni Comunità.

Rutter, Michael, Moffit, Terrie, and Caspi, Avshalom. 2006. Gene-environment interplay and psychopathology: multiple varieties but real effects. *Journal of Child Psychology and Psychiatry* 47: 226–261.

Sahlins, Marshall D. 2008. *The Western Illusion of Human Nature: With Reflections on the Long History of Hierarchy, Equality and the Sublimation of Anarchy in the West, and Comparative Notes on Other Conceptions of the Human Condition*. Chicago: Prickly Paradigm Press.

Sahlins, Marshall D. 2013. *What Kinship is and What is not*. London-Chicago: The University of Chicago Press.

Salardi, Silvia. 2010. *Test genetici tra determinismo e libertà*. Torino: Giappichelli.

Salardi, Silvia. 2014. The genetic foundation of human nature and the legal approach. Some philosophical-legal concerns. *Global Bioethics*. London: Routledge.

Scarpelli, Uberto. 1976. La definizione nel diritto. In *Diritto e Analisi del Linguaggio*, edited by Uberto Scarpelli, 183–197. Milano: Edizioni Comunità.

Scarpelli, Uberto. 1985. *Contributo alla semantica del linguaggio normativo*. Edited by Anna Pintore. Milano: Giuffrè.

Seneca, *De Beneficiis*, III, 18 2.

Touraine, Alain. 2013. *La fin des sociétés*. Seuil: La Couleur des Idées.

Wallace, William A. 1996. *The Modeling of Nature. Philosophy of Science and Philosophy of Nature in Synthesis*. USA: The Catholic University of America Press.

Part III
Language of Law

Alessio Sardo

Legal Philosophers, Meaning and Force

1. Introduction

Following the seminal work of J.L. Austin, we can consider speaking as a *social communicative interaction*: when we *say* something (for instance, 'Today I am in Zagreb' or 'Go home!') we also *do* something (*describing* in the first case, *prescribing* in the second case) and, normally, we produce certain effects on the audience (in the second case, maybe you will really follow my order). The action is threefold (Austin 1975):[1] 1) We *say* something, that is we put forward a representational content – glossed also as the 'locution', or the 'sense' of an utterance; 2) We do something *in* saying something (ordering, suggesting, asserting, asking, etc.) – and this is the 'illocutionary force' (or simply 'force' of the utterance); 3) We do something *by* saying something: that is, we produce psychological or behavioural consequences by means of our utterance (which are *imputed* to our speech) – Austin called this third element 'perlocution'. Austin's minimal scheme can be enriched with more levels, in order to map further salient features. For instance, following Grice, we can introduce in our picture 4) the notion of *conversational implicature*, in order to describe *what is meant* by the speaker (a content that is inferentially constructed by virtue of the so-called *conversational maxims*). We can also add 5) the notion of *linguistic presupposition*, which can provide a powerful tool for the analysis of those contextual elements which are taken for granted by the participants to a communication process, and implicitly associated to certain linguistic expressions. Progressive refinements are possible, but, generally speaking, legal philosophers do not get so far. There are just a few exceptions. For instance, see Marmor (2005) and Poggi (2012, 2013).

It is commonly thought that Austin's account or, more often, the reformulation offered by Searle (1969) can be profitably used also for the analysis of law, starting from the assumption that legal phenomena can be considered as a peculiar form of *institutionalised normative speech*. This move requires important theoretical choices. One of them is really puzzling: we have to take a stand on the complicated relations between *what is said* (the locution, or, if you prefer, the *sense* of an utterance) and *what we do in saying something* (the illocutionary force: ordering,

1 For a detailed discussion on the relation between locution and illocution in Austin's theory see Recanati (1987, § 9) and Sbisà (2006; 2013).

asking, saying, etc.). The boundaries of this relation are far from being clear: analytic philosophers have proposed many alternative solutions, reaching a very high level of complexity. In spite of the great variety of proposals, all legal philosophers seem to adopt one of the following two strategies:

A) *First Strategy.* The author claims that sense (i.e. the semantic, or – if your are not an inferentialist – representational, content) and force are sharply separated. Illocutionary force cannot be considered also as part of the representational content: the former can be perfectly understood (or grasped) even without taking into account its force (i.e. it is force-neutral). The same holds for logical relations between different contents. Accordingly, every speech act embeds only one type of invariant 'assertive' content, which is commonly presented as a *proposition*. Propositions, on their turn, are defined in terms of *truth-conditions* (this is why they are often labelled 'assertive', and not 'neutral' contents).[2] The author who chooses this first strategy will maintain, for instance, that an assertion such as 'Alejandro is in Zagreb' expresses the proposition 'ALEJANDRO $_{\text{(in Zagreb)}}$', which is true *if and only if* Alejandro is really in this marvellous city, and that the very same proposition will be expressed by the command 'Alejandro, go to Zagreb!' and by the question 'Is Alejandro in Zagreb?' This strategy is similar to the one implied by Searle in his early writings (see ibid.).

B) *Second Strategy*. The author maintains that sense and force are deeply connected at the semantic level: the latter is attached to the representational content of the speech act, for we cannot fully understand semantic contents without taking into account their force. Accordingly, it seems necessary to distinguish (at least) between *two kinds of semantic content*: a prescriptive (or directive) content, and a descriptive content. Semantic meanings can be either propositions, or proposition-like entities; the latter are supposed to be not truth-apt, for they lack any connection with the categories of reality and truth. The author who chooses this second strategy will consider, for instance, that an utterance such as 'Go to Zagreb, Alejandro!' expresses a *directive-meaning*, which cannot be understood as a description of portions of reality; therefore, it doesn't make sense to consider them as truth-functional entities (or truth-functional abstractions).[3] Our representations (corresponding to what we might be tempted to call 'mental scripts') normally contain, along with the idea of a certain action, or event, also the thought that a certain action *is real* or, alternatively, that it *ought to be real.*

---

2 I think that this linguistic use is, to a certain extent, improper, because a certain content can be truth-functional without being necessarily asserted.

3 An abstraction need not necessarily also be considered as an 'entity'.

Now, many legal philosophers (Alchourrón and Bulygin 1981, 1984; Raz 1990; Marmor 2005; Villa 2012) follow the first strategy. They have basically three reasons for playing this move. First, it provides a very simple and elegant solution: apparently, it satisfies Ockham's razor – there is only one kind of content, not two or even more – and avoids any confusion between meaning and force. Second, it can be used in order to justify a division of labour between semantics – conceived as the (logical) analysis of truth-functional meanings – and pragmatics – conceived as the study of the different illocutionary forces. The consequence of this division is a tremendous simplification of the tasks assigned to legal philosophers: these fellows are not obliged to tackle with pragmatics in order to talk about normative (legal) systems. Third, starting from these premises, it is really easy to defend the idea that there is a logic for the normative discourse, which applies only to the contents, without telling us anything at all about the relations between genuine normative components (i.e. illocutionary forces): to be sure, it has to be conceded that it makes no sense to talk about logical relations between norms *qua* speech acts. However, after this quick clarification, it can be maintained that propositional logic applies straightforwardly to the contents, without any serious concern about the nature of implication, the role of deontic operators in the sentence and so on. Actually, it is well known that logical connectives have been traditionally defined by means of tables of truth-values.

As far as I know, only a handful of authors have defended the second strategy: it is worth mentioning at least Ross (1941, 1968), Weinberger (1958, 1985a, 1985b, 1987, 1988), Tarello (1974) and Poggi (2012, 2013). See also Muffato (2007) on this point. I think that their preference is mainly determined by two convictions. On the one hand, they consider that what is done in saying something has a deep impact on the inferential treatment of what is said. On the other, they manifest a strong distrust toward the idea of giving priority to assertion (and truth) over prescription (and will). Moreover, it is clear enough that this second strategy assigns a methodological (and, perhaps, logical) precedence to pragmatics over semantics. This consideration is present with the highest degree of awareness in the works of Francesca Poggi, a radical contextualist.

My contribution to this wide debate will be very modest:

1) I will present the dominant position, very briefly.
2) I will sketch out the most sophisticated version of the minority view, proposed by no less an authority than Alf Ross.
3) I will introduce a couple of arguments which can be used by the 'minority party' to defend the idea that illocutionary force has a deep inferential impact,

by pointing out that this element cannot be sharply distinguished from sense (and representation).

4) I will maintain that these arguments are not sufficient to settle the dispute: first, we need further arguments; second, possible alternative strategies shall be explored.

2. The first strategy

As I have already said, the first strategy is the most common among those legal philosophers who are willing to consider law as *a real* (i.e. not *ideal*) institutionalised form of linguistic interaction. According to this 'popular' conception, law is to be understood as a *peculiar social phenomenon*, constituted by *legal norms. Legal norms*, in turn, are conceived as *prescriptive speech acts*, that is, *sentences uttered with a normative pragmatic-function*. They are *deliberative acts of command* issued by a normative authority (i.e. the legislator) as the *expression of a wish, or a will*, directed to the *addressees* of the norms. Legislators can be identified either through a descriptive analysis of the 'social sources' within a certain normative system, by using the notion of the *rule of recognition*, or by reverting to the hypothesis of the *fundamental norm*, which stems from a transcendental argument. The first solution is generally preferred.

Any *act of commanding* is thus considered as a (more or less) *binding* combination of two radically different elements: a *descriptive factor* (conceived as a *proposition*) and a *prescriptive factor*; the latter is elliptically defined as a 'purely pragmatic indicator'.[4] *Propositions*, on the other hand, are defined as *truth-evaluable contents*: they constitute the *representational side* of *every* kind of speech act – also the 'normative' (or 'prescriptive') ones. *Illocutionary force* ('F'), instead, is considered as a pragmatic variable: it is neither an alethic modality, nor an intensional operator. For these reasons, it cannot be iterated and implied in order to generate other propositions. Perhaps, this very assumption is the reason why the combination of illocutionary forces is considered implausible in this literature. Using Hedenius' lexicon, we would say that the content is the same: only the 'factor of publication' changes.

Several defenders of this first strategy embrace *meta-ethical non-cognitivism* – a theoretical position that rejects the very idea that norms are truth-functional entities (Alchourrón and Bulygin 1981, 1984). From their perspective, normative

---

4 The expression 'pragmatic indicator' obviously calls for a definition, but defenders of the dominant position assume that this is neither the business of the legal philosopher, nor of any other academic figure that is interested in the development of a theory of meaning.

propositions can only be true or false, for they are genuine descriptive statements. In contrast, it wouldn't make any sense to consider a norm as true or false, for norms are not to be considered as descriptions of empirical features. Following Reichenbach, some author is willing to add that illocutionary acts have no truth-conditions, simply because they are *acts* (Reichenbach 1947, 337). However, ethical non-cognitivism should by no means be considered as a stumbling block to genuine propositions about the *existence of a* norm. These propositions are conceived as *meta-descriptions*, which can be equated to purely cognitive-contents. In the lexicon used by Alchourrón, Bulygin and their disciples these meta-descriptions are called 'normative propositions'. Normative propositions are often formulated using deontic words; nonetheless (*pace* Kelsen) their deep logical structure should be a proposition of the form 'The norm *N* belongs to the normative system NS_X'. For this very reason, we cannot consider the presence of a *deontic syntactical element* on the 'surface' of a certain deontic formulation as a *sufficient condition* for the conclusion that the content expressed by the formulation at stake is a norm. On the other hand, we should realise that it is very well possible to express norms even without relying on deontic words. For instance, I can command something using a future indicative tense ('You will not smoke marijuana!' said by me to Alejandro, now, in this room should be interpreted as a norm, if we presuppose my authority).

Legal authorities issue three different kinds of commands: i) *Prohibitions* or *Rejections* ('It is prohibited to smoke marijuana'); ii) *Obligations* ('Smoking marijuana is obligatory'); iii) *Permissions* ('Smoking marijuana is permitted'). Somebody could be willing to add a further kind of normative speech act: iv) *Derogations*. ('The norm that states that the prohibition of marijuana is derogated'). Most of the time legislators issue *conditional norms* ('If there is a medical prescription, then smoking marijuana is permitted').

The first strategy is affected by huge problems. First of all, we cannot assume without further arguments that the legislator commands, prescribes or uses propositions: the legislator prescribes *realising* (or *refraining from*) a certain action – or a certain state of affair – which is not necessarily a proposition. Second, if we define propositions in terms of truth-values – that is, we have what we may call an 'assertive' notion of a proposition, and not a 'neutral' one – it is hard to see how we can maintain, at the same time, that norms contain propositions and that they are not truth-functional abstractions: this would strike any reasonable man as a contradiction! Third, we might ask these theorists how we can attach the so-called 'pragmatic indicator' to the truth-functional component, for this remains completely obscure.

3. The upstream view defended in *Directives and Norms*

Alf Ross goes directly against the mainstream, endorsing the thesis that *meaning is entirely derivative from use*. Accordingly, *semantics* (i.e. the analysis of linguistic expressions *qua* bearers of meaning) and *syntax* (i.e. the logical and grammatical principles that govern the structure of the language) are to be considered as abstractions from *pragmatics* (i.e. the use of linguistic tools in human acts). Such abstractions are acceptable *if and only if* they reflect (empirical) facts of linguistic behaviour.[5] Let us consider, for instance, the following slogan written at the beginning of his masterpiece *Directives and Norms*: 'It is only through speech that we know language' (Ross 1968, 4). Ross then splits all the *possible uses* of language – or, in Austin's lexicon, illocutionary acts – in two broad *categories*, corresponding to different *pragmatic functions*: 'indicatives' and 'directives'.

Ross uses 'indicatives' to denote a large container, which includes an entire series of *speech acts* that are all connected with the *ideas of truth and knowledge*. This large group is constituted by: acts of saying, assertions, conjectures, and so on. All these different acts have in common the *typical function* of presenting some topic as *real* ('Smoking a joint by Alejandro – so it is'). By the same token, Ross uses 'directives' to denote a second, albeit of more or less the same size, container of *speech acts* that includes: suggestions, requests, orders, supplications, entreaties, invitations, recommendations, warnings, and similar. All these acts have in common the *typical function* of presenting a topic as something that *ought to be*: i.e., they express an 'action idea', conceived as a 'pattern of behaviour' ('Smoking a joint by Alejandro – so it ought to be' (ibid., 34)).

The content of an indicative speech is a *proposition*, symbolised as 'i(T)', where 'i' stands for the idea of reality ('so it is'); the content of a directive speech, instead, is a *directive*, symbolised as 'd(T)', where 'd' stands for the idea of obligation ('so it ought to be'). Propositions are conceived as representations of facts and can therefore be treated as truth-bearer sentences. The opposite holds for directives. Directives *qua meaning-contents* are *type-entities*. The *idea of a topic* ('T') is the element that directives and indicatives have in common. Accordingly, the main

---

5 Ross does not assume that a semiotic theory has to distinguish a full range of different contents – one for each function of our language. If he were to assume the controversial view that every function of language points to a corresponding kind of content, he would expose his theory to the strong objection of 'hypostatized-functions', which, armed with Ockham's razor, goes directly to the jugular of an excessively crowded metaphysical constellation. Moreover, Ross analysis is deeply behavioristic. We cannot consider meaning as something that could be fixed by the power of mind alone.

difference between directives and indicatives is located in the operators, 'i' (the thought of reality), and 'd' (the thought that something ought to be).[6]

Legal systems are *sets of heteronomous quasi-commands* whose authority derives from the legal order conceived as an impersonal system of norms (ibid., 50).[7] The *legal order* is an institutional system. This means that it is not composed only by rules that establish a certain pattern of behaviour, but also by many constitutive rules, i.e. norms that provide necessary conditions for the existence of legal institutions ('agencies empowered to create or enforce the law'), such as legislative assemblies and courts of justice (ibid., 51). These institutions appear to the individual mind as 'public authorities', being part of 'the machinery of the law'. Every constitutive rule of a certain legal system is established by a social convention, which comes into existence through contextualised linguistic interactions (ibid., 54ff). Nevertheless, the ultimate ground for a social convention– and its ultimate source of effectiveness – is settled by a subjective moral judgment, which is purely subjective and irrational, being determined only by *emotions*. Legal norms are thus considered not as illocutionary acts, but as *perlocutionary effects* produced by directive speech acts, issued by normative authorities.

As we have already said, the first, 'popular', strategy is committed to the following theses: every speech act expresses the very same kind of representational content; the dimension of thought is co-intensive with the dimension of truth; pragmatic elements have no implication on semantics, irrespective of whether we are inclined to consider semantics as a formal analysis of logical and truth-functional inferences or whether we are inclined to consider this field as an inquiry into the mechanism used by human beings to represent the reality. Ross uses (at least) four arguments in order to demonstrate that the 'popular' account is wrong and to show that *illocutionary force* has a strong impact on our systems of representation, and on their logic. The first argument focuses on the acceptance of meaning, the second relies on the distinction between internal and external negation of a directive, the third is the well-known *Ross's Paradox*, and the fourth is the opposition 'internal v. external consequence'.

---

6 In this respect, Ross still remains very close to the Kantian approach that characterised his early writings: *Sein* and *Sollen* are conceived as sharply separated categories of thought.

7 These entities (or abstractions) are similar to propositions with respect to the following: i) they are language-dependent; ii) they should not be confused with the sentences expressing them; therefore, iii) their existence depends on two linguistic facts: formulation and interpretation; iv) in order to be correctly produced they have to respect syntactic rules; v) both can be mentioned without making use of them; vi) both can be used in therapeutic speech exercises; vii) both can be considered without being used.

1. Argument from Acceptance. According to Ross's view, both propositions and directives have an *adjudicative function*: they are subject to 'acceptance' and 'rejection', which are attitude-deciding acts. However, the acceptance/rejection of a proposition is radically different from the acceptance/rejection of a directive: the former is a declarative and cognitive attitude-deciding act ('true' and 'false' are assumed to be intrinsic properties of the content); the latter is an act of volition, which has a non-cognitive nature. For this reason, it makes no sense to consider true and false as predicates of a directive.

This claim is supported by an analysis of the basic features of human action. In Ross's opinion, a directive is a practical content characterised by the dispositional property of being *action-determining*. A directive-content is incapable of determining human action on its own for a further act of acceptance is always required; however, if accepted by the addressee, a directive-content can provide what we might call – departing from Ross's lexicon – a 'sufficient reason' for action. In this respect, cognitive (or descriptive) contents are completely different: even if we accept a proposition (or a set of propositions), this piece of information about the world is not even potentially capable of being action-determining by its own.

Under normal circumstances, a directive issued by the legislator will be felt as a valid claim mainly because it generally comes with the threat of some sort of sanction (ibid., 40). However, the feeling of obligation can also derive from other factors: intrinsic respect for the authority of the commander, consistency with our personal view on the morals, and so on. This is simply because human minds have different motivational processes: legalistic, conformist, opportunistic, etc. These processes can be either categorical (derived from a pure feeling of obligation) or teleological (derived from a mean-ends interest-based reasoning).

We can easily see that the non-cognitivist alternative proposed by Ross is primarily a speech act semantic account of directive discourse. The author suggests that the primary meaning of a directive consists in the speech act performed through the expression of a particular attitude. In other words, he holds that to express a mental state *just is* to perform a speech act of some sort. What it is to think that 'T' does not directly bear upon the question of what 'T' means. The route for grasping what 'T' means must include the previous step of explaining the conditions under which thinking that 'T' *also counts as* doing *S*, where '*S*' is a speech act of some sort.

2. Opposition 'External/Internal Negation'. Alf Ross demonstrates that while internal and external negation are equivalent in propositional (but not in modal) logic, the opposite holds in deontic logic. As far as indicative speech is concerned, external negation (symbolised as follows: '– i(T)') expresses the refusal to accept that things stand in the way described by 'i(T)' – the negation is thus embedded in the second-order proposition. By contrast, internal negation (symbolised as follows: 'i(–T)') is embedded in the first-order proposition which states that things in the world are not in a certain way (ibid., 144ff). These two propositions are clearly equivalent: external negation '–i(T)' is the rejection of the proposition 'i(T)'; assuming the principle of non-contradiction ('one must not at the same time accept and reject the same proposition'), if a proposition is not accepted, its complement – in this case 'i(T)' – shall be accepted. Therefore, '–i(T) ≡ i(–T)'.

Now, deontic speech is a completely different story: 'to say that *A* is under no obligation to stay at home is not the same as to say that he is under the obligation not so stay at home, that is, to go out' (ibid., 150f). If one accepts a certain directive, one must not, at the same time, reject the same directive. Moreover, if one accepts the directive, one must also accept its complement. But this does not hold for rejections: 'rejection of a directive is compatible with rejection as well as acceptance of its complement' (ibid., 152). For instance, from the external negation of the directive 'Stay at home!' does not follow the obligation to go out (On the negation of conditional norms see Ratti 2013, 81ff)

3. Opposition 'External/Internal Disjunction' (Ross's Paradox). According to Ross, 'O(p) v O(q)' is totally different from O(p v q) – even if we are not usually conscious of this distinction in everyday discourse. The former disjunction means that there is an obligation to choose between *p* and *q*, while the latter means that there is either an obligation to perform *p*, without any choice, or to perform *q*, again with no choice (Ross 1968, 158ff). Moreover, whereas in indicative logic 'p → p v q' is valid, in deontic logic Op does not imply O(p v q). Here goes the famous example: the obligation to post a letter does not imply an obligation to either post it or burn it (Ross 1941, 53ff)

4. Opposition 'External/Internal Consequence'. Internal implication is expressed by the formula O(p→q), while external implication is expressed by the formula O(p)→O(q). They are not equivalent, and they shall not be confused (Ross 1968, 166ff). The latter states that a certain obligation is tied up with a second obligation (for instance, 'if Alejandro is under the obligation of smoking a joint, he is also under the obligation of sharing it with his friend Luka'); the former states that if someone has made something, then he is also obliged to something else, without implying the obligation of the first action (for instance, 'if Alejandro is rolling a joint, he is under the obligation of lighting it').

Ross's account is not free from pathologies. The logical and semantic states of what Ross calls 'the idea of a topic', for instance, remain obscure. If we read the first chapters of *Directives and Norms*, we have the impression that the idea of a topic (T) in the formulas 'i(T)' and 'd(T)' should be considered as (something like) a definite description, or a verbal name, while the semantic abstraction from illocutionary force (either 'd' or 'i') should be understood as a peculiar predicate, which is attached to the definite description in order to obtain a well-formed sentence. Accordingly, we shall conclude that, without force-predicate, no inference is possible, for definite descriptions (or verbal names) are singular terms and no inference is possible if we only have a singular term (from 'the action of smoking' I cannot infer anything at all!).

In some passages taken from the last chapter of the book, Ross's scheme seems to be completely overturned, and this is a terrible surprise: the cognitive part of a directive clearly becomes a proposition, which, by definition, can be object of truth-functional inferences. Moreover – and this is truly astonishing – this very proposition is assertive and not neutral for it is defined in terms of truth-conditions (as something that 'ought to be true'). The model becomes basically indistinguishable from the one that belongs to the dominant view. I honestly do not understand why but even the symbolisation changes – for instance, 'd(T)' becomes 'Op' (ibid., 155). I do not see any simplification in this move. We might very well ask ourselves what happened. All of this is completely inconsistent for it goes directly against Ross's fundamental assumptions – especially against the idea that directives have nothing to do with reality (ibid., 35). To crown it all, Ross does not even explain whether 'i' and 'd' are connected to '(T)' in the same way or whether the connection is different; the notion of 'content' itself is obscure and Ross does not make any argument against non-assertive versions of the notion of proposition.

I think that these pathologies can be cured. First of all, we could solve the ambiguities by pursuing consistency in our stipulations. Second, we can assume that directives have *compliance conditions*, instead of truth conditions: the command 'Alejandro, smoke some marijuana!' is complied if and only if Alejandro smokes some marijuana. Third, we can revise Ross's notational apparatus, to avoid further confusions between directive contents, propositions, definite descriptions, etc. Fourth, we can specify whether force is a sentential operator or not.

4. Adding some fuel to the minority account

4.1 Contradictions and incompatibilities for contraries

In order to demonstrate that illocutionary force has a deep impact at the level of semantic contents, we can try to restate a puzzle proposed by Ota Weinberger in the early '80 (Weinberger 1985a, 1985b). I have developed this reformulation together with Alejandro Calzetta (Calzetta and Sardo 2014)[8].

If all speech acts were just pragmatic operations on propositions, lacking any semantic relevance whatsoever, and if propositions have logical priority on their uses, we should want to say that from a *contradiction* between two propositions *p* and *–p* a whole series of *incompatibilities for contraries* between speech acts will obtain. From *p* and *–p* we obtain the following: a) Assertions '⊢p' / '⊢-p'; b) Commands: '!p'/ '!-p'; c) Rejections: '¡p' / '¡-p'; d) Positive Permissions: '*Per*p' / '*Per*-p'; e) Questions 'p?' / -p?'. If we want to stick to some *basic assumptions* of the standard view, we shall conclude that all these speech acts yield *incompatibilities for contraries*. However, it is possible to demonstrate that this is not the case for *p* and *–p* do not generate incompatibilities in all the speech acts in which they are embedded:

1) The presence of *p* and *–p* does not imply any incompatibility when they are embedded in the act of rejection (c). Let us take, for instance, 'Smoking marijuana is rejected.' 'Not smoking marijuana is rejected.' We can issue both of them at the same time and, surprisingly, the result of these two speech acts is not a contradiction but, at best, a normative gap. The rejection of a contradiction is no contradiction at all.
2) The two speech acts '*Per*p' and '*Per*-p' are likewise not incompatible. If, for instance, my mother tells me 'You are permitted to smoke marijuana' and 'You are permitted not to smoke marijuana' or, if you prefer, 'You are permitted both to smoke marijuana and not to smoke marijuana', she is basically saying that I can do whatever I want to: once again, no contradiction is implied.
3) Finally, the same kind of consideration holds for questions: 'p?' and '-p?' are not incompatible at all and they can be answered with the very same answer. 'Does Alejandro smoke marijuana?' is compatible with 'Does not Alejandro smoke marijuana?' Indeed, I can even ask: 'Does Alejandro smoke marijuana or not?' And the answer to both questions can always be the same: 'Alejandro smokes marijuana.'

4.2 Paraphrases and illusions

A second series of arguments can be drawn from Baker and Hacker's radical (and Wittgensteinian) criticism of the distinction between sense and force in order to demonstrate the flaws of truth-functional semantics and compositionality. The gist of Baker and Hacker's argumentation can be summed up as follows: every

8 In our demonstration we assume the validity of the conglomeration principle.

attempt to demonstrate that sentences in different moods share a common descriptive content is either 'nonsensical' or 'vacuous' (Baker and Hacker 1984, 81):

1. We have to consider that *describing* is a language-activity directed to certain objects. A typical description generally requires more than one sentence. Furthermore, 'not every sentence which is about something which might be an object of description is itself either a description or necessarily a part of description' (ibid., 82). For instance, it is impossible to describe a ceremony of the Catholic Church with a single sentence.
2. If we use 'description' in an ordinary sense, then the thesis that all sentences describe (or *partly* describe) something is completely false. Imperatives, optatives, interrogatives and explanations are not commonly used as description units. *Wh-questions* do not describe anything ('What did you do yesterday?'). The same holds for exclamations and ejaculations ('What a day!'), imperative sentences ('Give me some marijuana!') and optatives ('If only I could have some marijuana!') (see ibid., 83–84).
3. If we want to use 'description' in a philosophical sense, then the thesis that all sentences 'describe' something is empty because it is based on arbitrary stipulations. It is not a discovery about the nature of sentences but rather a 'piece of legislation' that establishes a new way of talking about sentences. Moreover, it is still hard to see how a logical truth ('Nothing can be red or green all over') or a self-contradiction can be understood as a description of something, or as having a descriptive content (ibid., 85–86).
4. The demonstration that all the different sentences of a language have a descriptive part in common is based on a 'weird' strategy, which is methodologically questionable: choosing two intuitively similar unasserted sentences, and rephrasing them in a way that split their 'common cognitive part' and their variable pragmatic part.

For instance, according to a strategy adopted by many authors, the following sentences:

[1] 'You smoke marijuana.'
[2] 'Do you smoke marijuana?'
[3] 'Smoke marijuana.'

could be reformulated in the following way:

[1'] 'It is the case/that you smoke marijuana.'
[2'] 'Is it the case/that you smoke marijuana?'
[3'] 'Make it the case/that you smoke marijuana.'

And this shall be considered as a clear demonstration that force and meaning are sharply separated, and that every speech act expresses a cognitive content. According to Baker and Hacker, these strategies are 'pure nonsense'. Leaving aside the fact that the objects of these reformulations are not clear at all (are they *type* sentences or *token* sentences?) the apparent uniformity of these sentences is an illusion that masks their logical differences. Moreover, in many cases the paraphrases fail, and this is by no means a merely formal problem (ibid., 95–96): the aim of these paraphrases is to represent the deep logical structure that lies behind the grammatical surface of ordinary language sentences. Their point is that the logical structure of ordinary language sentences cannot be captured by intrinsic paraphrases for it is entirely dependent on their use. This is easy to demonstrate. Let us take, for instance, the following cases:

[4] 'Everybody smokes a joint.'	[4'] Make it the case that everybody smokes a joint.
[5] 'Let A be an isosceles triangle!'	[5'] Make it the case that A is an isosceles triangle.
[6] 'If it rains, smoke a joint.'	[6'] Make it the case that if it rains, you smoke a joint.
[7] 'Let me smoke!'	[7'] Make it the case that I will smoke.

In each of these cases the result of the paraphrases is a complete failure:

- [4'] and [5'] obscure, or mask, the addressees of the command.
- [6] is a conditional command, while [6'] is a command to make a conditional true.
- [7'] would be equivalent to 'Make me go', which is very different from 'Let me go!'

The examples could, of course, be multiplied. However, Hacker and Backer's arguments do not come for free: the price is the rejection of the idea that compositionality can be used to explain the unity of meaning and the need to explain what the 'glue' that keeps the different parts of a sentence together is. In this respect, their approach is incompatible with Ross's theory. If we add this argument to the minority view, we should also, in order to avoid any contradiction, revise many of its tenets.

5. One step beyond

Are these arguments sufficient to demonstrate that sense and force, locution and illocution are not sharply separated? Once I would have answered 'Yes' – basically due to ignorance of the recent philosophical literature on this topic – but now my answer is 'No' for several reasons:

1. Further arguments shall be adduced in favour of the view that there are two semantic contents at hand (instead of one propositional content qualified by non-truth-conditionally conveyed contents), one non-descriptive, pertaining to the speech-act performed by virtue of issuing or uttering a directive, and one descriptive which is further qualified by a deontic/illocutionary force operator. Actually, it does not immediately follow that the descriptive counterpart must be a pragmatically enriched proposition. For instance, it could very well be a descriptive (non-normative) proposition about the creation of a norm, or the issuing of a command. This thesis can be the result of a cognitivist 'paratactic approach' (Jørgensen 1937/38, 293; Davidson 1979 and, with some caveats, Lewis 1970 – the last one cannot be considered as a 'paratactic approach' *sensu stricto*). Consider the following example: we could claim that an imperative sentence such as 'Close the door!' can be easily paraphrased using an explicit performative such as 'I order you to close the door', where 'I order' shall be considered as a description of the speech act, which can be subject to a truth-functional analysis. This is a reductionist approach, because it tries to explain use-conditional features of meaning through categories that belong to the classical truth-conditional semantics; and – as Josh Parsons points out – is now commonplace among the 'Australian cognitivists'. We can sum up what we have just said as follows: 'The thesis of cognitivism, then, is that imperatives are equivalent to the corresponding performatives, and the performatives in turn are true iff it is so commanded' (Parsons 2012, 52).

What kind of arguments can we bring in favour of our case? A nice way to begin is to demonstrate, as Josh Parsons brilliantly does, that several flaws affect this sort of cognitivist approach (ibid., § 3).

First of all, there is plenty of room for 'unwanted validities', because this model ends up by transforming arguments that are patently invalid into perfectly valid arguments. Here goes Parsons's example. Consider the following argument (S): (S1) 'Attack at dawn!' – Therefore (S2) 'Someone commands something'. According to this kind of cognitivism, this argument shall be translated in (S'): (S1') 'I command that you attack at dawn' – Therefore (S2') 'Someone commands something'. Bearing in mind that the argument S' is valid, if cognitivism is true, then also the argument S should be valid. Unfortunately (for them) this is not the case: in (S) the premises and the conclusion have a different subject matter.

Secondly, cognitivism also produces 'unwanted consistencies'. In this case the demonstration given by Parsons is very close to the one implied in our reformulation of Weinberger's puzzle. Let us take an inconsistent set of commands: (1) 'Attack!'; (2) 'Do not attack!'. It is very likely that the cognitivist will offer the following paraphrases: (1') 'I command that you attack'; (2') 'I command that you do not attack'. Now, the problem is the following: (1') and (2') are not inconsistent, 'for it is not inconsistent to report that an inconsistent set of commands has been made'. Actually, I can say (3) 'I commanded that you attack and I commanded that you do not attack' without any worry of falling into contradiction because I am just 'describing'.

2. Another option worth subjecting to critical scrutiny claims that the meaning of a directive is a modal/deontic proposition in the sense that the deontic modal does not operate on the proposition but figures into its content. This is not a reductionist account of directives, precisely because the proposition associated with the meaning of a directive is not the proposition expressed by the corresponding declarative descriptive sentence, but a deontic or normative proposition. Hilpinen and Aloni defend accounts of this sort (Hilpinen 2006; Aloni, 2007). The analysis of this proposal goes beyond the aims of this modest paper.

3. The Frege-Geach objections to noncognitivist accounts of directive speech – objections that are connected with the complicated relations between predication and assertion – should be rejected (Geach 1960, 1965). There is still a heap of problems pertaining to how we are to explain the inconsistency of speech-acts (or attitudes) that are not reducible to each other: in other words, we have to show how certain attitudes, other than beliefs, are 'inconsistencies transmitting' (Schroeder 2008, 43ff). Mark Schroeder has recently developed a possible line of defence (Schroeder 2008).

Acknowledgements: I would like to thank Mauro Barberis, Alejandro D. Calzetta, Riccardo Guastini, Nicola Muffato, Francesca Poggi for their precious comments on an earlier version of this paper.

References

Alchourrón, Carlos Eduardo, and Bulygin, Eugenio. 1971. *Normative Systems*. Wien, Springer.

Alchourrón, Carlos Eduardo, and Bulygin, Eugenio. 1981. The Expressive Conception of Norms. In *New Studies in Deontic Logic*, edited by Risto Hilpinen. Dordrecht: D. Reidel Publishing Company.

Alchourrón, Carlos Eduardo, and Bulygin, Eugenio. 1984. Pragmatic Foundation for the Logic of Norms. *Rechtstheorie* 15: 453–464.

Aloni, Maria. 2007. Free Choice, Modals and Imperatives. *Natural Language Semantics* 15: 65–94.

Austin, John L. 1975. *How to Do Things with Words*, 2nd ed. Oxford: Clarendon Press.

Baker, Gordon P., and Hacker, Peter M.S. 1984. *Scepticism, rules and language.* Oxford: Basil Blackwell.

Calzetta, Alejandro D., and Sardo, Alessio. 2014. Una nueva visita a la concepción expresiva. *Doxa* 37: 45–63.

Davidson, Donald. 1979. Moods and Performances. *The Southwest Journal of Philosophy* 10: 7–20.

Geach, Peter. 1960. Ascriptivism. *The Philosophical Review* LXIX: 221–225.

Geach, Peter. 1965. Assertion. *Philosophical Review* 74(4): 449–465.

Grice, Paul. 1957. Meaning. *Philosophical Review* 66: 377–388.

Hilpinen, Risto. 2006. Norms, Normative Utterances and Normative Propositions. *Análisis Filosófico* 26: 229–241.

Jørgensen, Jorgen. 1937/38. Imperatives and Logic. *Erkenntnis* 7: 288–296.

Lewis, David. 1970. General Semantics. *Synthese* 22: 18–67.

Marmor, Andrei. 2005. *Interpretation and Legal Theory.* Oxford – Portland (Oregon): Hart Publishing.

Muffato, Nicola. 2007. *La semantica delle norme.* Genova: Ecig.

Parsons, Josh. 2012. Cognitivism about Imperatives. *Analysis* 72: 49–54.

Poggi, Francesca. 2012. Contextualism, but Not Enough. *Revus* 17: 55–65.

Poggi, Francesca. 2013. The Myth of Literal Meaning in Legal Interpretation. *Analisi e Diritto* 2013: 313–335.

Ratti, Giovanni Battista. *Studi sulla logica del diritto e della scienza giuridica.* Madrid: Marcial Pons.

Raz, Joseph. [1975] 1999. *Practical Reason and Norms.* Oxford: Oxford University Press.

Recanati, Francois. 1987. *Meaning and Force. The Pragmatics of Performative Utterances.* Cambridge: Cambridge University Press.

Reichenbach, Hans. 1947. *Elements of Symbolic Logic.* New York: The MacMillan Company.

Ross, Alf. 1941. Imperatives and Logic. *Theoria* 7: 53–71.

Ross, Alf. 1968. *Directives and Norms.* London: Routledge & Kegan Paul.

Sbisà, Marina. 2006. Speech Acts Without Propositions? *Grazer Philosophische Studien* 72: 155–178.

Sbisà, Marina. 2013. Locution, Illocution, Perlocution. In *Pragmatics of Speech Actions,* edited by Marina Sbisà and Ken Turner, 25–75. Berlin: De Gruyter Mouton.

Schroeder, Mark. 2008. *Being For. Evaluating the Semantic Program of Expressivism.* Oxford: Oxford UP.

Searle, John. 1969. *Speech Acts.* Cambridge: Cambridge University Press.

Stalnaker, Robert. 1970. Pragmatics. *Synthese* 22: 272–289.

Stalnaker, Robert. 1974. Pragmatic Presuppositions. In *Semantics and Philosophy*, edited by Milton K. Munitz and Peter K. Unger. New York: New York University Press.

Stenius, Erik. 1967. Mood and Language Game. *Synthese* 17: 254–274.

Villa, Vittorio. 2012. *Una teoria pragmaticamente orientata dell'interpretazione giuridica.* Torino: Giappichelli.

Tarello, Giovanni. 1974. *Diritto, enunciati, usi.* Bologna: Il Mulino.

Weinberger, Ota. 1958. *Die Sollsatzproblematik in der modernen Logik.* Prag: Verlag der Tschechoslowakischen Akademie der Wissenschaften.

Weinberger, Ota. 1985a. The Expressive Conception of Norms – An Impasse for the Logic of Norms. *Law and Philosophy* 4: 165–198.

Weinberger, Ota. 1985b. On the Meaning of Norm Sentences, Normative Inconsistency, and Normative Entailment. A Reply to Carlos E. Alchourrón and Eugenio Bulygin. *Law and Philosophy* 4: 465–475.

Weinberger, Ota. 1987. *Logik, Semantik, Hermeneutik.* München: Beck.

Weinberger, Ota. 1988. *Norm und Institution. Eine Einführung in die Theorie des Rechts.* Wien: Manz.

Silvia Zorzetto

On Impossibility in Law

1. Introduction

The concept of impossibility in law has multifaceted applications. Legal scholars and judges are familiar with a wide range of cases in which it appears relevant, while many statutory laws and legal acts take into consideration impossible situations. Moreover, in contemporary legal systems there are cases of nonsense norms and prescriptions that either seem absurd or bear only a symbolic significance in point of fact. There are also cases in which norms presuppose or depend on impossible requirements. It is impossible, for example, to obey when the law prescribes something that cannot take place. It is sometimes beyond our means not to infringe a norm imposing an obligation. Furthermore, the fact that an action is impossible may also be a reason for applying or not applying norms, remedies and punishments. It follows, therefore, that many excuses and exceptions depend on impossibility. And there are instances when being in compliance with the law clashes with cases of legal antinomies, i.e. when acting in obedience to one norm entails infringing another. Impossibility also occurs when provisions cannot be implemented because of technical gaps.

Impossibility also has a multitude of sources. At times it depends on logic and language or human intellectual faculties, while on other occasions it is basically related to nature and the human capacity for action. But it may also be a side effect of living circumstances or originate in mistakes in laws. It is therefore very common to postulate impossibility in relation to norms, obligations, concrete human actions, natural events, etc., while there are actually many different kinds of impossibility – logical, conceptual, practical, empirical/factual, and so on.

The aim of this paper is therefore to clarify the most relevant uses of impossibility by illustrating what legal impossibility is and presenting a typology.

While very many philosophical and moral studies deal with the question if ought implies can (see Vranas 2007), impossibility tends to be a neglected subject in current analytical legal thinking.[1] In ethics there is, however, much debate about the principle (see Kramer 2004), which often furnishes the implicit general

1 Some exceptions are Rabel 1907, Brecht 1941, Stockhammer 1959, Capozzi 1996 and Conte and Di Lucia 2012.

framework of discourse on impossibility in law, even though a wide gap normally exists between concrete legal issues and analysis in ethics and jurisprudence.

Here I will be presenting only a few aspects of my research,[2] and will be putting aside any discussion of deficiencies by jurists as well as the contentious methodological and philosophical issues arising from the ought-implies-can principle in ethics.[3] For the moral debating does not seem to contribute to clarifying the use of impossibility in law, which has specific features absent from other practical domains.

Impossibility in law depends essentially on what laws provide as well as the concept of law held by judges and jurists. For instance, many natural law theories show evidence of this by deriving impossibilities from natural general principles and/or the very nature of things (see Schermaier 2006, 5). From a descriptive perspective, legal thinking and practice define what is legally impossible, far more than facts, logic, language or moral principles themselves. It cannot be denied that factual/logical impossibilities may be indeed legally relevant, but the last word belongs to the law. This approach is, in fact, rooted in a constructivist conception of law that considers it an intellectual artefact, i.e. a conventional domain defined by constitutive rules and governed by authorities and its own pragmatics (Roversi 2014).

In legal thinking and practice the implication contained in the ought-implies-can principle has the same structure as that found in Charles I. Lewis's strict formulation.[4] This means that according to the bench and legal doctrine, what is laid down needs to have the possibility of becoming an obligation or, in other words, an obligation must have a possible content. The issue is, of course, what sense is given to possibility and that is precisely what the law decides.

However, a version of the ought-implies-can principle is relevant to the present analysis, namely the idea that a norm must be practically realisable or it is pointless. As some philosophers observe, this is a general idea in law often expressed by the maxim *impossibilium nulla obligatio est*, which means that nobody can be obliged to perform what they find impossible. A leitmotif in legal thinking is that the law always obliges actions on the assumption that the actions are possible.

2 This paper is the continuation of a preliminary analysis (see Zorzetto 2014).

3 The principle is interpreted in many ways: it is considered a logical/conceptual/metaphysical entailment, a presupposition, a conversational implicature, and a first- or second-order meta-theoretical moral principle. It has been traced back to Pelagius and Augustine, but is usually associated with Kant, though there is much disagreement about how he understood it (see Stern 2004).

4 For an introduction to strict implication and the related notion of impossibility see Kenny 2007, 116–120.

Failing that, the legal world would become 'a kind of buffoonery' (Zimmermann 1996, 687).

To illustrate and test these hypotheses, I will be focusing my discourse on three points. The first will present some paradigmatic uses of the most renowned maxims on impossibility such as the principle *impossibilium nulla obligatio est*, while the second will discuss specific features of impossibility in law and the final point will outline a preliminary typology of very common meanings of impossibility in legal reasoning.

2. Legal maxims

The idea that an impossible obligation cannot exist is a common place in legal thinking, as the many maxims or principles routinely used to express it show. Besides the Celsus maxim *impossibilium nulla obligatio est,* there are similar tenets like *nemo potest ad impossibile obligari, ultra posse nulla obligatio, ultra posse nemo obligatur, ad impossibilia nemo tenetur, lex non cogit ad impossibilia, lex non cogit seu ad vana aut impossibilia, lex non intendit aliquid impossibile, quia impotentia excusat legem* or *in potentia excusat legem.*

These maxims, of Classical origin, were all in current use in the Middle Ages, and are present everywhere in Anglo-American and continental legal thinking and practice, both in higher court case law as well as private and public law.

In particular, the maxims *lex non cogit ad impossibilia* and *lex non intendit aliquid impossibile* are currently applied in the construction of statutes in Anglo-American law.

> As English case law shows, according to the bench, the administration of law must yield to that which everything must bend, to necessity. The law is understood to disclaim all intention of compelling injunctions to impossibilities, so that the administration of law must adopt that general exception in the consideration of particular cases. The law is not so unreasonable as to require the performance of impossibilities […] and when legislators use language so broad as apparently to lead to such results, the courts say that the legislature cannot have intended to include those cases in which, by the act of God, a literal obedience to their mandate has become impossible. Hence, if a statute apparently requires the performance of things which cannot be performed or apparently bases its commands upon the assumption of an impossible state of affairs, the court must seek for some interpretation of its terms not too strained or fantastic, which will avoid these results. If the legislature does direct or require an impossibility, in language too plain to be mistaken or to be explained away the act will simply be rendered inoperative thereby, and it becomes the duty of the court to pronounce accordingly. (Campbell Black 2008, 99–100)

Views like this date back to 17th and 18th century precedents in the Chancery Division of the English Court, to be found with illustrious judges like Sir Edward

Coke (Co. Litt. 231, b: Broom 1882, 242–251). Nowadays common law judges still follow these leading cases and apply the above tenets in many fields of law, like possession, property, real estates, contracts, and so on.

As the quotation shows, the idea that impossibility is a legal limit is a common assumption, which leads to a teleological interpretation of texts against the *littera legis* and in favour of the *spirit* of the law. In particular, the *ad impossibilia* argument is very close to the line of thought of reasonable/rational legislation.

The same point of view is also present in continental law. A good example of how strong its impact is within the EU legal system is the doctrine according to which national laws can derogate from European legislation only if the differences in treatment are justified by a legitimate aim and the means are appropriate and necessary. In European Court of Justice case law, practical impossibilities are clear cases of legitimate derogation as 'it is impossible for the states to set up a subsequent unilateral measure against a legal order which they have accepted on a reciprocal basis' (Judgment of the Court of 15 July 1964, Case 6/64: *Flaminio Costa v E.N.E.L.*).

Legal concepts and categories such as some kinds of contracts are also construed on assumptions about what is practically possible or impossible. A good example is the aleatory contract, whose distinctive feature is its uncertain outcome at the time of the agreement. It is a kind of contract that works for situations where it is impossible to evaluate a feasible distribution of risks.

Many legal systems give much weight to the lack of basic necessities, and therefore provide the specific measures needed.

Remedies also depend on assumptions about practical possibilities of proof and defence. Both civil and criminal rules of procedure, for example, provide different *loci standi,* which take into consideration the possibility of identifying the class of agents and victims.

As is well known, the excuses for offences such as a state of necessity and legitimate defence are typically justified on the grounds of the idea that *ultra posse nemo obligatur.* This type of justification also exists in the area of political conflicts and disagreements among States.[5]

---

5 See e.g. The Trial of German Major War Criminals sitting at Nuremberg, Germany, 16–27 July 1946, spec. on 19 July 1946:
To be obliged on pain of punishment to murder the head of the State? A soldier should do that? And in war time? Those who have committed such crimes have always been punished, but to punish them for not doing so would indeed be something new. Naturally there are limits to legal obligations for the jurists too, but in a state of conflict which offers only this kind of solution, the old saying applies: *Ultra posse nemo obligatur*.

Moreover, the maxims *nemo tenetur se detegere*, *nemo tenetur contra se edere* and *nemo tenetur se ipsum accusare* are usually recognised as corollaries of the due process of law and the right to resist (Reggio 2012, 211–214). They can, however, also be interpreted as occurrences of the principle ought-implies-can, for they are in fact based on the assumption that it is impossible to expect people to tell the truth *contra se*.

Generally accepted legal principles, such as that of reasonableness and precaution together with *homo homini* presumptions, rely on what is practically possible/impossible. It is interesting to note that some feel these principles are grounded in the above maxims, which are seen as tokens of a very general principle of law deriving from both common sense and equity.

However, for all these principles to be applied, the circumstantially relevant possibilities and impossibilities need to be identified, and the criteria for doing so may be generally held beliefs and convictions, basic standards of conduct or the best scientific knowledge.

How to identify what is materially impossible lies indeed at the heart of the matter. A telling emblem is the termination of contract tenet, both in civil and common law traditions, where many statutes and precedents establish that the debtor is no longer obliged to take action when performance becomes objectively impossible (Wade 1940, 519ff; Hellner 1969, 705–720). According to bench and legal doctrine, the concept of impossibility must not be interpreted *stricto sensu* as denoting only logical or absolute impossibilities for all. The parameter is not an ideal agent, but a normal person in the same situation as the debtor. Common factors for defining what is impossible are the skills and awareness of the parties, the content of their agreement, the nature of the contract, contingences, acts of Gods, changes in law, etc.

The maxim *actus dei nemini facit iniuriam* expresses therefore a particular case. This was illustrated in 1579–1581 *Wolfe v Shelley* in these words:

> if a lessee covenants to leave wood in as good a plight as the wood was at the time of the lease, and afterwards the three trees are blown down by the tempest, he is discharged from his covenant, *quia impotentia excusat legem*.

In 1869 *Baily v De Crespigny* the maxim *lex non cogit ad impossibilia* was also applied to free a defendant from his covenant not to build or permit anything

---

See also the discussion about the European policy initiative for the new monetary system at the 30 November 1978 Bundesbank Council meeting with Chancellor Schmidt (assurances on the operation of EMS) [http://www.margaretthatcher.org/document/111554, accessed on 20 August 2014].

to be built on the land for an agreed term due to a subsequent act of Parliament revoking his power to perform the covenant.

In particular, judges usually evaluate if the contract is of such a nature that its performance was contemplated as dependent on the persistence of the object in question. If, for example, the parties could not reasonably have contemplated a contingency making the performance impossible or the event causing the impossibility was of such a kind that it could not reasonably have been foreseen by the parties at the time of the agreement (Eisenberg 2009).

The idea *ad impossibilia nemo tenetur* also has a significant impact on the causation issue both in tort and criminal law (Pisani 2011/2012, 118). It is particularly interesting as it plays two opposite functions by justifying the *condicio sine qua non* theory of causation, based on necessity, as well as the alternative concept known as the adequacy theory that gives relevance to deviations. In tort law, liability for damages, especially in the case of dangerous activities, often tends to be excluded where damage occurs, though not as a consequence of the normal course of events.

For some legal theories, all laws need to be interpreted according to a pragmatic general assumption that they are to be followed as long as there are no factual obstacles or normative limitations. The fundamental premise of this view is that legal rules are reasons for action which are essential for interacting with others and planning our lives, so that the law is seen as a naturally designed domain, which takes into account normal factual conditions which do not irrationally interfere with the realization of social order.

Supreme Courts usually explain that *lex non cogit ad impossibilia* expresses a general legal principle that 'derives from the principles of justice and equity' and over the years has been applied to avoid, for instance, time bar provisions in statutes (South Africa Supreme Court, *Barkhuizen v Napier* Case CCT72/05, decided on 4 April 2007).

The ought-implies-can principle and its corollary *ad impossibilia nemo tenetur* are also implicit in many concepts of rules like defeasible or *prima facie* tenets that have to be applied *rebus sic stantibus* and/or under normal circumstances, but are nevertheless open to exceptions: 'The law is understood to disclaim all intention of compelling to impossibilities and the administration of laws must adopt that general exception in the consideration of all particular cases' (Rajasthan High Court *State of Rajasthan v Tara and Others* on 7 February 2001).

Sometimes the view that laws essentially regard normal situations leads to the impression that only major cases are ruled in written provisions, while marginal ones have to be settled on the ground of principles.

Some feel that the principle *ad impossibilia nemo tenetur* is also a criterion of rationality in legal reasoning. And in his theory of fundamental rights, Alexy defines principles as 'norms which require that something be realised to the greatest extent possible, given the legal and factual possibilities' (Alexy 2003, 135). This definition can also be applied to rules, though it is more important to note that it calls for a very active judicial practice since Alexy's theory calls for judges to make clear-cut interpretations and applications in order to realise as far as possible the values embedded in the law.

As anticipated at the beginning, the ought-implies-can principle and its corollary *ad impossibilia nemo tenetur* are commonly related to conflicts in law. From an extreme point of view, in the case of legal antinomy no genuine prescription exists at all, which means that consistency is an essential feature of law (Feis 2012). However, it is more common to think that legal systems may be, and in fact are, inconsistent. In case of legal antinomies, therefore, it is impossible to be in compliance with the law, unless a meta-criterion comes to the rescue by establishing the sole rule to be applied in the case.

Rules may also prescribe to a general class of persons a conduct that some of its members are unable to perform. Such partial impossibility is usually discussed under the name of over-inclusiveness, as for instance with the ruling 'Sons and daughters must obey their own parents', which clearly cannot be applied to orphans (Gentili 2013, 172). Speaking of orphans obeying their parents is nonsensical, unless one assumes a broad concept that includes obedience to the will expressed by the dead in their lifetime. On the contrary, the rule 'Sons and daughters must respect their own parents' is also applicable to orphans since respect towards parents includes looking after their memory, and thus remains after death.

Over-inclusiveness is usually neutralised in re-interpreting the rules. Going back to our example, a more specific rule that calls for non-orphans alone to obey their parents can be created by distinguishing between orphans and non-orphans. It is however open to debate whether in this way a complementary rule on non-orphans is also generated, or the situation of non-orphans becomes simply irrelevant (un-ruled).

Finally, impossibility is related to legal and, more precisely, technical gaps in Kelsen's lexicon (Kelsen 1970, 127–128). When rule A presupposes rule B, but the latter does not exist, following rule A is impossible. Conte calls this situation a 'praxeological gap' to denote the absence of a first rule whose validity is a necessary requirement for the efficacy of a second one (Conte and Di Lucia 2012, 167–178). The same gap in construction exists when rules are addressed to elective judges, but no rule exists for the election of judges.

3. What is impossible according to the law?

The above examples show that the key issue in ethics, i.e. whether a person can be morally obliged to do something that is logically impossible, has little pertinence to legal impossibilities, which are more related to requirements whose fulfilment is physically unfeasible.

In fact, while the law is interested in what people can do in reality, abilities, choices, and opportunities together with obligations are also indexed to times, facts and laws themselves. In the legal domain 'can' depends both on personal ability and opportunity: a person can do *p* as they have both the ability and the opportunity to do so (Vranas 2007; Gardner 2013). Abilities require skills, physical capacities and knowledge, while efficacy or success in achieving aims and unreasonableness in expecting someone to do something is of little count. A person has the opportunity to do *p* if the situation allows them to exercise their ability.

In abstract terms there are three general kinds of impossibility.

First, a rule has no sense for linguistic/conceptual reasons. A trivial example is the rule 'One ought to paint the absolute blue'. Not all cases of impossibility are so easy to understand. For instance, the rule 'Children are allowed to paint the town red during carnival' is far from being meaningless, for as native English speakers know, painting the town red means engaging in a wild spree.

Second, a rule cannot be infringed because it prescribes a necessity for logical/conceptual or practical/factual reasons. For instance, 2 + 2 famously = 4, and humans cannot not observe the laws of physics and neither can they control unconscious emotions.

Third, a rule cannot be observed because it prescribes an impossible action for all concerned. This is the most problematic case, as the following example shows. Let us consider articles 3, 13 and 1 of the Nice Chart of Human Rights: 'Everyone has the right to respect for his or her physical and mental integrity'; 'The arts and scientific research shall be free of constraint'; 'Human dignity is inviolable. It must be respected and protected'. Are these genuine or hollow rules? Are they declarations with a purely symbolic meaning or do they impose any duties or obligations?

Let us now consider that when laws say something impossible, a basic option exists. We can think that (i) no law, no obligation exists at all, or that (ii) a law actually exists but cannot be respected (Cohen 2008, 251–254). Though the attitude of legal operators is not up to now clear, the former option is usually chosen where impossibility is very manifest.

In fact, legal impossibilities are context-dependent, as the above uses show. What is legally impossible depends on both the specific context of application as well as the abstract content of each rule.

Another specific feature of impossibility in law is that the abstract meaning of the Latin maxims is not the basic problem; what is controversial is how they are implemented in each case. It is therefore essential to identify which impossibilities are legally relevant and therefore which criteria must be established. Judges have a wide discretion in identifying them as they are seldom explicitly stated in legal texts. According to the bench and legal doctrine, these criteria are usually to be found in common sense or specific branches of knowledge.

Moreover, the concepts of impossibility and possibility can be construed as all-or-nothing: one thing is possible or impossible, *tertium non datur*. But they can also be more-or-less concepts since we can conceive an infinite spectrum of different degrees of possibilities/impossibilities. In logic, impossibility is an all-or-nothing concept, while both in natural and legal language it is relative and continuous, though not measurable.

Impossibilities also depend on how conduct and events are described and hence the concepts used to express laws. It is of course true that people are able to conceive and speak about possible worlds different from the real one we live in. Good examples are conditionals and counterfactuals (Hage 2013). But in our world a train cannot arrive before its departure as a time constraint makes this impossible, assuming the concepts of 'train', 'arrival' and 'departure' have their common meanings.

In other words, our way of thinking is influenced by the meaning of words, and words also play an important part in determining our thinking. Therefore, something may or may not be possible depending on concepts (both ordinary and legal). In particular, our definitions and conceptual distinctions are not fixed, but are related to the pragmatic context and the purposes embedded in them. Many legal cases show this kind of interplay. For instance, destroying business documents, not delivering them or not keeping them appropriately are very different actions according to common sense and many laws. But in the case of fraudulent bankruptcy such actions are considered equally relevant, with the result that according to Italian case law, the difference between the three is lost when one has been proven to have damaged the company irreparably.

In the same way, whether an impossibility exists or not depends on how obligations, duties, prohibitions are described. And also what personal abilities are relevant according to the law as well as moral/internal motives.

So an issue that frequently arises is that of whether a person initially able to fulfil an obligation still has to carry it out even when fulfilment becomes impossible (Kramer 2003, 28–29). Two very run-of-the-mill examples are the following: an employee idles his time away and is unable to finish his work by the deadline;

a debtor is robbed on the way to the bank and thus is unable to repay the loan by the deadline. In the first example there is culpability, while in the second, an act of God. In neither case can the obligation be performed, but the concept of 'cannot' goes beyond physical impossibility and what is relevant is the level of due care and precautions adopted by the debtor. In the same way, a mountain climber might not be able to avoid a fall even if he climbs a slope cautiously, yet he could have avoided the accident by not mountaineering. A driver has a general duty to avoid accidents, but though he drives carefully, an accident still occurs. He/she could have avoided it by not driving at all. The overarching standard is the determination of impossibility or reasonableness in the situation in question.

In fact, though not mentioned in the laws of many countries, reasonableness is the main criterion for identifying relevant impossibilities. Both in civil and common law courts it is frequently used jointly with a principle of equity or justice as fairness. A basic intuition that motivates judges to accept the ought-implies-can principle and related maxims is the sense that it would be unfair to require of people to remedy situations beyond their control or those which they have striven hard to avoid.

It is interesting that laws sometimes create fictions to conceal impossibilities and save fairness. For instance, in English law there is a general rule requiring *profert* of a document pleaded, which means that the document must be duly produced to the court. But there are some exceptions that arise from necessity: when the document has already been pleaded in another court, destroyed by the opposite party or is in his/her hands, it is presumed to have been submitted to the bench. The reason given by the Court of King's Bench is that *lex non cogit ad impossibilia* (1789 *Read v Brookman* case).

When a law decrees something impossible, a general problem is whether only a purely nominal duty exists to follow it. A correct approach is to verify if within the legal system there are remedies, sanctions or other laws that can be applied to enforce such duties anyway. In addition, an unenforceable law may exist as a fact in that it influences conduct, motivation and attitude towards the law. For this reason, for instance, the futility argument against the laws of war is spurious, though most wars are indeed conducted with little regard for the rules (Lamb 2013, 6–7).

The artificial nature of legal impossibilities, i.e. that they depend on what the law itself prescribes, is also demonstrated by the fact that debtors often suffer constrictions although they cannot perform their obligations. Well-known examples are cases of strict liability in torts and the rules on termination of obligations in countries like Italy and Croatia. The latter's Civil Code provides that:

> An obligation shall be terminated when its performance becomes impossible due to circumstances for which the debtor is not responsible (art. 208);
>
> A debtor is also liable for partial or full impossibility to perform although the impossibility was not due to his fault, if the impossibility occurred after the delay the debtor is liable for (art. 342.4);
>
> In case of limitation of the maximum amount for compensatory damages, the creditor shall be entitled to full compensation if the impossibility to perform the obligation results from the intention or gross negligence of the debtor (art. 346.4);
>
> Should, after entering into a contract, extraordinary circumstances arise, that cannot be foreseen at the time of entering into a contract, making it excessively onerous for one party to perform, or if under such circumstances a party were to suffer an excessive loss as a result of the performance, variations or even the termination of the contract may be requested (art. 369).

Individual intention, will and feeling may be relevant to legal impossibilities. It is frequently said that 'can' means being able to act in compliance with the law through the scrupulous exercise of care and good will, and 'cannot' therefore means being *un*able to act. People are usually presumed to be free and capable of choosing what they want. In 1885 J. Maule, in *Canham v Barry*, observed that a man may, no doubt, for a good consideration contract to do that which he cannot be sure he will be able to do: 'a man may, if he chooses, covenant that it shall not rain tomorrow'.

Thus, an obligation, albeit impossible, does not cease to be in case of fault or folly. And these situations may depend on the physical capacities of the parties. For example, kleptomaniacs may be presumed by the law unable to control their impulses. And this though they can regularly control them (for instance, they generally avoid stealing when immediate arrest is probable, as when they are in full view of a police officer: DSM-5 2013, 478).

Let us consider that feelings and emotions can also be relevant for the law. As has been observed, it is commonly said that a person ought to feel in a certain way, e.g. be grateful, in spite of the fact that feelings cannot be voluntarily controlled. However, we can interpret duties or obligations concerning feelings/emotions as prescriptions to follow them since people can control their behaviour and cultivate feelings over time, so we can express gratitude in thanking or helping others.

4. A typology of impossibilities

The several meanings of impossibility existing in the legal domain can be summed up as follows.

(i) *Impossibility as a lack of rights or duties*: for instance, it is impossible for everybody to have the right of free speech if the law does not ascribe free speech to everybody. Likewise, we cannot all have the duty to testify if testimony is not recognised by the law. This kind of impossibility is compatible with both the static and the dynamic conception of rights/powers,[6] and such cases of impossibility may be seen as normative gaps, or not depending on the conception of the legal system and its completion.

(ii) *Impossibility as a lack of obligation or power*: for instance, in the case of personal exemption from paying taxes, it is impossible to be obliged to pay taxes. The same is true of the case of personal immunities, for it is impossible to file lawsuits and/or impose sanctions or punishments (Nwapi 2014, 35). This kind of impossibility does not denote any normative gap and is based on a relational and inter-dependent concept of legal positions in line with Hohfeld's table of deontic modalities.

(iii) *Impossibility as a lack of claim or power to enforce law*: for instance, it is impossible to carry out a judgment where there is a legitimate justification, or obtain extradition for alleged crimes where no rights have been infringed. The difference with this meaning is that impossibility is here related to the application of the law and is thus a property relying on the circumstances of cases rather than the sole definition of rights/duties or obligations/powers.

(iv) *Impossibility as a lack of evidence*: impossibility is directly related to proof in trials too, where 'impossible' means 'unproven' and/or 'improvable' according to the specific information available and the relevant rules on evidence.[7] For instance, it was impossible to say that there was a real danger of Lord Hoffmann being biased against Pinochet. This kind of impossibility is not related to the content of the law or its normative gaps, but rather to the arguments given for establishing or helping to establish a fact or the truth of a statement. To give another example, in an Italian case of defamation for the publication of offensive messages on Facebook, the court decided not to proceed as it was impossible to identify the sender/s of messages due to unsuitable evidence and the fact that a Facebook profile cannot be monitored all the time (see the Italian Court of Cassation, criminal section V, No. 18887, 18 April 2014).

---

6 About the static and the dynamic conception of rights/powers see for an introduction Poggi 2013, 23–82.

7 As has been observed in judicial matters and decision-making 'the articulation of all logical propositions in a probability space' is an impossible task 'when the probability space ranges over all human affairs' (Leiter and Allen 2001, 1509).

(v) *Impossibility as unacceptability*: behaviour is said to be impossible when it is totally ungrounded and insufferably offensive. This meaning of impossibility often occurs in everyday speech, and also in law. For example, according to Italian case law husbands/wives have the right to abandon the marital home in cases of intolerable/impossible cohabitation (Falzea 2010, 33).

(vi) *Impossibility as unreasonableness*: another use shared by legal parlance and ordinary language is 'impossible' meaning very unreasonable. In common parlance this use is informal, as for example when a mother complains about her difficult child and says 'John is being impossible'. In the legal domain this sense of impossibility is highly sophisticated and influenced by the 'reasonable man' concept. Moreover, it is both value-laden and fact-based. For instance, in 1675 *Hayes v Bickerstaff* it was said that a man's covenant shall not be strained so as to be unreasonable, or that it was improbable to be so intended, without necessary words to make it such; for it is unreasonable to suppose a man should covenant against the tortious acts of strangers, impossible for him to prevent, or probably to attempt preventing.

(vii) *Impossibility as uncertainty*: with regard especially to factual beliefs and fact-finding, 'impossible' may also mean 'uncertain', i.e. not absolutely ascertainable. It is close in meaning to impossibility as a lack of evidence (see iv), but quite distinct. Let us consider the standard of reasonable doubt that is grounded on our knowledge that it is impossible to determine innocence or guilt with absolute certainty. Impossibility in this case depends both on what is considered reasonable and the evidence available. However, a certain situation can be impossible to prove due to a lack of evidence in the legal process. Much evidence is in fact inadmissible in the courts, though it might be useful in reaching certainty in some circumstances (e.g. the hearsay rule).

(viii) *Impossibility as a lack of any plausible belief*: i.e. impossible as incredible or far-fetched. A defence based on alibi is a typical example that renders accusation unsubstantial.

(ix) *Impossibility as excessive difficulty*: according to European case law procedural rules cannot make the exercise of EU rights practically impossible, i.e. extremely difficult. The principle of effectiveness, for example, is violated by short time-limits that make 'the exercise of rights conferred by EU law impossible or excessively difficult.' The concrete application of this principle shows that the expression 'impossible or excessively difficult' is a hendiadys.

(x) *Impossibility as unavailability or deficiency of effectiveness*: 'impossible' also means 'ineffective' as many important uses are related to the effectiveness of the law, i.e. the entire legal system or some of its rules. For instance, with the collapse of the Rwandan legal system in 1994 it was impossible to carry out investigations and prosecutions. The implementation of a rule or contractual clause may well be impossible due to acts of God.

(xi) *Impossibility as unfitting/unfulfilling*: from a teleological point of view, 'impossible' may also mean 'not efficacious' or 'inefficient', that is to say not managing to produce the intended result. For instance, according to the bench (see the Italian Court of Cassation, criminal section III, No. 11835, 19 February 2013), a formal delegation of powers is superfluous and must be assumed *in re ipsa* within large-scale companies characterised by extensive delegations of activities. This tenet is consistent with the principle *ad impossibilia nemo tenetur* which excludes a single person from overseeing over many diverse activities. To give another example, the regulation for aggregating mountain farmsteads in Italy needs to be applied case by case and can be derogated where, according to the principle *ad impossibilia nemo tenetur*, it would be unfitting, as in the case of a proprietor possessing only one farmstead and not finding anyone interested in aggregating with him (Regional Administrative Tribunal Bolzano Trentino-Alto Adige section I, No. 258, 2 September 2010).

(xii) *Impossibility as inescapability/unavoidability*: this sense is common in cases of acts of torture or necessity.

(xiii) *Impossibility as a moral dilemma*: it is said that there is a practical impossibility in 'cases of desperation', that is situations where 'somebody resorts to contravening somebody else's moral rights in order to avert a dire fate for himself or for another person' (Kramer 2003, 64). So the decision to sacrifice other human lives in order to defeat some terrorists is a moral dilemma, i.e. a situation of moral conflict. Such a dilemma presents moral requirements which cannot all be resolved satisfactorily for a morality based on the supreme value of human life.

(xiv) *Impossibility as a conflict of legal duties*: in 1997 appeal case *Prosecutor of the Republic of Croatia* v. *Blaškić* it was said that the state official had been ordered by his superiors to refuse to surrender the documents and the state official would have been unable to disregard the instruction of his government: '*ad impossibilia nemo tenetur.*'

(xv) *Impossibility as (un)fairness*: in the 1787 *Pollard v Shaaffer* case the alleged breach was that the defendant had not paid the whole rent, or given back the house in good order. The defendant pleaded that the British army had invaded Philadelphia, taken possession of the house and committed acts of waste and destruction.

The Supreme Court of Pennsylvania declared the defendant had to pay the rent for the period of the army's occupation but was

> excused from his covenant to deliver up the house in good repair because a covenant to do this, against an act of God or an enemy, ought to be special and express, and so clear that no other meaning could be put upon it.

The defendant

> had no premium for this risk and it was not in the contemplation of either party. And, lastly, because equality is equity, and the loss should be divided [...]. Suppose, when the lease was executed, that the lessee had been asked, Is it your meaning, that, in case the buildings shall be destroyed by an act of God, or public enemies, you are to rebuild or repair them? His answer would have been unquestionably, 'No; I never entertained such an idea.' Should the like question have been put to the lessor, his answer would certainly have been, 'No, I do not expect anything so unreasonable'.

It is interesting to note that the principle *ad impossibilia nemo tenetur* is also used to avoid strict liability and impose fair instrumental duties (e.g. of information), instead of general duties of control. Italian courts state that it is impossible to oblige internet providers to control that privacy rights are duly observed for all the images uploaded on web sites. But they must take care and inform users of the privacy rights and supply all instructions for minimizing the risk of violation (Tribunal of Milan section IV, No. 1972, 12 April 2010).

(xvi) *Impossibility as necessity*: in the 1951 *Rex* v. *Canestra* case it was said that the maxim *lex non cogit ad impossibilia/nemo tenetur ad impossibilia* 'can only be applied to prohibition by translating them into the language of necessity, namely, that it was impossible to refrain from doing the prohibited act because it was necessary to do it'. In other cases, it is said that the maxim applies when there is an 'invincible disability to perform the mandatory part of the law, or to forbear the prohibition.'

5. Conclusion

The typology illustrated above is an initial review of some paradigmatic cases of apparent impossibility, each of which calls for further investigation and analysis. As can be seen, while most of the cases overlap, they all still have distinct connotations.

Some primary conclusions can however already be drawn. Though we speak about impossibility in law, it is in fact a most rare occurrence. What emerges strikingly is the association with issues of justice and equity and the call to standards of reasonableness and normality in each case. The concept of impossibility is used by judges at their discretion in order to adapt general rules to particular circumstances. In cases of original impossibility, situations are most often re-interpreted so as to have meaning and consequences on a legal level.

References

Alexy, Robert. 2003. Constitutional Rights, Balancing, and Rationality. *Ratio Juris* 16: 131–140.

American Psychiatric Association. 2013. The Diagnostic and Statistical Manual of Mental Disorders, Fifth Edition – DSM 5. Arlington: American Psychiatric Association.

Brecht, Arnold. 1941. The Impossible in Political and Legal Philosophy. *Canadian Law Review* 29: 312–331.

Broom, Herbert. 2000 [1882]. *A Selection of Legal Maxims, Classified and Illustrated.* Clark (New Jersey): The LawBook Exchange, Ltd.

Bundesbank Council meeting with Chancellor Schmidt (assurances on operation of EMS). 30 November 1978. *Bundesbank Archives (N2/267)* [http://www.margaretthatcher.org/document/111554, accessed on 14 May 2015].

Campbell Black, Henry. 2008 [1896]. *Handbook on the Construction and Interpretation of the Laws.* Clark (New Jersey): The LawBook Exchange, Ltd.

Capozzi, Gino. 1996. La possibilità giuridica. *Rivista internazionale di filosofia del diritto* 73: 418–449.

Cohen, Gerald A. 2008. *Rescuing Justice and Equality.* Cambridge MA: Harvard University Press.

Conte, Amedeo Giovanni, and Di Lucia, Paolo. 2012. Adýnaton. Four Dichotomies for a Philosophy of Impossibility. *Phenomenology and Mind* 2: 167–178. [http://www.phenomenologyandmind.eu accessed on 06.08.2014].

Eisenberg, Melvin A. 2009. Impossibility, Impracticability, and Frustration. *Journal of Legal Analysis* 1: 207–261.

Falzea, Angelo. 2010. La separazione personale. In *Ricerche di teoria generale del diritto e di dogmatica giuridica. III Scritti d'occasione*, 25–36. Milano: Giuffrè.

Feis, Guglielmo. 2012. "Dovere implica potere" a tutela dei diritti? [http://www.openstarts.units.it/ accessed on 20.08.2014].

Gardner, John. 2013. Reasons and Abilities: Some Preliminaries. *American Journal of Jurisprudence* 58: 63–74.

Gentili, Aurelio. 2013. Scienza giuridica e prassi forense. In *Il diritto come discorso*, 139–182. Milano: Giuffrè.

Hage, Jaap. 2013. Rules as Soft Constraints on Possible Worlds, 1–10. [http://www.jaaphage.nl/RULES%20AS%20SOFT%20CONSTRAINTS%20ON%20POSSIBLE%20WORLDS.pdf, assessed on 21.08.2014].

Hellner, Jan. 1969. The Influence of the German Doctrine of Impossibility on Swedish Sales Law. In *Ius privatum gentium: festschrift fur Max Rheistein zum 70. Geburtstag am 5 Juli 1969*, edited by von Ernst von Caemmerer, Soia Mentschikoff and Konrad Zweigert, 705–720. Tübingen: Mohr.

Kelsen, Hans. 1934. *Reine Rechtslehre. Einleitung in die Rechtswissenschaftliche Problematik*. Italian trans. by Renato Treves, *Lineamenti di dottrina pura del diritto*. Torino: Einaudi.

Kenny, Anthony. 2007. *Philosophy in the Modern World. A New History of Western Philosophy*, Vol. 4. Oxford: Oxford University Press.

Kramer, Matthew H. 2004. Moral Rights and the Limits of the "Ought"-Implies-"Can" Principle: Why Impeccable Precautions are No Excuse. In *Where Law and Morality Meet*, 249–294. Oxford: Oxford University Press.

Lamb, Antony. 2013. *Ethics and the Laws of War: The Moral Justification of Legal Norms*. New York: Routledge.

Leiter, Brian, and Allen, J. Ronald. 2001. Naturalized Epistemology and the Law of Evidence. *Virginia Law Review* 87: 1491–1550.

Nwapi, Chilenye. 2014. Jurisdiction by Necessity and the Regulation of the Transnational Corporate Actor. *Utrecht Journal of International and European Law* 78: 24–43 [http://dx.doi.org/10.5334/ujiel.cb, accessed on 20.08.2014].

Pisani, Mario. 2011/2012. Beccaria y el principio de humanidad. In *Cahiers de Defense Sociale. Pour une Politique Criminelle Humaniste*, 118–122. [http://www.defensesociale.org/CAHIERS_2012/Cahiers_2011-2012_PDF.pdf, accessed on 20.08.2014].

Poggi, Francesca. 2013. *Concetti teorici fondamentali. Lezioni di teoria generale del diritto*. Pisa: ETS.

Rabel, Ernst. 1907. Origine de la règle "impossibilium nulla obligatio". In *Mélanges Gerardin*, 473–512. Paris: L. Larose & L. Tenin.

Reggio, Federico. 2012. Nemo tenetur se detegere. In *Il diritto come processo. Princìpi, regole e brocardi per la formazione*, edited by Paolo Moro, 211–214. Milano: Franco Angeli.

Roversi, Corrado. 2014. Legal Metaphoric Artifacts (March 18, 2014). Available at *Social Science Research Network* [http://ssrn.com/abstract=2410790, assessed on 06.08.2014].

Schermaier, von Martin Josef. 2006. Impossibilium nulla obligatio. Vorverständnis, Begriff und Gegenstand der Unmöglichkeit der Leistung im römischen Recht. In *Annali del Seminario giuridico dell'Università degli*

Studi di Palermo – AUPA, 1–15. [http://www.unipa.it/~dipstdir/pub/annali/2006/Schermaier.pdf, assessed on 20.08.2014].

Stern, Robert. 2004. Does 'ought' imply 'can'? And did Kant think it does? *Utilitas* 16: 42–61.

Stockhammer, Morris. 1959. Ultra posse nemo obligatur. *Rivista internazionale di filosofia del diritto* 36: 25–35.

Vranas, Peter B. M. 2007. I Ought, Therefore I Can. *Philosophical Studies* 136: 167–216.

Wade, H. W. R. 1940. The Principle of Impossibility in Contract. *Law Quarterly Review* 56: 519ff.

Zimmermann, Reinhard. 1996. *The Law of Obligations: Roman Foundations of the Civilian Tradition*. Oxford: Clarendon.

Zorzetto, Silvia. 2014. Thinking of Impossibility in Following Legal Norms. Some Brief Comments About Bartosz Brozek's Rule Following. *Revus – Journal for Constitutional Theory and Philosophy of Law* 20: 47–60.

Legislation

Chart of Fundamental Rights of the European Union. 20 March 2010. In *Official Journal of the European Union* 2010/C 83/2.

Civil Obligations Act of the Republic of Croatia. Provisional English translation [http://www.lexadin.nl/wlg/legis/nofr/eur/lxwecro.htm, accessed on 14 May 2015]. Official version published in Official Gazette of the Republic of Croatia no. 35/2005.

Court rulings

Canham v Barry case. 1885. In 15 *C.B.* 597, 619 (1855). Quoted in Compulsory Reference in Actions at Law. Harvard Law Review 34/3 (1921): 321–325.

Court of Justice Judgment 15 July 1964. Case 6/64. *Flaminio Costa v E.N.E.L.* In InfoCuria – Case-law of the Court of Justice [http://curia.europa.eu/, accessed on 14 May 2015].

Coke, Sir Edward. 1826. 1579–1581 Wolfe v Shelley case. Part 1, Fol. 88, Vol. 1, 219 ss. In *The Reports of Sir Edward Coke, Knt. [1572–1617]: In Thirteen Parts, Volume 1*. London: Joseph Butterworth and Son.

High Court of Justice Baily v De Crespigny case. 1869. In *Law Reports 4 Queen's Bench Division*. Quoted in Impossibility as a Defense to the Performance of a Contract. Harvard Law Review 19/6 (1906): 462–463.

International Criminal Tribunal for the former Yugoslavia. 1997. Appeal case Prosecutor of the Republic of Croatia v. Blaškić. *Official database ICTY* [http://www.icty.org/x/cases/blaskic/acdec/en/71029JT3.html, accessed on 14 May 2015].

Italian Court of Cassation, criminal section V, No. 18887, 18 April 2014. In *Jusexplorer* [http://www.iusexplorer.it/, accessed on 14 May 2015]

Italian Court of Cassation, criminal section III, No. 11835, 19 February 2013. In *Jusexplorer* [http://www.iusexplorer.it/, accessed on 14 May 2015].

Rajasthan High Court State of Rajasthan v Tara and Others. 7 February 2001. In 2007 (3) *WLN* 491 [http://indiankanoon.org/doc/1479729/, accessed on 14 May 2015].

Read v Brookman case. 1789 In 3 *Term Reports* 151, 100 *English Reports* 504.

Regional Administrative Tribunal Bolzano Trentino-Alto Adige section I, No. 258, September 2, 2010. In *Jusexplorer* [http://www.iusexplorer.it/, accessed on 14 May 2015].

Supreme Court of Pennsylvania Hayes v Bickerstaff case. 1675. In *Reports and cases ruled and adjudged in the Courts of Pennsylvania before and since the revolution* (by A. J. Dallas). Vol. 1. Second Edition. 1806. Philadelphia: P. Byrne.

Supreme Court of Pennsylvania. Pollard v Shaaffer case. September Term, 1787. 1 *U.S.* 210 (1 Dall. 210, 1 L.Ed. 104).

Supreme Court of South Africa. Barkhuizen v Napier Case CCT72/05. 4 April 2007. In [2007] *ZACC* 5; 2007 5 *SA* 323 [http://www.saflii.org/za/cases/ZACC/2007/5.html, accessed on 14 May 2015].

Supreme Court of South Africa Rex v. Canestra case. 1951(2) SA 317 (A). Quoted in Administrator of Cape of Good Hope and Another v Ntshwaqela and Others (165/89) [1989] ZASCA 167; [1990] 2 All SA 34 (A) (30 November 1989) [http://www.saflii.org/za/cases/ZASCA/1989/167.html, accessed on 14 May 2015].

Trial of German Major War Criminals sitting at Nuremberg, Germany. 16–27 July 1946. In *The Nizkor Project*, [http://www.nizkor.org/, accessed on 14 May 2015].

Tribunal of Milan section IV, No. 1972, 12 April 2010. In *Jusexplorer* [http://www.iusexplorer.it/, accessed on 14 May 2015].

Part IV
Constitutional and EU Law

Fruzsina Gárdos-Orosz

Judicial Review of Constitutional Amendments: A Theoretical Approach

1. Introduction[1]

> How can we 'put marriage, religion, and private property solemnly under the protection of the constitution, and in the same constitution offer the legal means for their elimination'? (Schmitt 2004, 46)

In 1978, the year I was born in, George W. Carrey of Georgetown University published an article in the *American Political Science Review* challenging "the commonly held proposition that Madison advocated separation of powers as a means of thwarting majority rule, or, conversely, of protecting identifiable minority interests". The author claims that

> Madison's chief purpose in advancing the doctrine of separation of powers – one which was shared by the majority of his contemporaries – was to prevent governmental tyranny whose characteristic feature was seen as arbitrary and capricious rule resulting in government of men, not of laws. (Carey 1978, 151)

Abbé Sieyès from France constructed the idea of the constituent power as the fourth power outside Montesquieu's triad realm of the separation of powers. In his later writings on the *Thermidorian Convention*, he also raised the idea of a judicial body that would defend the constitution (see Sieyès 1822, ch. 5). The notion of the constituent power is definitely a good means of preventing the tyranny of established government and at the same time of guaranteeing popular control over government. But at what cost? Is it not finally a "capricious rule resulting in government of men, not of laws"? Does it mean losing legal, normative control over one actor, the unlimited constituent majority, in the name of democratic legitimacy? If the separation of powers is not a procedural, but a substantive concept, the substance to be reached by this idea is worth revisiting, although today it belongs strictly to the concept of the rule of law.

---

1 This paper could be regarded as the continuation of the CEE Forum's earlier discussions on constitutional review and the separation of powers (see Brodocz 2014; Hein and Ewert 2014; Belov 2014).

I argue that, when extending or reconsidering the separation of powers (see Möllers 2013) and the constituent power (Loughlin 2013) as concepts, it is essential to render the principle of checks and balances, and the relevance of discourse, interaction between institutions – highly relevant. I argue that the constituent power in the contemporary state cannot functionally be fully separated from the institutional power (*pouvoir constituée*). This understanding helps to answer questions of substance in terms of what limited government means today (see Loughlin 2005).

Although there are plenty of new state actors and new problems concerning the exact allocation of powers and concrete solutions for an effective interaction between the actors, the substance of the idea of the separation of powers has not necessarily changed (see Troper 1992, 1). Taking account of the core ideas of the constitutional state, it might become possible in constitutional law of the 21st century to respect the constituent power and at the same time authorise constitutional courts to review unconstitutional amendments to constitutions.

Focusing on the justification of the judicial review of constitutional amendments, this study revisits several theoretical questions about the separation of powers, and the role and competence of the constituent power. I claim that, in a system where so-called eternity clauses do not help to identify the limits of changes to the constitution, constitutional amendments can be subject to substantive constitutional review only if it is possible to justify this review, justify certain limited constraints on the constituent power. In this paper, I argue for a path that promises results in this field.

2. A brief overview of the practice of European states as a starting point

The purpose of looking at the real-life issue from a European perspective is limited to gathering information and providing some examples on the possible practical solutions in the text of constitutions and in case law (see more in Gárdos-Orosz 2015).

Interestingly, constitutional courts in Europe do not exercise their power to annul unconstitutional amendments to constitutions, not even in states whose courts have otherwise declared that such reviews are within their competence.

The French *Conseil Constitutionnel*, emphasising the sovereignty of the French people, has always rejected the possibility of a substantive review of constitutional amendments. The *Conseil* defends this position firmly despite the eternity clause of the French Constitution, which itself restricts amendment powers and has an eternal-effect provision, namely that it is impossible to change the republican form of government (see Baranger 2011, 389–428), but the *Conseil* does not permit the review of constitutional amendments.

The German Constitutional Court, for instance, has declared that it is possible to review constitutional amendments if they do not affect the provisions protected by the eternity clause. However, whenever it conducted a review (during the sixties and the seventies of the last century), it declined to annul the provision being reviewed, even when the Court was given a legitimate opportunity to do so. The German Constitutional Court has also highlighted that, when reviewing constitutional amendments, the main task of the Court is interpretation. Interpretation means that it has to define the meaning of the new text by taking into consideration the Basic Law as a whole and the structure, the basic order of fundamental values. By contrast, the practice of the Austrian and Czech constitutional courts includes cases in which constitutional amendments were declared substantively unconstitutional (see Pfersmann 2012, 98–103).

In *a priori* constitutional review procedures, constitutional courts reviewing constitutional amendments is quite rare in Europe. However, the Romanian Constitution makes it possible in an *ex officio* procedure. The Turkish Constitution[2] explicitly allows *a posteriori* reviews of constitutional amendments, but only in a procedural sense. The Russian Constitution[3] and the Constitution of Bosnia and Herzegovina[4] make reviewing the constitutions of members of the federation possible so as to make sure that they are coherent with the federal constitutions. This is, however, typical of federal states and, therefore, does not affect the theoretical foundations of the possibility of reviewing constitutional amendments.

What is more relevant for the perspective of this study is the practice of states that allows the judicial review of constitutional amendments, although not through developing specific competencies codified in the constitution, but through decisions of the constitutional courts themselves. In France, Spain, Austria, Cyprus and Germany, for example, it is possible to check whether the constituent power has followed procedural rules (see Gözler 2008). When developing their practice, the constitutional courts of Austria, Cyprus and Germany were quite uncertain whether it was possible to conduct substantive reviews of constitutional amendments in addition to formal reviews. The relevant decision of the Austrian Constitutional Court claims that amendments affecting fundamental issues have to be differentiated from amendments that can be regarded as more technical in

2 Article 148(1) of the Turkish Constitution.

3 Article 125(2)(b) of the Russian Constitution.

4 Article 6(3)(a) of the Constitution of Bosnia and Herzegovina.

nature. The Austrian Constitutional Court does not review amendments of the latter category. However, when amendments concern fundamental changes to the Constitution, the Constitutional Court should have more say in reviewing such amendments.[5]

Consequently, a constitutional court declaring a constitutional amendment unconstitutional is rather rare in Europe.[6] In constitutional democracies, this does not happen even if constitutional courts have this power based on an explicit authorisation or interpretation of their competence. However, this trend only shows that, in established democracies, there has not been a particularly strong need for this (see Troper 2003, 105–107).

3. Theoretical guidelines for revisiting judicial reviews of constitutional amendments

Many legal and political theorists and constitutional lawyers have dealt with the question of unconstitutional amendments to constitutions and the limits of judicial review. In this section, I do not aim to summarise all the literature available (see Levinson 1995; Jacobson 2010, 34–83; Gözler 2008), but will rather test a new idea.

Much time has passed since Montesquieu and Madison wrote their theses on the separation of powers. One problem is certainly the growing number of actors. State actors that have come into existence without a real change, a real movement in the field of the separation of powers are part of this group. One member of this group was identified by Benjamin Constant and later developed by Carl Schmitt. This is the presidential power. Another one was *pouvoir constituant* (see Klein 1998, 8). The notion of *pouvoir constituant* emerged as a concept to counterbalance *pouvoir constitué*, i.e. all other state actors. The name originates from the works of Abbé Sieyès, but could date from earlier times if the works of Jean Jacques Rousseau or John Calvin are looked at (see Klein 98, 7–8). This power has the right to check all the other branches of power, adopts the constitution and, with this act, shares competencies (see Bibó 1986, 386–387). This theory had the capacity to reconcile the idea of the separation of powers with the idea of popular sovereignty

5 The decision G-12/00, G 48–51/00 of the Austrian Constitutional Court of 10 March 2010.

6 See, for example, the decision of the Constitutional Court of Turkey on the interpretation of democracy, Islam, secularism and headscarves (no. E.2008/16 and K.2008/116), or the decision of the Austrian Constitutional Court (G-12/00, G 48–51/00 of 10 March 2010) on the interpretation of the rule of law.

in a way that made the people become the source of the constitution, the final source of all state power (see Győrfi and Jakab 204). Given that 19th century Parliamentarism[7] could hardly be spoken about, it has to be highlighted that the original idea of the constituent power is now advocated within the concept of parliamentary democracy (see Goldsworthy 2010). Although the constituent power appeared as a concept to counterbalance *pouvoir constitué*, i.e. the institutional side of the state, the role that this concept may have in constitutional law theory of the 21st century is today debated (see Mouton 2014).

I agree that the people as the possessor of sovereignty do not denote the totality of each and every individual, but rather an existing factor that the sovereign must take into account when specifying the purposes of and organising the state's activities (see Troper 2012, 353–354). Many mainstream authors believe that the act of adopting a constitution as a whole is an act of the constituent power, and that the power that amends a constitution does not act in the name of the constituent power, but in the name of the parliament, i.e. elected representatives (see Petrétei 2009, 78–80). In spite of the strength of this argument, I agree more with other acknowledged authors who say that it is not possible to make this distinction in theory (see Takács 2011, 64). When identifying the frontiers of the constituent power, it is impossible to rely only on procedural grounds. More specifically, it is impossible to say that the constituent power is necessarily something related to the constitution. Nor can it be said that a clear-cut dividing line between constitution-making and constitutional amendments can be identified.

All in all, popular sovereignty remains the well-known foundation of constitutional democracy, which is why many authors are concerned about the so-called 'total constitution' transforming today's parliamentary legislative states into juristocracies (see Kumm 2006, 345). However, basic law is the constitution of the people, and representation of the constitution of the people against the legislative power, government and courts is one of the reasons that legitimise constitutional courts and judicial reviews.

As to legitimising constitutional adjudication, Michel Troper relies on the theory of Riccardo Guastini. According to him, two types of decision-making processes have to be distinguished: one based on 'interpretation as an act of will' and the other 'interpretation based on knowledge'. Interpretation based on knowledge presupposes that the text analysed has some meaning. It is, accordingly, an

7 Parliamentarism changed the original concept of the separation of powers immediately due to popular sovereignty (parliament) having been fused with government (see Győrfi and Jakab 2009, 204).

exercise in deciding between true and false. On the other hand, interpretation as a function of will defines interpretation as a prescriptive task in which the person carrying out the interpretation decides on the meaning of the text. This allows for the existence of a final interpreting authority (see Troper 2003, 103–108).

However, even if constructing a final interpreting authority becomes possible, whether courts are the most competent constitutional institution to make justified decisions – necessarily based, in part, on 'interpretation as an act of will' – still requires justification.

Parliaments are products of popular vote and are, hence, necessarily better at aggregating the needs and preferences of societies. They are not, however, the most capable organs for collecting individual justices. Representatives go for re-election, appealing to potential voters and not to everybody, which means that they wish to justify their reasons only to them and not to everybody. This is why the aim of decision-making – if not bound by constitutional constraints, such as the rule of law, the separation of powers, checks and balances, etc. – is strictly related to majority rule. Ordinary courts reason primarily for the litigants, while constitutional courts reason for all members of the society and the state. This is why the construction with the function of separate constitutional adjudication is the most suitable one for balancing the operations of the state and society. In addition, if Alexy's view is taken and constitutional principles accepted as 'optimisation commands',[8] I assume that 'balancing' as a method of constitutional interpretation must remain the basis of final interpretations of matters of state and law. Thus, competencies in efficient balancing must also be taken into account when deciding on the legitimacy of the final interpreter.

For the purposes of identifying the frontiers of the constituent power, we should also bear in mind the fact that today, besides constitutional issues, daily policy issues are also commonly regulated in constitutions. This is why we can talk about the core and the penumbra of constitutions. Consequently, there arises the question whether the constituent power extends necessarily to every regulation included in constitutions. The decisionist answer to this question would certainly be positive, but from a normative standpoint, this presumption cannot necessarily be proven.[9] A good illustration of this dilemma is the following: if the constituent

8 Alexy states that "principles are norms commanding that something be realised to the highest degree that is actually and legally possible" (see Alexy 2004, 295).

9 Decisionists may argue that the constituent power decides about what amounts to be a matter regulated at constitutional level. Normativists, by contrast, dispute this view arguing that not all constitutional provisions have necessarily a fundamental value. For a more detailed explanation, see Loughlin (2014, 218–237).

power decided to regulate all forms of pension entitlement or all detailed rules of waste collection in the constitution, would such provisions automatically have a constitutional value or grade through their inclusion in the constitution?

I claim that, from a normative standpoint, not all provisions of the constitution receive a constitutional value automatically. As a consequence, even in the case of constitutions without eternity clauses, differentiation has to be made between rules in the constitution, their justifiable limits, and the nature and scope of interpretation and deference with regard to them. Finally, the constitution, amendments to it and interpretations of the same are on an equal footing in a system of balanced rules and principles, which forms the groundwork of a well-functioning constitutional democracy.

People are represented in the best possible way if all three of these functions are carried out by their actors in a coordinated manner. Conflicts might be as beneficial as cooperation, there is no cooperation without conflicts, but it is neither the constituent nor the amending constituent power, nor the final interpreting authority that has the final word in operating constitutional rules and principles. The final say is a product of this system in each and every individual case.

4. A possible six-step route to the justification of substantive reviews of constitutional amendments[10]

According to certain normative theories, which I draw on in my argumentation presented below, the essence of law and democracy (democracy under the rule of law) is that the basic concepts of rights cannot change from one day to the other according to the current will of the people. They can only develop organically, and courts responsible for constitutionality reviews have to be aware of this principle when interpreting constitutions (see Jacobson 2010, ch. 2, esp. p. 77). Constitutional amendments to the constitutional principles and rules of a legal system cannot be implemented unconditionally by majority power. The normative balance of the political will in a state operating under the rule of law is the condition. In what follows, I aim to outline an argument to justify the above claim.

4.1 Background

Supporters of procedural democracy argue that the substantive restriction of the democratic decision-making process must not create a 'Rule of Platonic

10 This part of the paper is based on a chapter of a study of mine published in a Hungarian volume (see Gárdos-Orosz 2014).

Guardians'. More specifically, it may not assign 'unjust privilege to the views of judges'. This is because imposing substantive limits on the will of the constituent would necessarily lead to preference being given to one interpretation of justice over some other. Giving preference to the justice of one over the justice of another systematically limits equal political rights and, consequently, the general implementation of equality. What is meant by political equality here is that every person's considerations are taken account of equally in the course of the state's operation. Without procedural equality, the existence of the state as such cannot be justified (see Győrfi and Jakab 2009, 204). A basic manifestation of this procedural equality is the joint effort of the political community at adopting a constitution. The possibility of unjust outcomes in the decision-making process must be managed as rare side-effects and can, thus, be disregarded.[11]

By contrast, John Rawls argues that a judge assessing constitutionality issues must, in addition to procedural justice, also apply a substantive test. However, this substance is not morality (see Rawls 1973, 85). The judiciary's competence extends to passing judgements under the rules of constitutional interpretation, which might be regarded as another special procedural rule whose sole purpose is achieving a decision in line with the interpretation principles generally accepted in constitutional democracies. In this sense, the principle of the rule of law and the exercise of fundamental rights do not impose an *a priori* limit on procedural democracy, but offer another level of procedure and can, therefore, also be managed within the framework of the terminology of procedural democracy.

The outcome of the judicial decision-making process in constitutionality issues is acceptable (legitimate in a legal sense) only if the procedural rules of constitutional reasoning have been followed. Normative theories point out that, as constitutions themselves are not merely political, but also legal documents, acts of the constituent should also belong to this realm in which constitutional interpretation is a natural part of law (see Dworkin 1986, chs. 6–7).

4.2 The restricted nature of the constituent power

Martin Loughlin, following Max Weber's theory about the three sources of legitimacy, claims that the constituent power is a modern, rational concept that no longer fits the traditional and sacred (authoritative) concept of the sovereign. Going back to the Enlightenment's secularisation and rationalisation of power, it

11 Tamás Győrfi himself argues for an interim solution, although he provides an excellent description of the arguments for both simplified procedural democracy and the material rule of law (see Győrfi 2013, 321–324).

is very difficult to believe that there could be a power in the modern concept of the state, i.e. the constituent, which is not obliged to obey the force of rationality, i.e. the power of justified public reason. The constitution is an expression of the constituent power of the people to make and remake the institutional arrangements through which they are governed. However, ultimate power (the author's note: sovereignty) resides "neither in the people nor in the constituted authorities; it exists in the relation established between constitutional imagination and governmental action" (see Loughlin 2014, 222).

The constituent power is, therefore, bound by the need to create an opportunity for the government to act, as well as the requirement of upholding constitutional ideals. This theory, if substantiated in depth, may be a starting point for proving that acts of the constituent power are not taboos. It is unclear, however, what constitutional ideals are in a state under the rule of law. Such ideals could include the constitutional justification of decisions or compliance with the rules of constitutional argumentation, as reflected in the ideas of Rawls, Jacobson or Dworkin.

4.3 Constitutional interpretation as a barrier to the constituent power

Rawls's concept is further explained by other approaches to political liberalism. The basic concept has recently been analysed by Tamás Győrfi. Political liberalism accepts that there are multiple publicly justifiable arguments within a political community and that somebody needs to decide between these views. The choice can be justified through constitutional reasoning. Public justification is a constraint on the exercise of any kind of power. Each process of justification means that the decision-maker must refer to reasons that are available to the addressee of the justification. A constitutional decision is justifiable and, thus, legitimate only if citizens can understand it on the basis of reasonable expectations. According to this approach, there must be substantive public reasons behind each decision. This facilitates not only avoiding both the tyranny of the majority, and the ultimate and uncontrolled rule of the legislative power or the judiciary, but also the protection of minority rights (see Győrfi 2013, 321–322).

4.4 Constitutional interpretation and courts

Even if we accept the above, there still remains the question why supreme judicial forums or separate constitutional courts giving ultimate interpretation is better than parliaments giving it. According to some criticism, the implementation of the concept of 'total constitution' almost carries the threat of constitutional dictatorship, with parliamentary legislative states being transformed into juristocracies (see Kumm 2006, 341–369).

There is no doubt whatsoever that constitutional interpretation is a special task that all constitutional institutions must carry out in the course of their decision-making activities. However, states usually set up special or specialised high courts authorised to review state decisions (see Ely 1980), as their main task is interpretation in the above sense. I have argued above that there is, indeed, theoretical groundwork on the basis of which it can be concluded that, in constitutional democracies, the position of the constituent power is today no longer special as compared to the traditional concepts of constituent power and popular sovereignty. The constituent power is neither in a special, completely exempt situation, nor is it separate from the constituted state and law.

Regular courts promote and protect the principle of the rule of law by interpreting and applying legal regulations within their own competence. If there is a conflict, they also decide which regulation to apply, decide on the basis of the principles of interpretation which are defined in advance and publicly accessible. Institutions carrying out constitutional reviews do something very similar when interpreting the constitution. The best way to uphold and protect the constitution is to have the guarantee that, in the case of conflict, the decision is made based on publicly (open to and contestable by all members of a polity) and formerly justified interpretation principles and rules. In the case of constitutional adjudication, if the result of interpretation is unacceptable to the constituent power, the constituent power may change, through amendments to the constitution, the norm incorporated in the constitution.[12]

It seems that, in addition to regular courts, the possibility of introducing constitutional courts is also justifiable. Accordingly, it is an acceptable interpretation that, when the constituent power assigns the task of interpreting and applying the constitution to an entity separate from parliaments, this empowerment includes constitutional courts also assessing constitutional amendments.

---

12 If unconstitutionality is established, the next question is whether constitutional courts are allowed to annul the unconstitutional norm or whether this can only be done by the constituent power. The situation is somewhat similar to that of the European Court of Human Rights which can establish that a constitutional norm violates the Convention, but has no power to annul the same.

4.5 What standard could be used for review?

The rule of law means that the state is governed by law. It must be presupposed that law – which most certainly includes a system of norms that define the basic rules of the political community and the lives of individuals – must be based on publicly justifiable arguments.

If there is no content that may be discovered in the course of constitutional interpretation (e.g., if a state adopts a new constitution and none of the provisions of that constitution correspond to any provision of any previous constitution in a given state), the will-based interpretation referred to above will prevail. However, this does not mean that the entity engaged in the interpretation is given absolute freedom. It means that this entity may, on the basis of publicly justifiable arguments, demonstrate that the rule included in the constitution or in its amendment does not meet the requirement of public justification.

Here is one example to support this train of thought: if a constitutional amendment or a new constitution reintroducing the legal institution of slavery were adopted tomorrow, state institutions whose task is interpreting the constitutional rule (e.g., the constitutional court) would have the competence to declare that the introduction of slavery does not meet the condition of public justifiability. This is because the essential content of the right to human dignity forms a part of all publicly justifiable arguments. The constituent power may, accordingly, choose freely from all publicly justifiable arguments, but its power is limited due to the necessity of public justification. This means that it cannot choose a solution that cannot be explained in accordance with the above criteria to all members of the political community. The requirement of constitutional reasoning is, therefore, a procedural guarantee whose character is substantive.

However, most cases do not deal with brand new constitutions. Consequently, in the course of constitutional interpretation, constitutional courts can rely on the already justified rules and principles either of domestic or international law.

The argument can certainly be reversed: if the content of a constitutional norm as determined by the constitutional court does not meet the above criteria, the constituent power may make its justifiable position clear through a constitutional amendment.

4.6 The result

According to this procedure, a dialogue may develop between the constituent power and the institution having competence to issue the ultimate interpretation of the constitution. The constituent power and the power to amend the constitution may decide at any time to cease this dialogue. However, in this case, ordinary courts applying law on a daily basis would certainly carry out the duty of constitutionality review by applying the constitution or, as a last resort, by excluding the application of rules that are publicly not justifiable. And, ultimately, the effort to eliminate this practice of ordinary courts could hardly be publicly justifiable in constitutional democracies.

5. Conclusion

I have argued in the paper for the revision of our basic concepts of the limits of the constituent power and the possibility of constitutionality reviews of unconstitutional amendments.

Many claim that functionalism is not a school of thought, but rather a way of thinking (see Loughlin 2006, 563). The rules of social coexistence and the organisation of the state are constantly evolving, and classic theories further developed. The basic functions identified in the course of exercising state power are possibly carried out by different constitutional institutions within the framework of a different set of rules at different times. The set of issues related to judicial reviews of unconstitutional amendments is a perfect case study as a number of fundamental questions need to be reconsidered to gain an overview of the problem. Such issues include the theory of the constituent power, the justification of constitutionality reviews or the principles of the rule of law, democracy and the separation of powers. In my paper, I have shown that it is essential to reflect on a number of related topics to understand and assess the current circumstances of adopting and reviewing constitutional rules and case law on this issue. Political and social factors, however, may also influence the way in which constitutional ideas are applied in everyday practice (see Stone 2000, I). I have argued that, today, judicial activism is not a negative notion in Europe's continental jurisprudence (see Kovács 2014) and that even judicial reviews of constitutional amendments may be theoretically justified if some basic notions of constitutional law are reconsidered.

References

Alexy, Robert. 2004. On the Structure of Legal Principles. *Ratio Juris* 13: 294–304.

Baranger, Denis. 2011. The Language of Eternity: Judicial Review of the Amending Power in France (or the Absence Thereof). *Israel Law Review* 44: 389–428.

Belov, Martin. 2014. Separation of Powers Reconsidered: A Proposal for a New Theoretical Model at the Beginning of the 21st Century. In *Law, politics, and the constitution. New perspectives from legal and political theory*, edited by Antonia

Geisler, Michael Hein and Siri Hummel, 47–62. Frankfurt am Main et al.: Peter Lang GmbH.

Bibó, István. 1983. Az államhatalmak elválasztása egykor és most [Separation of Powers in Government in the Past and Today]. In *Válogatott tanulmányok II* [Selected Papers 2], edited by Bibó István Jr., 367–399. Budapest: Magvető.

Brodocz, André. 2014. Constitutional courts and their power of interpretation. In *Law, politics, and the constitution. New perspectives from legal and political theory*, edited by Antonia Geisler, Michael Hein and Siri Hummel, 15–30. Frankfurt am Main et al.: Peter Lang GmbH.

Carrey, George W. 1978. Separation of Powers and the Madisonian Model: A Reply to the Critics. *The American Political Science Review* 72: 151–164.

Colon-Rios, Joel. 2012. *Weak Constitutionalism. Democratic Legitimacy and the Question of Constituent Power*. New York: Routledge.

Dworkin, Ronald. 1986. *Law's empire*. Cambridge: Harvard University Press.

Ely, John Hart. 1980. *Democracy and Distrust: A Theory of Judicial Review*. Oxford: Harvard University Press.

Gárdos-Orosz, Fruzsina. 2014. Az alkotmánymódosítások alkotmányossági felülvizsgálata: elméleti koncepciók, nemzetközi trendek és magyar kérdések. In *Alkotmányozás és alkotmányjogi változások Európában és Magyarországon*, edited by Fruzsina Gárdos-Orosz and Zoltán Szente, 167–184. Budapest: Nemzeti Közszolgálati Egyetem.

Gárdos-Orosz, Fruzsina. 2015. Judicial review of constitutional amendments: The Hungarian case in context. In *Challenges and Pitfalls in the Recent Hungarian Constitutional Development*, edited by Zoltán Szente, Fanni Madák and Zsuzsanna Fejes, 97–112. Paris: L'Harmattan.

Hein, Michael, and Ewert, Stefan. 2014. What is 'politicisation' of constitutional courts? Towards a decision-oriented concept. In *Law, politics, and the constitution. New perspectives from legal and political theory*, edited by Antonia Geisler, Michael Hein and Siri Hummel, 31–46. Frankfurt am Main et al.: Peter Lang GmbH.

Klein, Claude. 1998. *Theorie et pratique de pouvoir constituant*. Paris: Presse Universitaire de France.

Kovács, Ágnes. 2014. New trend in the debate on justifying judicial review: considering the benefits of judicial reasoning. In *The Rule of Law and Challenges to Jurisprudence*, edited by Péter Cserne, Miklós Könczöl and Marta Soniewicka, 101–112. Frankfurt am Main et al.: Peter Lang GmbH.

Kumm, Mathias. 2006. Who's Afraid of the Total Constitution? *German Law Journal* 4: 341–369.

Loughlin, Martin. 2005. The functionalist style of public law. *University of Toronto Law Journal* 55: 361–403.

Loughlin, Martin. 2014. The Concept of Constituent Power. *European Journal of Political Theory* 13: 218–237.

Loughlin, Martin, and Walker, Neil (eds.). 2008. *The Paradox of Constitutionalism: Constituent Power and Constitutional Form*. Oxford: Oxford University Press.

Levinson, Stanford (ed.). 1995. *Responding to Imperfection: The Theory and Practice of Constitutional Amendment*. Princeton, New Jersey: Princeton University Press.

Jacobson, Jeffrey. 2010. *Constitutional Identity*. Harvard University Press.

Goldsworthy, Jeffrey. 2010. *Parliamentary Sovereignty: Contemporary Debates*. Cambridge: Cambridge University Press.

Gözler, Kemal 2008. *Judicial Review of Constitutional Amendments: A Comparative Study*. Bursa: Ekin Press.

Győrfi, Tamás, and Jakab, András. 2009. 2. § Alkotmányos alapelvek, ellenállási jog [Article 2: Basic principles, the right of resistance]. In *Az Alkotmány kommentárja* [Commentary on the Constitution.], edited by András Jakab, 127–237. Budapest: Századvég.

Győrfi, Tamás. 2013. Between common law constitutionalism and procedural democracy. *Oxford Journal of Legal Studies* 33: 317–338.

Mouton, Stéphane. 2014. *L'apport de la théorie du pouvoir constituant de Condorcet au droit constitutionnel contemporain.* [www.droitconstitutionnel.org/congres Nancy/comN9/moutonTD9.pdf, accessed on 30 August 2014].

Möllers, Christoph. 2013. *The three branches: a comparative model of separation of powers*. Oxford: Oxford University Press.

Paine, Thomas. 1995. *Az ember jogai* [The Rights of Man]. Budapest: Osiris-Readers International.

Petrétei, József. 2009. *Az alkotmányos demokrácia alapintézményei* [Basic notions of constitutional democracy]. Budapest-Pécs: Dialóg-Campus.

Pfersmann, Otto. 2012. Unconstitutional constitutional amendments: a normativist approach. *Zeitschrift für öffentliches Recht* 67: 98–103.

Rawls, John. 1973. *A Theory of Justice*. Oxford: Oxford University Press.

Sieyes, Abbé Emmanuel Joseph. 1922. *Qu'est-ce que le Tiers-État? precede de l'Essai sur les privileges.* [http://classiques.uqac.ca/classiques/sieyes_emmanuel_joseph/qu_est_ce_que_tiers_etat/que_est_de_que_le_tiers_etat.pdf, accessed on 5 August 2014].

Schmitt, Carl. 2004. *Legality and Legitimacy*, translated by Jeffrey Seitzer. Duke University Press.

Stone Sweet, Alec. 2000. *Governing with Judges: Constitutional Politics in Europe*. Oxford: Oxford University Press.

Takács, Péter. 2011. *Az alkotmány legitimitása* [Legitimacy of the constitution]. *Alkotmánybírósági Szemle* 2: 64–78.

Troper, Michel. 1992. Development of the notion of separation of powers. *Israel Law Review* 26: 1–15.

Troper, Michel. 2003. The Logic of Justification of Judicial Review. *International Journal of Constitutional Law* 2: 105–107.

Troper, Michael. 2012. Sovereignty. In *The Oxford Handbook of Comparative Constitutional Law*, edited by Michael Rosenfeld and András Sajó, 350–369. Oxford: Oxford University Press.

Domenica Dreyer

The Substance and Effects of EU Law and Jurisprudence under the Social Constructivist Research Agenda

1. What are the puzzles with respect to legislation and jurisprudence?

Legislation is an essential mechanism in the constitution of social reality that is complemented by guiding jurisprudence. Law creates political, economic and societal structures, be it via legal frameworks or detailed demands. The law is perceived as self-evident constitutional part of a society. Thereby it is ignored that the law was created by the people. The significance of self-evidence is termed by German sociologists as 'Verdinglichung' [reification] which implies that man is capable of forgetting his own creatorship in the human world (Berger and Luckmann 2010 [1980], 94; Krell 2009, 360). The legal system seems contingent but is at the same time dynamic and it could change or be quite different. Yet, the rule of law has become the key criterion as an indicator of good governance (Bingham 2011).

The rule of law implies regulation by law with effects on the social order of societies. In the integration process of the European Union (EU), regulation plays a key role in building social circumstances (Dingwerth et al 2010, 84ff). The latest treaty reform of 2009 sets the agenda for secondary law-making. Hence, European law is the framework for the social reality to be established by legislative processes at the European level. Of course, the subsidiarity principle guarantees to address policy challenges at the European level only if they cannot be solved nationally, but still: there is a wide scope for policy-making (Art. 5 I TEU). The Union is the sole law-maker in the policy fields of tariffs and competition rules for the common market, currency policy and trade policy (Art. 3 I TFEU); it furthermore shares the competences with the member states in the common market, social policy, agriculture, environment, consumer protection, transportation, energy and the common area of freedom, security and justice (Art. 4 II TFEU). EU treaty law is drafted in intergovernmental procedures with the support of diplomatic staff. Wordings leave margin for interpretation on the terms and conditions codified. Even secondary legislation processes result in specific rules drafted in phrasings which leave considerable scope for translation into national law and practices. In the case of the EU, though, the law is subject to the jurisprudence of an independent supra-national European Court of Justice. This creates a significant tension at the European level, because the advantage of a sanctioning authority that binds member states to fulfil their obligations under European law at the same time limits the scope of the once diplomatically drafted treaties. The moment that the highest judges agree on an understanding of a passage of law, this one interpretation becomes binding for all the member states. In this sense, the Court of the European Union constitutes a very powerful actor in the harmonisation of European law and thereby plays a critical role in constructing social realities. Judgments of the ECJ furthermore enjoy a very high standing and acceptance rate. It is established custom for the academic sphere to observe closely, analyse in detail and interpret exactly the meaning of jurisprudence. At the same time, the significance for legal practice on the national and regional level is analysed. This positivist approach takes laws and jurisprudence for granted. It leads to cases in which jurisprudence as a matter of course leads to adjustments in legislation. Obviously, the reasoning and justification – or more general: the discourse – of the European Court of Justice contributes significantly to reification in law-making. Accordingly, the discourse towards law-making and jurisprudence both contribute to the social reality and need scholarly attention. This discovery leads us to a different pathway of investigation. Since both legislation and jurisprudence are seemingly taken for granted – *Verdinglichung* [reification] – it is even more important to point to the fact that both legislation and jurisprudence are created by man and constitute norms and interpretations which construct social reality in the political entity of the EU. In order to uncover the processes which lead to the specific discourses in legislation and jurisprudence, it is therefore suggested to use the social constructivist research framework. Such a research agenda is substantiated with the argument that legal norms embody moral attitudes and values of an existing society – through both their genesis and application (Cottier 2010, 157).

2. The social constructivist research agenda

2.1 Understanding the objectives of social constructivism

Constructivism is a meta theory which is constituted of general 'claims about the nature of social life and social change' (Finnemore and Sikkink 2001, 393). One of the few general assumptions of constructivism is the idea that there are collective, intersubjective understandings that are agreed upon, for example by rules or language (Adler 2013, 121). These intersubjective meanings are similar to self-evidently perceived phenomena. Therefore, constructivism may serve to provide a framework for research questions directed at political and legal discourses in order to uncover their self-evident implications. Constructivists ask *how* things *became what they are*, instead of asking for their emergence (ibid.). Identities and ideas as well as their development are important for constructivists in their aim to understand what induces processes of change (Finnemore and Sikkink 2001, 394). The institutional setting or the constitution of political entities is similarly relevant, since such settings contribute to political behaviour (Wendt 1999). Another one of the ideas of constructivism is that speech is persuasive: it can change people's minds and their idea of 'what goals are valuable and about the roles they play (or should play) in social life' (Finnemore and Sikkink 2001, 402). Accordingly, discourse processes like political debates and legislative processes but also the explanations in judgments contribute to what is perceived as right and lawful.

2.2 Methodological approaches in social constructivism

Several scholars have compared the research design of different constructivist research projects and found that there are quantitative, qualitative and multi-methods designs (Adler 2013, 122; Finnemore and Sikkink 2001, 392). Some scholars use conventional case studies, others apply process, narrative or discourse analysis. Some focus on the actor-structure investigation, while others look at macro-historical comparisons or framing effects (Adler 2013, 122). Constructivists strive to uncover what lies underneath the surface of speech, legislation, jurisprudence or action. Interpretative methods like content and discourse and document analysis help to uncover the conceptions, perceptions and supremacies of legislation and jurisprudence. With this approach, constructivists are united in their 'theoretical arguments', not in their 'empirical research strategies' (Finnemore and Sikkink 2001, 392). It is the core aim of these researchers to examine the social background for acceptance of seemingly self-evident phenomena (Adler 2013, 122), or to put it into social constructivist terminology: to apply the 'interpretive practice of uncovering intersubjective meanings' (ibid.).

2.3 Added value

While it is not possible to make predictions about the future with this meta-theory of social constructivism, the theory is a vehicle to help uncover structures within social realities – structures which contribute to the specific social reality. Social constructivist research enables reflective thinking of supposedly self-evident processes like legislation and jurisprudence. Of course, the reflective perspective of the researcher to think with these meta assumptions also contributes to the interpretation of social reality, but this does not change the fact that constructivist research comes closer to uncovering social processes and the creation of social reality – especially in uncovering the *contributions* to the creation of social reality. This sets the foundation for the criticism of developments in society: if it is possible to detect the justification discourses for specific policy developments, it is feasible to counter-argue against such processes. Or at least to point to the fact that ideas, identities and intersubjective perceptions are in progress which may not be as rational or reasonable as perceived. According to this understanding, the law has a straightforward political dimension, especially in jurisprudence (Burley and Mattli 1993, 41–42). It is not just legalism. The law is rather an expression of settled 'ideas, experiences and social relationships' which form 'part of the cultural memory' of a society and which henceforth need scholarly attention (Bast 2012, 140).

3. How to uncover the effects of legislation and jurisprudence in EU law

The aim of the social constructivist research agenda with respect to European legislation and jurisprudence is to uncover the significant influence of discourse, legislation and jurisprudence in the cycle of policy-making processes. Challenging something as self-evident as legislation and jurisprudence enables the researcher to uncover underlying mechanisms: What interests and legitimising justifications are used in legal rhetoric and discourse? Or, in constructivist terminology: what are the intersubjective beliefs hidden in jurisprudence?

Decision-making on the supra-state European level in the context of the EU is a legitimated process based on the treaties that the member states have signed. Jurisprudence of the European Court of Justice fulfils a pre-eminent position due to its precedence over national law and jurisprudence. This precedence was established by the Court itself in a few case law decisions in the 1960s among which one judgment is outstanding (ECJ, Costa/ENEL 1964). It was a seemingly minor case brought forward by an individual Italian stockholder on the question whether Italy had the right to nationalise the energy sector. The judges ruled that the European Economic Community is different and advanced in comparison to traditional international treaties and that it constitutes an original legal order (ECJ, Costa/ENEL 1964, Rn 8). Accordingly, national law has to comply with the duties that the member states have committed themselves to with the foundation of the European Economic Community (ECJ, Costa/ENEL 1964, Rn 9f). The decision upheld that the member states have partly constrained and to some extent delegated their sovereignty in specific policy areas and that in this context European law precedes national law (ECJ, Costa/ENEL 1964, Rn 8, 11, 12). The Court concluded that the Italian stockholder was right in claiming that the nationalization of the energy sector was contrary to the provisions of Art. 37 I and II of the Treaty on the European Economic Community. This decision with its far-reaching impact – namely, the supremacy of European law – was accepted as such in the judiciary sphere, by academia and society as a whole. And without any contestation, the supremacy of the European Court of Justice within the European Union system has become a foundational part of the system. Even though some National Constitutional Courts at times challenge the constitutional jurisprudence of the highest European Court, like for instance the German Federal Constitutional Court, the supremacy of the highest European Court is widely accepted. It has become an intersubjective and general understanding that the jurisprudence of the European Court of Justice constitutes a good system to guarantee order. This is demonstrated, for example, when the Court reaches the highest rate of approval in Eurobarometer surveys (European Commission 2012, 69). The European Court of Justice is *the* European institution which European citizens trust the most – followed by the European Parliament, the European Commission, the European Central Bank and, lastly, the Council of the European Union (European Commission 2012, 69).[1] Yet, jurisprudence and legislation remain a dynamic process: specific provisions that are translated into secondary law are generally a question of negotiation, they are not static. This is a dynamic process within an established institutional setting. Therefore it is all the more worth examining this intersubjective understanding of the role and authority of legislation and jurisprudence actors, their discourses and actions.

Constructivists are convinced that people derive their self-evident understandings, normative ideas and epistemic ideals from a framing background which is not obvious at first sight. The contextualised understanding contributes to the reproduction of self-evident understandings which become intersubjective and general understandings (Adler 2013, 121; Gould 1998, 81). For constructivists, the social context of actors is very important, hence scholars ask: 'How does this shaping happen and with what results?' (Finnemore and Sikkink 2001, 394). In the case of European law and jurisprudence this means that it is necessary to uncover the background for the acceptance of European law. This is a research question which not only addresses the decisions in the first decades of the European Economic Community that established the supremacy of European law and jurisprudence and was sustained by lawyers who contributed to the formalization of 'new social

1 Unfortunately, the Court and the Council were excluded from Eurobarometer surveys, at the time citizens were only asked about their trust in the European Parliament, European Commission and European Central Bank. Therefore, the numbers are based on the 2012 survey.

facts' (Burley and Mattli 1993, 41–42 and 76). It gives reason to examine current developments in legislation, jurisprudence and the associated discourses. Such a research agenda recognises the discourse effect attributed to the institutions of legislation and jurisprudence and attempts to uncover its social constructivist potential. In order to connect the theoretical points to actual jurisprudence and to emphasise both the importance of discourse but also the political effects of jurisprudence, the following part of this paper shall focus on two case study examples on shaping European social reality.

3.1 The Charter of Fundamental Rights as a social constructivist research opportunity

The first example illustrates the relevance of discourse during the legislative process. It is particularly interesting to look at the protocols that document how the Charter of Fundamental Rights (CFR) and the Draft for a Constitution Treaty became what they are. By means of document analysis it is possible to see which rights and affirmations were suggested, what kind of discussions took place and which of these rights were actually codified.

Given the drafting of the Charter of Fundamental Rights, social constructivists would ask: What are the intersubjective meanings hidden in the developed rules of the Charter of Fundamental Rights? What are the ideas behind the Charter? How come that the Charter was drafted in the beginning of the 21st century? What kind of institutional set-up enabled the drafting process of the Charter? To what extent did the institutional setting influence the political behaviour of delegates? What importance can be assigned to speech during the drafting process? The relevance of speech is particularly obvious given the procedural set-up of the Convention meetings: the delegates had to consent on the fundamental rights and freedoms that should be granted to citizens of the European Union and those under jurisdiction of the European Union.

In investigating how the Charter became what it is today, it is possible either to combine methodological approaches or to focus on any of the following options. Process analysis responds to the question of how the Convention emerged. This may involve an analysis of the process leading up to the calling of the Convention into existence, but it is also possible to zoom in on the Convention paper itself: How did it become what it is now? This links up with the second methodological option: narrative analysis would clarify the justifications used during the drafting process of the Charter. It implies a close examination of the fundamental rights and values brought forward by different delegates and their positions in reaching a common position. Possible guiding research questions focus on moral principles and justifications, the 'plot' of the Charter which holds the drafting story, and furthermore significant symbols, descriptions, and key words (Viehöver 2011, 209–210). Such narrative analysis may be combined with systematic discourse analysis which detects the exact statements of different delegates and the ways in which it is possible to categorise specific opinions or arguments. It may partly overlap with narrative analysis. Guiding research questions include an examination of the appearance and disappearance of specific discourses, symbolic and linguistic strategies and means, determination of incidents during a discourse, resources, interests and strategies of actors in relevant speech positions, and connections between this discourse and other discourses (Keller 2011, 70).

Another option is to focus on the actor-structure connection and significance with respect to the Charter: Who are the relevant actors involved? Are there other relevant 'invisible' actors apart from the official delegates in the Convention? What are the institutional settings that pre-structure the Convention? What significance is there to the attachment of the delegates to specific institutions? The key to this approach is to aim to unveil the interpretations of values and rights hidden in the drafting process towards an inter-subjective understanding of fundamental rights and freedoms. Why is it relevant to examine this? The Charter is a fundamental document for the EU because it confirms the European value consensus (Lerch 2005, 237). The Charter codifies the European fundamental freedoms and is essential for EU values in general (Jarass 2012, 457). The TEU refers to the Charter of Fundamental Rights in Art. 7 and thereby incorporates the Charter into the primary treaties of the EU (Jarass 2012, 458). Hence, the Charter is a fundamental and very meaningful treaty document that has its place as integral part in the European legal system. Looking at how the Charter became what it is makes it necessary to investigate the delegation that drafted the Charter and also to address the discussions about the exact wording of the rights and freedoms to be codified during the drafting process. Just giving one example emphasises the significance of the social constructivist research project for the Charter: human dignity is codified in Art. 1 of the Charter of Fundamental Rights and in Art. 2 of the Treaty on the European Union. This expression is in line with the 1948 Universal Declaration on Human Rights of the United Nations. But in the European Convention on Human Rights and Fundamental Freedoms, there is no such equivalence. In the Convention, there was a lively discussion about whether *human dignity* qualifies as fundamental right. It was the president of the Convention, Roman Herzog, who managed to convince the Convention that human dignity is in fact the basis of all fundamental rights (Calliess 2011, Art. 1 GRCh Rn 4; Jarass 2013, Art. 1 GRCh Rn 2). This is why Art. 1 of the CFR qualifies as pivotal for and the focal point of the Charter and is also the key for the general principles of the EU (Jarass 2013, Art. 1 GRCh Rn 4). Accordingly, Roman Herzog had substantial influence on the fundamental starting point not only of the Charter of Fundamental Rights but also on the general understanding of values in the EU (Art. 2 TEU). What this means in translation to daily practice is a wholly different question. This will mainly depend on the interpretation of the European Court of Justice. It seems that, again, only the jurisdiction of the Court will really show what is understood by abstract and general fundamental rights and freedoms codified by member states. Even the most distinguished EU lawyers cannot estimate the extent to which the Charter will be binding and relegate to the upcoming decisions of the Court of Justice that will define the scope of the Charter (Jarass 2012, 457–459; Calliess 2011, Rn 17). So far, few decisions point to the European Court of Justice seeing itself as a Constitutional Court and there are already some cases in which the Court decided in favour of fundamental rights and on the costs of secondary European law, such as the Dublin-II-decision or the recent decision on data preservation (ECJ, Cases C-411/10 and 493/10, 21.12.2011; ECJ, Cases C-293/12 and C-594/12, 8.04.2014). This is a development that will shape fundamentally the social reality of European societies and the constructivist research approach provides us with the tools and the approach to reveal such processes. The added value of the social constructivist research agenda lies in the possibility of uncovering structures within social realities with reflective research on seemingly self-evident processes like the drafting of the Charter. The political dimension of the legislative process needs to be uncovered: it is not just that the Charter of Fundamental Rights was drafted. With the Charter, the EU received the heart and soul that are displayed in the constitutional fundamental freedoms. This is a significant step forward in the political integration process of the EU. It codifies that the EU is much more than an economic community. Particularly it implies that the European Court of Justice now also relies on interpreting the Charter of Fundamental Rights when judging on cases. The Charter provides even more scope of interpretation. This leads us to consider jurisprudence as research opportunity.

3.2 Jurisprudence in asylum law as a social constructivist research opportunity

Jurisprudence of the highest courts is generally an interesting subject area for social constructivist research since it implies the highest authority and is associated by citizens with the highest levels of trust (European Commisison 2012, 69). How would social constructivists approach jurisprudence? They would ask: How do judgments emerge? What kind of justifications are given? Are there specific ideas that one can single out in the process? What relevance does the institutional set-up have for the decisions of the judges? This relevant question is substantiated by the fact that there is little option to contest a decision of the European Court of Justice. Since judges know that there is not much possibility to correct a judgment, they are supposedly aware of their responsibility and are careful with their decisions (Höpner 2014, 11). At the same time, the lack of corrective options implies a great extent of authority. If member states find that a judgment of the European Court misinterprets the content of regulated legislation, then there is only the option of changing the law through the legislative process (ibid.). In practice this means: in order to correct a judgment by the European Court of Justice on a directive, the European Commission would have to start an initiative and would need a qualified or even unanimous majority of the Council and the consent of the European Parliament in order to change the directive. Hence the obstacles to changing secondary law are already high but in situations in which the European Court of Justice decides on the application of primary law with reference to the Treaty on the European Union (TEU) or the Treaty on the Functioning of the European Union (TFEU), the political correction of an error judgment would imply the need to change or amend the treaties. Such an amendment would have to be consented to by each of the 28 member states and would then lead to ratification procedures in several member states where the constitutions require referenda. In view of the recent experiences and a visible populist mood swing in the electorate since the 2014 elections to the European Parliament, nobody would initiate a treaty amendment imprudently. It is more likely that member states will find a way to *muddle through* the decisions of the Court. This hypothesis is substantiated by the fact that the European Court of Justice always leaves some margin for interpretation in its judgments in order to acknowledge cultural characteristics in the member states' judicial systems. So there is no doubt about the significance of judgments and this significance directs the attention of the social constructivist scholar to the persuasiveness of written judgments as discussed in the literature of member states: how do judgments influence political debate and further political decisions and reformed legislation? The methodological approach can vary and combine different strategies: an investigation of European Court of Justice decisions might then focus on content, narrative and discourse analysis, in order to reveal conceptions and perceptions. Case studies of decisive judgments could be the starting point of an investigation based on the narrative and discourse analyses. Subsequently, it would be necessary to look at the reasoning within the judgments which contain justifications for the specific decision. The idea is to unveil intersubjective meanings that occur with the judgment and which may be in contrast to the political actions of the executives of the member states. This is illustrated by the January 2014 decision of the European Court of Justice relating to asylum law. In that case, the Court was asked by Belgium to define the term *domestic armed conflict* in connection with *serious harm*. Those terms are in a causal relationship when the determining authorities of the member states decide whether an asylum seeker qualifies for international protection status (ECJ, Case C-285/12, Rn 34). Hence, the interpretation of the exact wording is relevant for asylum-seekers and their social reality during and after an asylum procedure. The Belgian Court had defined the term *domestic conflict* in line with the interpretation of the International Criminal Court but the European Court of Justice found that the legislator of the European Directive used a terminology different from that of international law and hence international humanitarian law could not be considered a synonymous legal basis for the interpretation of the terms in question (ECJ, Case C-285/12, Rn 21, 24). In order to find out how the legislator intended the term 'conflict without international character' to be understood, the Court looked into the law-making process of the directive and actually process-traced the intention of the Commission when it suggested the directive (ECJ, Case C-285/12, Rn 34, 35). The Court found that the European legislator deliberately chose a different terminology. Contentwise this meant that the organisation, intensity or length of a conflict are irrelevant for determining that a domestic armed conflict is taking place (ECJ, Case C-285/12, Rn 32, 34, 35). Hence, the scope for interpretation was assessed by the Court to be wider in the European directive than in international humanitarian law. Furthermore, the Court extended the scope of protection to be granted in the EU by concluding that subsidiary protection exceeds the protection rights under the Geneva Convention and is intended to be a complementary instrument of protection, hence there must be substantially more protection than just according to international refugee law (ECJ, Case C-285, Rn 33).

It can be concluded from this that abstract-general norms still need a specific definition when confronted with reality. Even a very specific directive leaves a margin for interpretation when it comes to its day-to-day application (at the time of judgment applicable: Council Directive 2004/83/EC, OJ L 304/12, 30.9.2004; now applicable: European Union: 2011/95/EU, OJ L 337/9, 20.12.2011). In this case, the European Court of Justice contributed to an extension of protection rights of asylum applicants and thereby forcefully shaped the actual social reality of these people seeking protection in the EU. The emphasis on the broader terminology used by the European legislator creates an extension for substantial subsidiary protection. This is a case of advocacy for asylum protection. And it is not just one judgment: When investigating previous decisions of the European Court of Justice concerning the asylum-relevant secondary law corpus: Reception Directive (ECJ, Case C-179/11, 27.09.2012), Qualification Directive (ECJ, Cases C-199/12, C-201/12, 7.11.2013), Return Directive (ECJ, Case C-329/11, 6.12.2011) and Dublin-II-Regulation (ECJ, Case C-411/10 and 493/10, 21.12.2011), it is obvious that the decisions are taken clearly in favour of the protection of individual rights and the argumentative incorporation of the Charter of Fundamental Rights plays regularly a vital role. No matter whether the Court defines the extent to which reception conditions apply – even when Dublin procedures are in action – and decides for full coverage (ECJ, Case C-179/11, 27.09.2012) or whether the Court affirms that persecution based on sexual identity may count as persecution of a social group as understood under the Geneva Convention (ECJ, Cases C-199/12, C-201/12, 7.11.2013), such jurisprudence entails the extension of asylum-seekers' protection rights. In the given example, social constructivist research points to relevant actors who seemingly stand in the background of the political system but forcefully contribute to political processes and legislation reforms due to the interpretation of legislation. This shows how jurisprudence controls the application of enacted laws. And more than that it contributes to the understanding of legal norms and thereby influences profoundly the creation of social reality.

4. Conclusion

The social constructivist research agenda provides scholarly options to go beyond the usual research agenda and to understand processes in the creation of social reality. The given case study examples that refer to the emerging relevance of the Charter of Fundamental Rights (European Court of Justice becoming a Constitutional Court) and the policy impact of jurisprudence on the interpretation of legislation (advocacy for asylum-seekers) justify this meta-approach which allows us to better understand the underlying structures and accordingly the effect on social reality instead of taking legal and judicial processes for granted as self-evident.

References

Adler, Emanuel. 2013. Constructivism in International Relations: Sources, Contributions and Debates. In *Handbook of international relations*, edited by Walter Carlsnaes, Thomas Risse-Kappen and Beth A. Simmons, 2nd edition, 112–144. London: SAGE.

Bast, Jürgen. 2012. Das Recht als Archiv sozialer Konstruktionen der Migration. *Zeitschrift für rechtswissenschaftliche Forschung* 2: 139–171.

Berger, Peter L., and Luckmann, Thomas. [1980] 2010. *Die gesellschaftliche Konstruktion der Wirklichkeit. Eine Theorie der Wissenssoziologie*. 23rd edition [unaltered version of 5th edition]. Frankfurt am Main: Fischer-Taschenbuch-Verlag.

Bingham, Tom H. 2011. *The rule of law*. London: Penguin.

Burley, Anne-Marie, and Mattli, Walter. 1993. Europe Before the Court: A Political Theory of Legal Integration. *International Organization* 47(1): 41–76.

Calliess, Christian. 2011 onwards. Art. 1 GRCh. In *EUV/AEUV. Das Verfassungsrecht der Europäischen Union mit Europäischer Grundrechtecharta*; Kommentar, edited by Christian Calliess and Matthias Ruffert, 4th edition. München: Beck.

Cottier, Thomas. 2010. Das Völkerrecht im Spannungsfeld von Nationalstaatlichkeit und Universalität. *Zeitschrift für Politik* 2: 156–169.

Dingwerth, Klaus, Blauberger, Michael, and Schmidt, Christian. 2010. *Postnationale Demokratie: Eine Einführung am Beispiel von EU, WTO und UNO*. Wiesbaden: VS Verlag für Sozialwissenschaften.

European Commission. 2012. Standard Eurobarometer 78, Autumn 2012, Public Opinion in the European Union. Report. [http://ec.europa.eu/public_opinion/archives/eb/eb78/eb78_publ_en.pdf, accessed on 17 September 2014].

Finnemore, Martha, and Sikkink, Kathryn. 2001. Taking Stock. The Constructivist Research Program in International Relations and Comparative Politics. *Annual Review of Political Science* 4(1): 391–416.

Fischer-Lescano, Andreas. 2013. *Rechtskraft*. Berlin: August-Verlag.

Gould, Harry. 1998. What is at Stake in the Agent-Structure Debate. In *International Relations in a Constructed World*, edited by Vendulka Kubalkove, Nicholas Onuf and Paul Kowert, 79–98. Armonk (NY): M.A. Sharpe.

Höpner, Martin. 2014. Die Wucht der "Integration durch Recht". Befunde aus der MPIfG-Forschungsgruppe zur Politischen Ökonomie der europäischen Integration, Tagungsbeitrag 4. Tagung Themengruppe Politik und Recht, 27/28 März 2014.

Jarass, Hans D. 2012. Die Bindung der Mitgliedstaaten an die EU-Grundrechte. *Neue Zeitschrift für Verwaltungsrecht* 8: 457–461.

Jarass, Hans D. 2013. Art. 1 GRCh. In *Charta der Grundrechte der Europäischen Union*. Unter Einbeziehung der vom EuGH entwickelten Grundrechte, der Grundrechtsregelungen der Verträge und der EMRK: Kommentar, edited by Hans D. Jarass, 2nd edition. München: Beck.

Keller, Reiner. 2011. *Diskursforschung. Eine Einführung für SozialwissenschaftlerInnen*. 4th edition. Wiesbaden: VS-Verlag.

Krell, Gert. 2009. *Weltbilder und Weltordnung. Einführung in die Theorie der internationalen Beziehungen*. 4th edition. Baden-Baden: Nomos.

Lerch, Marika. 2005. Internationale Menschenrechte und europäische Identität. Eine konstruktivistische Analyse der EU-Grundrechtecharta. In *Konstruktivistische Analysen der internationalen Politik*, edited by Cornelia Ulbert and Christoph Weller, 215–245. Wiesbaden: VS Verlag für Sozialwissenschaften.

Viehöver, Willy. 2011. Diskurse als Narrationen. In *Handbuch sozialwissenschaftliche Diskursanalyse*, edited by Reiner Keller, Andreas Hirseland, Reiner Schneider and Willy Viehöver, 3rd edition, 193–224. Wiesbaden: VS Verlag für Sozialwissenschaften.

Wendt, Alexander. 1999. *Social Theory of International Politics*. Cambridge: Cambridge University Press.

Court rulings

European Court of Justice: Judgment of the Court: Case (C-6/64), Flamio Costa vs. ENEL. 15.07.1964.

European Court of Justice: Judgment of the Court: Case (C-329/11), Alexandre Achughbabian vs. Préfet du Val-de-Marne. Reference for a preliminary ruling: Cour d'appel de Paris – France. 06.12.2011.

European Court of Justice: Judgment of the Court: Joint Cases (C-411/10) and (C-493/10) Court of Appeal [England & Wales] [Civil Division], High Court of Ireland – N. S. (C-411/10)/Secretary of State for the Home Department und M. E. (C-493/10), A. S. M., M. T., K. P., E. H./Refugee Applications Commissioner, Minister for Justice, Equality and Law Reform. 21.12.2011.

European Court of Justice: Judgment of the Court: Case (C-179/11) Cimade und Groupe d'information et de soutien des immigrés (GISTI) vs. Ministre de l'Intérieur, de l'Outre-mer, des Collectivités territoriales et de l'Immigration. Reference for a preliminary ruling: Conseil d'État – France. 27.09.2012.

European Court of Justice: Judgment of the Court: Joined Cases (C-199/12) and (C-200/12). Minister voor Immigratie en Asiel gegen X (C-199/12) und Y (C-200/12) und Z gegen Minister voor Immigratie en Asiel (C-201/12), Reference for a preliminary ruling: Raad van State – The Netherlands. 07.11.2013.

European Court of Justice: Judgment of the Court, Case (C-285/12), Aboubacar Diakité versus Commissaire général aux réfugiés et aux apatrides, 30.01.2014.

European Court of Justice: Judgment in Joined Cases (C-293/12) and (C-594/12), Rights Ireland Ltd (C-293/12) v Minister for Communications, Marine and

Natural Resources and Others and Kärntner Landesregierung (C-594/12) and Others. References for a preliminary ruling: High Court – Ireland, Verfassungsgerichtshof – Austria. 08.04.2014.

Legislation

Council of the European Union: Directive 2004/83/EC (OJ L 304/12, 30.9.2004).

European Union, *Consolidated version of the Treaty on European Union*, 13 December 2007, 2008/C 115/01.

European Union, *Consolidated version of the Treaty on the Functioning of the European Union*, 13 December 2007, 2008/C 115/01.

European Union: Directive 2011/95/EU (OJ L 337/9, 20.12.2011).

Part V
Contemporary State

Martin Belov

Can We Still Drive the State Machine the 'Old School' Way? Structural and Functional Deficits of the Modern State

1. Introduction

We live in a time of turbulence and mass discontent with the political, social and economic systems of which we are supposed to be an integral part. There is a shared belief that the problems to which both the states and the people are exposed are caused by crises in leadership, morale, ideology and efficiency. Although such claims are to a great degree justified, it is not only the incompetence of politicians, the decline of ideologies, and the global financial crisis that have produced the permanent inability of the state to fulfil its typical tasks. Citizens are not only deeply dissatisfied with the results of policymaking and the way politics is done. They have also lost the belief that the system is made to serve them in good and bad times and that it is capable of representing their collective values and goals.

This article tries to outline and analyse the reasons for the failure of modern representative democracies to meet the expectations of nations and citizens generated by the 'supporting ideologies' of the 19th and 20th centuries. It poses the general question 'Can we still drive the state machine the old school way?' by analysing the structural and functional deficits of modern representative democracies.

There are three cornerstone constitutional and political ideas that have fundamental importance for the maintenance of the equilibrium between state and society; government and people; power, citizens and territory. These are the concepts of *representation*; of the *pyramid-like hierarchical structure of the territorial distribution of state power*, in which the power unites the people on a distinct and clearly defined territory; and the *transtemporal continuity* of the nation and the state, which leads to constitutional and political upgrading of the system *based on spiral-like political cycles*.

These three phenomena – the *lines of representation*, the *territorial pyramid of the state power*, and the *spiral of time that swirls the constitutional civilisation* – can be subsumed under the concept of *constitutional geometry*. There are profound problems regarding these three components of the constitutional geometry. They produce greater and greater malfunction both in constitutions and the political systems that they are intended to form and frame. Since the beginning of the 21st century, the societies that belong to the centre or the periphery of the European constitutional tradition have experienced an increasing crisis of parliamentarism, democracy, and representation. The *representation crisis*, the *territoriality crisis* (see Cuttitta 2006, 28), and the *temporality crisis* are the key factors that have produced the crisis of representative democracy in general, and of parliamentary democracy in particular. The crisis of representation consists in *broken lines of representation, trust, and responsibility*; the crisis of territoriality, in *broken pyramids of vertical distribution of public power*; and the crisis of temporality, in *the broken spiral of time* winding up political cycles and distorting the political rhythm of the system.

2. The crisis of political representation

Political representation is one of the most crucial elements of political governance. It is an inevitable component of the constitutional geometry of each political community, the state included. Since the late 18th and 19th centuries, representation has been cross-fertilized with democracy (see Brito Vieira and Runciman 2008, 29–63, who emphasise that representation is also possible in a non-democratic way). Since the end of the Cold War, representative democracy has clearly become the predominant regime on the European continent.

It seems that exactly this mirage of the ultimate and final victory of mass representative democracy planted the seeds for the crisis that has been advancing since the beginning of the 21st century. The reason for this is that a crisis of representation has undermined society's potential to sustain a democratic state regime. This crisis affects all main aspects of representation – its scope, type, and chain. As already mentioned, it results in broken lines of representation, trust, and responsibility.

The scope of representation concerns the issue of the basis of representation or, in other words, the question of who is or, more precisely, who gets represented. Here one can distinguish between *elitist representation* and *mass representation*. *Elitist representation* historically existed in three main forms: first, as the clear and structurally enshrined rigid representation of historically privileged classes; second, as less clear and less structurally enshrined representation schemes that are also open to new elites; and third, as diffuse and obscure, much more functional than structural lobbyist representation, which is still very much practiced. *Mass representation* first took the shape of national and then, with the full political enfranchisement of the population, that of people's representation. In theory, one can speculate about whether a representation of all human beings living in a distinct territory that is both postnational and not structurally enshrined and limited is possible and necessary.

There is a *reverse relationship between the broadening of the scope of representation and its density, efficiency, and feasibility*. The broader the scope of representation, the more fictitious, inadequate, and imaginary it is. The pre-modern forms of representation were tools in the hands of the privileged elites for the realisation of their political rights. The census-based representation of the white, male, property-owning elite ensured the protection of its dominant position in the system. In general, overt elite representation has a structural advantage in that it is clear whose interests are protected. There is a relatively straightforward line of trust and responsibility between the representatives and the represented that keeps the representation relation alive and functional. However, this is to the detriment of the inclusiveness and openness of the system of representation.

The problem with broad representation of the people is that it is based on several axiomatic stipulations that are very difficult to sustain in practice. The idea that the people are a single political unit and a feasible collective political entity, that they are capable of formulating a general will aiming at the common good, the stipulation that although unified the people are at the same time differentiated into individuals and groups with interests, values and goals that need to be represented in their own right (although that thesis contradicts to some extent to the previous ones) form the corpus of the so-called 'supportive ideologies' of the constitutionalism of the 18th, 19th, and 20th centuries.

The politicians of the constitutional age are expected to promise that they will serve the pantheon of the new divine commands of human kind that are explicitly or implicitly enshrined in nation state constitutions. However, to promise to serve everybody and to pursue an abstract general interest is sometimes, in practice, to have a preliminary blanket excuse that you will serve no one. If society activated as a political community is capable of at least broadly outlining the general shape of the common good, or in other words to formulate a set of values, aims, and institutions in the form of political and constitutional consensus, then this product of an implicit social contract may serve its main purpose. The common good has to function as a criterion for assessing the political decisions of state institutions and all other veto players (for the concept of veto players see Tsebelis 2002). Unfortunately, in the context of an increasingly pluralizing society with decreasing social awareness, social mobilisation, and political self-identification of a vast part of the citizens, the formulation of a coherent and feasible common good becomes more and more unachievable.

The hollowing out of the anyway abstract categories of the 18th and 19th centuries, which nevertheless maintain their pivotal status in the construction of the national constitutional statehood even in the 21st century, combined with the extinction of idea- and ideology-based party politics and the increase of lobbyism and demagogy, leads to the strange situation that the classical democratic instruments and lexica have begun to serve narrow elitist interests. *Representative democracy has committed suicide through the hyperinflation of the usage of formal democratic tools that almost never lead to the establishment of substantial democracy.*

Thus one may think about whether we should not reinvent segmented and group interest representation as an official version of political representation in order to give that representation real life and concrete shape, and to fix the broken and almost non-existent lines of trust, control and responsibility. This might diminish the instances in which the official version of general interest representation and the consequent pretention that policy is made in the pursuit of a common good serve as a veil for hiding individual or group special interests. Such strengthening of overt specific interest representation could and should be done only through enhancement of ideology and the reinforcement of ideology-based political parties. The structural introduction of special (class, guild, estate, strata, etc.) representation is doomed to failure, as the history of corporate representation clearly demonstrates. However, such functional reassessment of the scope of representation is not very likely to occur in the light of the progressive increase of catch-all and populist parties, paralleled by a decrease of ideological and coherent strategy-based political parties.

Let's now turn to the issue of the types of representation. With regard to the content and the substance of representation there are four main types of representation that have been elaborated in theoretical, constitutional and political discourses – the *territorial*, the *national*, the *party political* and the *social group interest* representation.

Territorial representation is constituency focused. It has been practiced since the late Middle Ages, beginning in pre-modern parliaments and in state and monarchical councils. Formally, it is also used in forums for representation of the constituent units of multilevel constitutional systems, such as Federal Councils, Senates, and regional committees, although in practice it is party politically biased.

Territory-fixed and constituency-focused representation has many disadvantages. It infringes upon the free mandate of the representatives and undermines the presumption of the existence of a transterritorial common interest. Furthermore, it may distort national integration through enhancement of the role of local elites and patronage schemes. This type of representation is fictitious and practically impossible in systems where there is an overall lack of stable linkage between elected politicians and the local electorate, a state of affairs that is to some extent due to the disintegration of local communities in the course of the establishment of the modern nation states.

National representation was the dominant type of representation during the phase of liberal constitutionalism. It is still the main formal target of most modern constitutions, although with the meaning of all-encompassing representation of the citizenry and not that of census-based privilege.

National representation raises several questions that need to be answered properly if the concept is to survive. These questions are: Is the holistic nation of the late 18th, the 19th and the early 20th centuries achievable in its maximalist version in the 21st century? Is the institutional design constructed for national representation still functional? Moreover, has the institutional design constructed for national representation ever functioned as per the 'law in books', and are the failures in the legislative, education, integration, and legitimation functions of the national parliaments (see Bagehot 2009; Schreyer and Schwarzmeier 2002, 165ff) remediable? The answers to the first three questions are rather negative, whereas the answer to the fourth one is: 'Maybe, to some extent and under specific circumstances'.

There is a vast literature on the issue of deparliamentarisation, which can be caused both by internal reasons (such as a crisis of representative party democracy) and by external reasons (EU integration, globalisation, global governance etc.). Thus I cannot exhaust the issue without entering into a multidiscursive and profound debate, which is impossible due to space constraints. Hence I prefer to jump to conclusions and suppose that without the recreation of the preconditions for parliamentary governance – strategic, programmatic, and idea-oriented political parties; media providing for substantial idea competition and pluralism; politically self-cautious citizens, etc. – the dysfunctionalities of the national representation will remain and even deepen.

Since the late 19th and early 20th centuries, the constitutional systems have (supposedly) guaranteed the people's representation, that is, *structurally national and functionally party political representation* (see Leibholz 1967, 112–114). However, observation of their actual functioning produces several additional questions to the issues mentioned above. First, how large is the mismatch between constitutionally enshrined people's representation and the pro-elitist bias of policymaking? Second, how can we reconcile the people's sovereignty with the elite-driven constitutional system? Third, how representative are the non-representative parts of the constitutional design, i.e. the judiciary and the administration? Due to space restraints I will allow these questions to remain rhetorical ones.

It is already self-evident, and has been thoroughly elaborated in the constitutional doctrine of the 20th century, especially after World War II, that the current type of representation is formally national but actually party political (ibid.). With regard to the crisis of representative democracy, the *party political representation* which is typical for the *Parteienstaat* (see Gabriel, Niedermayer and Stöss 2001) of the 20th century raises two groups of issues: first, issues concerning the political parties, and second, issues concerning the electorate.

The first group of problems comprises the crisis or lack of (real) party ideology, strategy oriented policymaking, policy continuity, and systematic social and political integration of the citizens by the political parties. The problem of the increase of populist and leadership-oriented parties instead of parties that are focused on ideas has already been mentioned.

The second group of problems concerns the political consumerism of the citizens, which stimulates populism; the electorate's preference of fast and pleasant policy outcomes; the political self-identification crisis on both the individual and group level; and the distortion of the integrative mechanisms that allow for systematic and idea-based political inclusion of the population.

Class, estate or professional representation is also not a viable alternative or solution to these problems. This is due to the fact that it preserves and perpetuates social fragmentation, creates a pillar-based society, enhances the oligarchic features of the political and social system, and usually produces either oligarchy or authoritarianism. Moreover, citizens participate in politics and are represented not as human beings and individuals but as members of robust social groups. These issues are widely discussed in the scientific literature.

Representative democracy is founded and depends on two antipodal but intertwined processes: social fragmentation and social integration. Social fragmentation consists in drawing lines of distinction, institutionalising cleavages, and accumulating political players with common interests. On the other hand, *social integration* is based on generating constitutional and political consensus, shaping common political projects, and finding a common ground for political cooperation. Both social fragmentation and social integration are of vital importance for the establishment and maintenance of representative democracy. *Democratic society needs to be permanently deconstructed and simultaneously reconstructed in order to be able to foster both constitutional and political conflict and consensus* as prerequisites for the creation and maintenance of a democratic state (about conflict and consensus see Randelzhofer and Süss, 1986).

Hence, dysfunctionalities in representative democracies emerge due to problems with both processes – social fragmentation and social integration. They lead to distortions of the fundamental chain of responsibility, trust and representation that starts from the people, the citizens, the electorate and the active citizens, goes through the political parties and ends up with the parliament and the other institutions of representative democracy.

3. The crisis of territoriality

The constitution needs a fixed territoriality. There should be clarity regarding the territorial scope of the application of the constitutional law in order to ensure its validity and legitimate expectations on the part of the citizens. This is an axiom of the nation state constitutionalism, which was the only type of constitutionalism until the end of the 20th century. The *territoriality of the creation and application of the law* is not limited to constitutional law. It is of crucial importance for all branches of law.

Globalisation and Europeanisation are sources of several issues pertaining to the *territoriality of law* (see Peters 2007, 251–308 and Osterhammel and Petersson 2003, 12). Some of these issues concern classical problems allocated in a supposedly postmodern context, others have their analogies in political history, whereas a third group of issues are absolutely new. Immigration and the integration of immigrants are issues that have been present since ancient times. However, a relatively new problem is whether and how the state can assure the representation and political participation of immigrants and 'new citizens'. The liberal approach allows for a simple decision from a legal point of view. Everyone who wants to get political rights should become a full citizen. Thus, the legal institution of national citizenship serves as the key inclusion/exclusion device for membership in the group of active citizens.

The great merit of the liberal approach is that it treats people as equal human beings and as equal citizens, leaving the burden of pre-political affiliations such as gender, race, religion, ethnicity, etc. in the realms of the private sphere and civil society. In practice, however, citizens cannot abandon their social, individual, and group diversity. They cannot set down their contextual burdens, and they cannot enter the temple of the state in the virgin white cloth of the pure citizen.

Hence all constitutional systems and regimes – national, subnational and supranational – are not, cannot, and maybe even should not be fully impartial, applying absolutely socially neutral criteria for inclusion and exclusion when it comes to political empowerment and political representation. The reason for this is that a community without a core constitutional and political consensus regarding its fundamental values, identities, and goals, as well as without a clear criterion for membership (allowing for the development of sufficiently strong feelings of both vertical belongingness to the referential polity and horizontal togetherness with the other participants in the project), is politically impotent or even doomed to disintegration.

Consequently there is a need for a common ideal, social and political project in order to maintain a coherent and politically vital community. On the other hand, it is necessary to systematically integrate the newcomers – 'new citizens' and immigrants – in the political project. This necessity is legitimate for two reasons: first, the imperatives stemming from human rights, human dignity and human nature, and second, the need to permanently revitalise the political community through the integration of its already present social parts.

The problem is that the blindness of the liberal approach towards social pluralism and its reflections on political participation, which can never be absolutely neutral from pre-political identities, can hardly be compensated by the proposals offered by multiculturalism. The establishment of a structurally fragmented society and the exposition of the pre-political diversity of the civil society in the sphere of the state can lead to irreconcilable social, political, and constitutional fragmentation and to the structural pillarisation of the state. This will diminish the transparency of the system, increase the role of the elites presiding over the social pillars, and possibly diminish the effectiveness and the problem solving capacity of the society. These are all classical concerns in constitutional and political science literature.

That is why typically constitutional systems allow for the guaranteed representation of minorities and the multicultural organisation of the constitutional infrastructure in two cases. The first case is when minorities are sufficiently small and thus their guaranteed representation cannot endanger the majority project. The second case is quite the opposite. It can be found in states with minorities that are so big and influential that they actually approach the status of the second or third majority. However, when it comes not to classical minorities but to newcomers to the systems such as immigrants or refugees, then constitutional law is not capable of giving a clear answer to the issues of their representation and political participation.

The second issue concerning the crisis of territoriality is caused by another mismatch between the personal and the territorial component of the state, namely the 'external compatriots'. The big question is whether and how they should be included in the political life of the mother-nation state. Whereas the issue of how and to what extent to politically integrate third country nationals living in the domestic territory is a problem for the countries of immigration, the question of how and to what extent to keep compatriots that have chosen to live for a long period or even permanently abroad is a problem for the states of emigration. The new opportunities created by EU integration, i.e. the free movement of people, have broadened the scope of the classical means of emigration. Hence some nations have disintegrated not due to war, foreign domination, or other factor producing loss of territory, but due to more or less voluntary movement of substantial parts of these nations to foreign territories.

If the constitutional legislator decides to allow for the extended political integration and representation of the 'external compatriots' in the national institutional design and policymaking process, then it has to reassess cornerstone ideas of modern nation state constitutional law, such as the territoriality of sovereignty. Many countries preserve some political rights for their citizens that live abroad. The full inclusion of external compatriots in the national political life, based on granting rights to election or appointment as MP, minister, president, judge, etc. – especially if those compatriots have double citizenship – creates situations of double loyalty and thus threatens national sovereignty. Such states have to accept the idea of open statehood (see Kirchhof 1999, 225–242) not only with regard to its legal but also to its factual aspect.

These two issues – the integration, political empowerment and representation of immigrants and emigrants, or, to put it differently, the new and the former compatriots – demonstrate clearly the crisis of the territoriality of statehood at the beginning of the 21st century (see Appadurai 2003, 337–349). This crisis consists in the *rapidly increasing mismatch between the three components of statehood according to the classical theory of Georg Jellinek – state power, state territory, and the people* (see Jellinek 2010). Thus the state of the 21st century is no longer the state of the 19th and the 20th centuries. Hence a conceptual decision regarding state sovereignty has to be made, namely *whether the state should be defined in terms of territory or in terms of people. The appropriate balance between the personal and territorial components of statehood should be recalibrated in order to preserve the vitality of the state power.*

This *partial divorce between the territory and the people* as constitutive elements of statehood could lead to a *redefinition of the concept of sovereignty and state power.* If the state is defined in terms of a nation that spreads outside of a certain territory, then immigrants should be excluded and emigrants included. In that case we might be confronted with a kind of *'virtual' or 'non-territorial' state* that is *physically fluid in its attempt to conform to and follow the nation.* On the other hand, if the state is defined as a territory-based phenomenon, then we might be pressed by circumstances to apply the idea of the political nation in order to preserve statehood and sovereignty. If that concept does not work, i.e.

because there is a very weak social, constitutional, and political consensus on the common values, goals, and institutions of the community, we might be pressed to walk the way of multiculturalism, or even to give up key concepts such as nation and sovereignty. However, apart from nationalistic concerns, the problem here would be *how to have a politically integrated and mobilized community capable of collective choice and action.*

Another aspect of the territoriality crisis is the *multiplication of the levels of policy making*. This process *per se* cannot be defined as a crisis of territoriality. On the contrary: the more levels of policymaking there are, there must be more territorial jurisdictions of public power. The fact that there might be two subnational – one local and one cantonal, state, or province, as well as national and European territories, jurisdictions and levels of policy- and decision-making – does not itself decouple the power from its territorial entrenchment.

However, *the more levels of policymaking there are, the less straightforward the representation and political participation of the members of the lower level are*. Multilevel governance (see Bache and Flinders 2004) diminishes the ability of the citizens and the institutions belonging to the lower level to influence and control the decisions that are made at the upper levels. Hence the proliferation of the number of territories reduces the importance of political power for the political players on the lower levels. The national political elites and the institutions they 'inhabit' are the main targets of democratic oversight. However, they are trapped in multilevel 'nested games' (see Tsebelis 1990) that shift the *locus of decision making upwards* and the *locus of control and accountability downwards*. That mismatch produces phenomena such as democratic deficit, deparliamentarisation, dedemocratisation, executive federalism (see Maurer 2002; Habermas 2011, 68), non-accountability and even non-governability that are supposed to be among the key problems of many multilevel political systems and of the EU in particular.

Finally, *deterritorialisation of politics is achieved through forms of e-governance and e-democracy*. The new opportunities that these create for launching policy initiatives, policy deliberation, policy adoption and broader policy participation *can broaden the political communities irrespective of their physical allocation* and *can set the deliberative and participatory veto players free from the constraints of physical presence*. Moreover, e-democracy and e-governance *reshape the channels of political communication, thus introducing structural changes in the ways political and policy campaigns are conducted and the state is practically managed.*

Once upon a time in the 19th century, many constitutions explicitly stipulated the *territorial locus of the central state institutions*. They demanded that the Parliament should be in session only in its building in the capital of the country, and that the head of state should be physically present in the state territory. He or she had to ask special permission from, or at least inform, the body of citizens, typically through the Parliament, before living the state territory. The purpose of such *territorial entrenchment* was *to safeguard the responsibility* of the key office holders to the people *by their physical presence in the area of the people's possible control.*

Naturally such clauses are obsolete and not necessary in the 21st century. However, I refer to them as a measure of how far *the process of decoupling of state power from state territory* has gone since the initial phase of modern constitutionalism. Indeed, the issue is not that the king is not always in his castle. The problem is that *political and economic elites have become so mobile that the state territory is no longer the policy constraint that it once was.* The fact that you can make profit in one country while investing it in another and using the benefits in a third *durably decouples elites from their electorates, political referential communities, or economic producers.* This leads to a *loosening of the popular responsibility of the elites. The inability of politicians*, even if they hold the most important nation state offices, *to reinforce the commitment of the economic and financial elites to the national territorial communities* becomes more and more obvious.

These phenomena demonstrate that we are presently living in a situation in which *the state territory still matters, but to a much lesser extent than in the constitutional civilisation of the 18th, 19th and 20th centuries. Policymaking has become partially decoupled from the state territory, or even from territory in general.* Moreover, *international and supranational regimes have shifted the real decision making centres far away from the territories and the capitals of the nation states. The population of the territory is no longer able to sufficiently control, not to mention effectively participate directly or indirectly in the proposition, adoption, and even implementation of the policies to which it is exposed. The agenda setters and the key veto players are increasingly freed from the constraints of territory in general, and from the state capitals, boundaries and jurisdictions in particular.* The head has been decoupled from the body. The hands and the feet cannot find where their (supposed) brain, heart, lungs, eyes, ears and tongue are. But they are free to belong to another body if they can manage to be transplanted.

4. The crisis of temporality

Policy- and decision-making is naturally embedded in time. Time is needed for the elaboration of draft acts and policy proposals, for thorough deliberation and for the adoption of legislative, executive, and other policy measures. Time is a crucial political resource and a precondition for social governance. Time is the frame of all constitutional competences and the political actions stemming from them. It is also simultaneously framed by constitutional law. That is why when analysing and evaluating the potential of state institutions and other political actors to influence and determine political practices that are efficient, transparent and responsible, we should not omit the temporal aspect of their governance potential. One should take into account that the parameters of the temporal context of constitutional competences and political action can be framed by the legislator but also by the socio-political practice itself.

The temporal context of the 21st century modifies to a great extent the modes of policymaking. This is particularly true for policy proposition and deliberation. Political leaders and political parties are supposed to be central communicative veto players as well as channels that simplify information and set guidelines for the electorate (see Geys and Vermeir 2012; Brader and Tucker 2010). The way they have accomplished this function from the late 18th until the late 20th century differs very much from the practice that has emerged since the end of the 20th century. Electronic media and new Internet media such as Facebook, Twitter, Google+, etc., have accelerated political communication about those social processes that are the object of policymaking. The party meetings at which permanent party members and sympathizers discuss, systematically and for a relatively long time, the content of policy, as well as the party newspapers that provided an ideology-based platform for information upgrade have been replaced by communication channels through which information is exchanged extremely fast and sometimes in a non-systematic manner (see Peters 2007, 280). Moreover, the addressees of the new media are potentially unlimited and very diverse. Televised political communication is closer to reality shows and quasi-commercial advertisements than to the systematic exchange of profound and ideology-based policy content. There is a flood of information that for the ordinary citizen is closer to disinformation. There are fewer clear information pillars that provide easily absorbed and reliable information.

Thus *political communication has become simultaneously more and less democratic and transparent.* The increased quantity and acceleration of dissemination speed of information through new, easier, faster, and more interactive means of data exchange have created huge potentials for the development of deliberative and participatory democracy. On the other hand, the same processes dilute the responsibility of the information sources and foster faster and more populist policymaking, very often to the detriment of the quality and durability of the results. The speeding up of the information current increases the transparency of the political system in general and of the political action in particular, sometimes to the detriment of its efficiency and responsibility.

Another aspect of the temporality crisis consists in the *speeding and winding up of political cycles* that lead to *distortions in the political rhythm* of the constitutional and the political system. There are structural and functional grounds for the speeding up of the political cycles.

The structural reasons are a by-product of the general formal (legal) democratisation of the constitutional systems during the 20th century. They consist of the replacement of the monarch with an elected republican head of state and of appointed office holders with elected office holders. The increase of the elected positions in the constitutional infrastructure of the state leads to frequent elections and – what is more important – to frequent electoral campaigns. In this case there are three types of elections – for MPs in the national Parliament, for president, and for local self-government institutions – and if they do not coincide, then they all serve the function of mid-term elections. The situation is even more complicated in multilevel constitutional systems that also provide for elections for supranational and subnational state bodies, such as the European Parliament and state, provincial, or cantonal parliaments.

The functional reasons for the speeding up of the political cycles are the frequent political crises that lead to pre-term termination of the mandate of different state institutions. Hence it is clear that politicians are expected by the people to provide long and mid-term solutions to social problems that have to be effective and responsible, even though they are in a situation of almost permanent electoral campaign.

In terms of democracy this is not a bad situation, since it allows for closer and more frequent control of the politicians by the electorate. The problem is that the electoral swirl in combination with the abovementioned influence of the new media dramatically increases demagogy masquerading as responsiveness and transparency, while decreasing the incentives and the chances for the politicians to make effective and responsible political decisions even if they want to do so. Hence several modern developments in the institutional design of constitutional and political systems – the emergence of new media, the increase in information flow, the electoral democratisation of the key political players etc. – *de facto* lead to a decrease in the problem-solving capacity of state institutions. Moreover, these innovations, although very positive in themselves, in practice produce new opportunities for lobbyist political action that does not correspond to the common good. Thus the *broken spiral of time* in combination with other factors *weakens the official institutions* of the constitutional system and *increases the capacities of the hidden elites*.

To conclude: the *temporality crisis* produces several issues that are of crucial importance for the survival of democracy and in some cases even of statehood. The most important of these concern the need and the institutional devices required for society (here I mean both the people and the elites) to maintain *temporal continuity of the general and sector policies* and the *democratic alternation of the ruling elites*. The aim is that political polycentrism, the efficiency of the state, and the rights of future generations should all be preserved. Indicators of the *temporal malfunctioning of statehood* are negative phenomena such as *cyclical financial and economic crisis, fluctuations of the political system between the extremities of anarchy and authoritarianism*, the emergence of *fluid and unstable party systems*, the *domination of demagogic over conceptual politics*, etc.

5. In place of a conclusion: What is the future of representative democracy?

Apart from the renouncement of democracy, which is obviously an undesirable solution, equal to political euthanasia for the demos, there are three general theoretical options for democratic reform. These are: first, the *reestablishment of the ideal, classical legal and social preconditions for a fully-fledged representative democracy*; second, the *establishment of a new type of representative democracy*; and third, the *establishment of a non-representative democracy*.

The reestablishment of the ideal, classical legal and social preconditions for a fully-fledged representative democracy would comprise several elements. There should be a politically active *tiers état* (see Sieyès 2009) independent of public power; stable lines of party political affiliation and clear and durable ideological preferences of considerable portions of the citizenry; ideology-based and strategically acting political parties; and effective parliamentary control also with regard to the EU and the international issues. Last but not least, there should be governments ruling on the basis of mid-term programs that are responsible and accountable to the parliament and via a feasible distinction between parliamentary majority and parliamentary minority also to the voters.

A new type of representative democracy can theoretically be based on three different forms of representation. These are *fragmented* representation, *charismatic* representation, and *pragmatic output-based* representation.

Fragmented representation consists in simultaneous inclusion of the organized social interests and groups by virtue of direct civic engagement and activism. It is a result of intense direct and participatory democratic actions by active citizens producing an overall representative effect. Although such a model is promising when it comes to enhancing the responsiveness and openness of the system, it might heavily undermine the responsibility, transparency, and efficiency of the system, making it hostage to the dispersed pressure of various overt and hidden interest groups. Another important issue is that fragmented representation could create serious policy coordination problems that might additionally endanger the effectiveness and the problem solving capacity of the state institutions.

Charismatic representation consists in the representation of the presumed holistic and homogeneous political community by a leader. This representation is based on the identification of the 'collective self of the nation' with the leader as a symbolic integrator of the people. Such representation *à la* Thomas Hobbes and Carl Schmitt requires as a precondition the elimination of social diversity, the alienation of political liberty in favour of the leader and his unrestrained, legal, and legitimate demand to require compliance by the population. Hence charismatic representation is irreconcilable with freedom and democracy and has to be discarded.

Pragmatic output-based representation can be described as non-ideological governance that should be accomplished by governments that are more expert than party political, by catch-all parties, and by democratically independent technocratic elites. In a broad sense it resembles Plato's ideal government by philosophers. In the axiological constitution of pragmatic output-based representation the values of expertise, expedience, and efficiency dominate over responsibility, participation, and transparency. The government is to a great extent replaced by governance. The only method for justifying the governance scheme is the popular satisfaction with its results.

Finally, a *non-representative democracy is impossible to establish in practice.* There have never been political systems organized as fully-fledged direct democracies. Moreover participatory democracy, deliberative democracy and e-democracy are possible supplements, extensions and variations of representative democracy, but do not constitute radical alternatives to it.

Hence the only way we can improve our representative systems while remaining in the realm of democracy is by fostering the conditions – both constitutional and social – for the reestablishment of party political representative democracy. Redefining ideologies in the light of the social context of the 21st century, reinforcing idea- and strategy-based party politics, and reassessing the territorial and personal elements of statehood with a view to the latest social and political developments are of crucial importance. Moreover the phenomena of time should be added to the coordinate scheme of constitutional law. However, this is just an abstract stipulation based on a preference towards representative democracy. It is not certain whether the trend of social, political and constitutional developments in the forthcoming years and decades will allow for its full or even partial realisation.

References

Appadurai Arjun. 2003. Sovereignty without territoriality: notes for a postnational geography. In *Anthropology of Space and Place: Locating Culture*. Edited by Setha Low and Denise Lawrence-Zuniga. Oxford: Wiley and Blackwell.

Bache, Ian, and Flinders, Matthew. 2004. *Multi-level Governance*. Oxford: Oxford University Press.

Bagehot, Walter. 2009. *The English Constitution*. Oxford: Oxford University Press.

Brader, Ted, and Tucker, Joshua. 2010. Follow the Leader: Party Cues, Policy Opinion, and the Power of Partisanship in Three Multiparty Systems. [http://www.upf.edu/dcpis/_pdf/2009-2010/forum/Tucker_paper.pdf, accessed on 24 March 2015].

Brito Vieira, Monica, and Runciman, David. 2008. *Representation*. Cambridge: Polity Press.

Gabriel, Oskar W., Niedermayer, Oskar, and Stöss, Richard (eds.). 2001. *Parteiendemokratie in Deutschland*. Bonn: BPB.

Geys, Benny, and Vermeir, Jan. 2012. Party Cues in Elections under Multilevel Governance: Theory and Evidence from US States. [https://www.gate.cnrs.fr/IMG/pdf/Geys2012-2.pdf, accessed on 5 February 2015].

Cuttitta, Paolo. 2006. Points and Lines: A Topography of Borders in the Global Space. *Ephemera* 6(1): 27–39.

Habermas, Jürgen. 2011. *On the Constitution of Europe*. Sofia: Kritika i humanizam (in Bulgarian).

Jellinek, Georg. 2010. *Allgemeine Staatslehre*. Nabu Press.

Kirchhof, Paul. 1999. The Balance of Powers between National and European Institutions. *European Law Journal* 5(3): 225–242.

Leibholz, Gerhard. 1967. *Strukturprobleme der modernen Demokratie*. Karlsruhe: C.F. Müller.

Maurer, Andreas. 2002. *Parlamentarische Demokratie in der Europäischen Union*. Baden-Baden: Nomos.

Osterhammel, Jürgen, and Petersson, Niels P. 2003. *Geschichte der Globalisierung: Dimensionen, Processe, Epochen*. München: Beck.

Peters, Anne. 2007. The Globalisation of State Constitutions. In *New Perspectives on the Divide between National and International Law*, edited by Janne E. Nijman and André Nollkaemper. Oxford: Oxford University Press.

Randelzhofer, Werner, and Süss, Albrecht (eds.). 1986. *Konflikt und Konsens. 35 Jahre Grundgesetz.* Berlin: Walter de Gruyter.

Schreyer, Bernhard, and Schwarzmeier, Manfred. 2002. *Grundkurs Politikwissenschaft: Studium der politischen Systeme.* Wiesbaden: Westdeutscher Verlag.

Sieyès, Emmanuel. 2009. *Qu'est-ce que le tiers-état?* Paris: Flammarion.

Tsebelis, George. 2002. *Veto Players. How Political Institutions Work.* Princeton/New York: Russell Sage Foundation/Princeton University Press.

Tsebelis, George. 1990. *Nested Games. Rational Choice in Comparative Politics.* Berkley: University of California Press.

Marco Stefano Birtolo

Privatising Law in Western, Multi-Faith and Multicultural Democracies

1. The neutrality of law in multicultural democracies

In the last decades, the coexistence of culturally different groups has resulted in unprecedented, although not completely new, problems which both political systems and contemporary political studies have tried to resolve in order to limit the impact of conflicting issues originating from potentially explosive clashes between individuals of different cultures. As a consequence, under the scenario of the 1990's Western political theory the current of multiculturalism has taken form as a sort of progression and overcoming of the long-standing controversy between communitarians and liberals (see Mullhalle and Swift 1992).

The word *multiculturalism* generally indicates a kind of political system and a legal solution for enhancing the cultural otherness and providing for its actual political and legal acknowledgement (see Modood 2007; Kukhatas 2003; Benhabib 2002; Shachar 2001; Parekh 2000; Okin 1999; Raz 1998; Kymlicka 1995; Gutmann 1994). Indeed, all theories relative to multiculturalism agree on the fact that in today's complex societies there is a high degree of cultural diversity which somehow needs to be protected and enhanced (see Crowder 2013; Murphy 2012; Monceri 2008).

In wider terms, the multiculturalist point of view asserts that the current functions of the modern nation-state should be re-elaborated taking into account the slant of a new multicultural reality. Primarily, due to the fact that it does not meet the expectations and needs of individuals and groups who are the carriers of traditions, habits and religions which differ from Western ones, and who do not identify themselves with mainstream culture. Due to external influences and the globalisation process, the contemporary nation-state could not work as a cohesive cultural institution and would be unable to base its unity on the homogeneity of its own citizens (see Parekh 2000, 194; Monceri 2008, 53).

Indeed, multicultural society questioned the alleged cultural homogeneity of modern states. Obviously, the state still plays an important role, but 'the old unity of territory, sovereignty and culture', which has so far provided the historical justification of modern state as well as been the engine of its development and stabilisation, is hastily falling apart (see Parekh 2000, 194).

Starting from these theoretical preconditions, multiculturalist theories claim that the modern state in its liberal democratic version should change its inner structure, granting recognition to individuals belonging to minority groups in the public sphere and in the legal system. From a theoretical point of view, multiculturalism criticises one fundamental element of the liberal democratic tradition: the possibility of a neutral political and normative sphere as a guarantee for a fair and equal treatment of each individual.

According to the most influential liberal theories (as the theories of John Rawls, Ronald Dworkin and Charles Larmore), the most libertarian-oriented theories (including those of Murray Newton Rothbard and Robert Nozick), or the deliberative democracy theory of Jürgen Habermas, the principle of neutrality of the political power is considered the fair solution for the conflicts generated from the so-called *fact of pluralism* (see Galeotti 1999, 5–6).

In criticising these perspectives, the multiculturalist asks a key question: is a neutral political power theoretically achievable? If it were, could it equally respond to the requests of acknowledgement purported by individuals, especially those of cultural minority groups?

Neutralists, like Rawls and Habermas, consider the principle of political neutrality as an instrument aimed neither to favour nor to prevent any idea of good, which ensures an equal treatment to each individual. According to this conception, we should firstly ignore the differences in choosing the principles of justice the political order is based upon. Secondly, we should repeat this process by applying it to the normative field. Indeed, in this perspective, political action could act neutrally only if it ignored differences, without siding with anyone (see Rawls, 1996; 1997; Habermas 2006).

Nevertheless, according to multiculturalists, this very same idea is not viable, because the effective belonging to a majority or to a minority group creates substantial differences between individuals, and the principle of neutrality could not reduce these differences. Indeed, in order to ensure a fair and equal treatment among individuals, the principle of neutrality helps to keep asymmetry between minority and majority stances, at their earlier stage, thus apparently fostering the *status quo* rather than assuring equality in treatment.

According to multiculturalists, it is impossible to separate the content of the normative sphere from the culture of the authors who produce laws, because all legal systems are the expression of a majority culture. So in the Western context, for instance, being fit, white, male, heterosexual and Christian is clearly different from being disabled, female, Muslim and homosexual; in the latter case, there are additional disadvantages and costs originating from a set of prejudices strengthened throughout the centuries, which are also reproduced in the normative field. Therefore, according to multiculturalists, the strict application of neutrality in the political and normative fields could not promote the path towards the inclusion of minority group individuals.

This is the most recent criticism of the idea of the institutions' neutrality advanced by multiculturalists who have been trying to elaborate a political theoretical solution more specifically focused on the differences: in order to grant equal treatment to both the individuals belonging to the majority groups and those belonging to the culturally disadvantaged minority groups, political institutions, especially the state, should accommodate minorities' request for recognition, even if this were to apparently result in violating the neutrality principle.

In other words, if in a liberal democracy the targets are the pursuit of equal freedom and equal treatment for everybody and the possibility for individuals to reflect themselves in the legal system, institutions should surpass the neutrality principle and specifically consider those requests for recognition coming from minority groups. Hence, democratic states and their legal systems could better meet the request of *representativeness* of different cultural and religious groups.

2. The conception of secularism in multi-faith societies

Instead of considering the problem, discussed above, as referred to the generic notion of cultural diversity, we could focus on a specific kind of diversity, namely the religious one. Thus, we could easily assume that criticism of the idea of neutrality has been similarly addressed by multiculturalists as the concept of secularism, which is usually intended as an attempt to eradicate or limit the influence of religious comprehensive doctrines from public and normative fields.

If the neutrality principle should generically serve as a parameter that aims at eliminating any kind of idea of the good in the political field, in the specific case of religious diversity, secularism should similarly target the removal of the religious element in the political and normative sphere.

It is, therefore, not by chance that in the last years secularism has been strongly disputed by scholars and academics of multiculturalism: starting from criticism of the neutrality principle mentioned above, then moving to a more specific criticism of the neutralist models of secularism, supported in the philosophical debate, for example, by Rawls and Habermas (Rawls 1997; Habermas 2006).

In neutralist secularism, the public and the normative fields are separated from the private one. This separation implies that religious expressions should be contained solely in the private field, since the public perspective should remain neutral in terms of religious ideas. Indeed, secularism is ideally meant to allow for an equal coexistence among religious diversities without favouring one over another.

This aim is feasible because, in politics and law, the secularist language should be neutral as regards religious diversities. Such secularist principles, at least as developed in Western contemporary times, is considered the fulfilment of the neutrality principle in relations between religion and politics and with the aim of creating a political space free from religious inferences, thus respectful to all religions.

However, in the recent philosophical and political debate, the effectiveness of neutralist secularism in including religious diversities has been questioned, especially since non-Christian individuals are now living permanently in the West. Indeed, European democracies – in particular after the massive immigration flows in the second half of the 20th century – have become multi-faith realities, compelled to face new problems, particularly when it comes to elaborating strategies to ensure a peaceful cohabitation among different groups.

With regard to multicultural and multi-faith societies, it is important to highlight that intercultural clashes occur primarily in the social areas of family and education. The major cause being that family and school represent the environment in which cultural identity is more strongly conveyed and where cultural and religious traits of certain social and legal institutions are more evident (see Walzer 1997).

Thus, minority religious groups, mostly composed of *newcomers*, are *de facto* in a social context where their position is certainly weaker than the cultural and religious position of the native majority and, above all, in a political and legal system they did not have the opportunity to create. In the law field, the problem is that citizens having a cultural background different from the Western and Christian one are forced to rethink their expectations and to adapt to a cultural and normative system, which is the expression of the 'national' majority culture and religion.

In addition, we must consider the difficulty, or the impossibility, of accessing political institutions capable of transforming the requests for recognition from individuals of non-Western religious and cultural groups, into legal decisions. Furthermore, traditional instruments of democratic policy such as the extension of the suffrage or the recognition of special representation do not seem to favour this kind of inclusion due to the fact that the demands of culturally disadvantaged groups require substantial time before they receive real, public and normative recognition and it is further accentuated by the composition of the current European democratic parliaments where the cultural and religious minorities of the *newcomers* are under-represented.

Nevertheless, if democracy is a political system whereby the recipients of the law can also consider themselves its authors, the difficulty of contemporary democratic states is the lack of institutions capable of quickly transforming into regulatory interventions the demands for recognition emanating from individuals of minority religious and cultural contexts.

Despite some exceptions, in European democratic states, a political and normative intercultural awareness of the new problems related to non-Christian citizens' lives is not adequately developed and, more specifically, of those problems that are not collocated in the political and legal context of host countries.

While democratic integration processes are still too weak to meet all the citizens' requests and turn them into regulatory interventions, political institutions, on the other hand, do not apparently realise that such a negligence could result in strong social conflicts.

However, if we acknowledge that the concept of secularism arises and develops from the influence of Western culture and Christianity, we should consider the possibility of re-evaluating the distinction between politics, religion and law in the Western multicultural and multi-faith democratic states.

3. Legal pluralism as a tool for integration

As I have explained above, the multiculturalist theory argues that the present classical channels of participation used by democratic states to integrate diversity, do not seem to meet the requests from individuals not fully identifying themselves into the majority culture. This would entail rethinking new strategies of political and normative inclusion so as to ensure the very value assumptions promoted by democracy – particularly in relation to the possibility for citizens to recognise themselves in the normative field. In particular, when the issues involve significant areas where the cultural influence of some institutions is more visible, including family, marriage and hereditary issues, the possibility that they can be regulated in a different way is taken into account.

Multiculturalist theories propose a wide range of solutions to get a better integration and ensure equal treatment. However, I will attempt to discuss and describe herein the theoretical proposal of cultural and religious diversity integration through the implementation of legal pluralism patterns in contemporary democratic states. I have chosen this proposal because it stands out as being a model in which individuals belonging to cultural and religious minorities can have their expectations in the legal field recognised more rapidly and effectively, solving the problem of political and normative under-representation.

Indeed, the proposal of integration through legal pluralism systems has been considered as a way to ensure greater and speedier inclusion of minority religious groups, particularly if we consider the difficulty for the *newcomers* to participate in the actual construction of the public, political and normative spheres.

Broadly speaking, legal pluralism is a method which considers a situation in which laws, including conflicting ones, that have different origins and contents are applied in the same territory or social environment. As a consequence, legal pluralism entails the possibility that in a given territory even a set of rules which are different from the state ones could be considered as normative orders. This aspect openly contrasts with the classical point of view of legal positivism, where the law is an exclusive prerogative of the state (see Edge 2013, 137–142; Shah 2005). There are many different examples in which legal pluralism can be enforced but 'there are two main ways by which this may be done: either as a completely parallel and separate system or as an accommodation within an existing system' (see ibid., 141).

In this context, I will specifically discuss the proposal of Ayelet Shachar, who focused most of her surveys on the elaboration of a model based on the pluralisation of sources of law in a multicultural context, as the title of her most important work – *Multicultural Jurisdiction* (2001) – suggests. Her proposal tries to elaborate a legal system in which individuals can reflect their expectations and multiple identities, even if this means to redefine the exclusive power of the state over some important areas in the private lives of individuals – in particular in family law (see also Shachar 2008).

Shachar elaborates, on the one hand, from the criticism of 'secularist absolutism' which supports the use of the principle of neutrality in the political and normative sphere (see Shachar 2001, 72); and on the other, she meditates on those models which deny the effectiveness of diversity policies because they are considered a source of discrimination of vulnerable subjects, such as women and children (ibid., 69).

The author proposes a 'paradigmatic shift' (ibid., 64) to surpass the forced choice among the current perspectives compelling towards an unconditional loyalty to the values of a particularistic community (as, for example, the theories of Chandran Kukathas and Micheal McDonald) or to the state (as the models of Amy Gutmann, Brian Barry, Stephen Macedo, Ian Shapiro and Susan Okin) (ibid., 88).

According to Shachar, the problem with the most influential multiculturalist theories is considering legal authority sources as *monolithic*, without taking into account that individuals with multiple belongings could refer to plural authority sources (ibid., 85). For these reasons, Shachar refuses both the multiculturalist theories which assume that 'the state must throw its weight behind the individual in any conflict between the individual and her minority group' (ibid., 64) and those theories that in order to support the collective rights of groups justify the domain of community over certain members' basic citizenship rights.

Thus, Shachar suggests to strengthen the 'ongoing interaction among different authority sources, as a means of improving the situation of traditionally vulnerable insiders' (ibid., 88). At the same time, those subjects should not be forced to face the difficult choice between loyalty to their culture and defence of their individual rights (ibid., 88).

Therefore, from a pragmatic point of view, this does not mean relegating all judicial power over some areas of the private lives of individuals into the hands of minority communities. This kind of choice does nothing but transfer the monopoly of authority from the government to the community, with potentially dangerous consequences for the more vulnerable members, and at the same time not providing an effective solution. Instead, the pluralisation of sources of law should be conceived as a resource: whereby individuals should be able to choose the authority source they want to refer to, in order to solve controversies in certain important fields of their lives.

Shachar suggests a pattern based on a fundamental rule, i.e. *no institution must have monopoly over authority* (ibid., 120–122). Actually Shachar states that legally disputed social fields, such as education and family, should not be under the full and sole jurisdiction of a single authority but, moreover, they should become the subject matter of actual competition. Thus, the non-monopoly rule should determine that no authority, state or group, can claim the right to acquire total control over the social fields that are subject to legal controversy (ibid., 121).

Nonetheless, Shachar stresses that, in order to have a pattern aiming at the safeguard of the individual, all possible choices should be clearly presented at an individual's discretion. In this way, individuals, especially the more vulnerable ones, can be aware of the consequences of being under a certain jurisdiction rather than some other.

In other words, if the aim of a liberal and democratic political order is also to assure individuals their cultural and religious diversity, urging them to definitely and permanently remain loyal to a certain community could not be ascertained as a good strategy; on the contrary, this could be a way of limiting the very same individual self-determination that is meant to be protected.

According to Shachar, this kind of pattern could potentially help what she defines as *transformative accommodation*, which is a possible inner transformation of both religious minority cultures and secular law. Such changes would be a result of the mutual influence of different jurisdictions and of the competition between state and community over the loyalty of individuals. As a consequence, this would enable them to feel both part of the civil society and members of a religious group at the same time (ibid., 126).

With regard to this theory, on 7 February 2008, Dr. Rowan Williams, Archbishop of Canterbury, gave a lecture – *Civil and Religious Law in England: a Religious Perspective* (2010) – destined to cause a great sensation. This lecture focused on the subject of the inclusion of religious minorities in the British political and juridical system. With particular emphasis on the situation of Muslim minorities permanently living in the United Kingdom for the last few decades, the Archbishop made a strong proposal: he suggested to include in the British legal order some principles of the Shari'a, the Islamic law, but *only in some areas of family law*, thus giving the Muslim community members the opportunity to settle some of their litigation in front of a court abiding to religious law.

Dr. Williams criticised the idea that the best way to ensure actual equality among individuals is to implement a uniform law, which is the same for everyone. He stated that his aim was simply to consider some of the most important themes related to religious minority rights in a secular state, and also to consider the consequences of creating a fair and productive relation between Islamic law and juridical law in the United Kingdom (see Williams 2010, 293–303).

At the same time, aware of the possible risks for the more vulnerable members of that religious community, primarily women, the Archbishop claimed that adequate protection against any kind of prejudice from the community itself should be ensured. He called for the recognition of a space to find a productive agreement with some parts of the Islamic law, in order to prevent stalemate situations in which the law clashes against religious conscience and in which, since it is impossible to control what communities do, individuals act as they like in private (ibid., 294).

This speech resulted in provoking several controversies among scholars and politicians, who dismissed the Archbishop's attitude as irresponsible, especially with regard to all those Muslim women living in a subordinate condition in their own communities, partially because of some specific traits of the Islamic legal culture. The English Prime Minister, Gordon Brown, quickly dissociated himself from the proposal. Similarly, and perhaps still haunted by recent fears following the terrorist attacks to the London underground in 2005, many influential press organisations labelled the Archbishop's opinions as heralds of a dangerous kind of multiculturalism, which is unable to fully understand the risks of possible discriminatory actions caused by his proposal.

Hence, the main criticism against Dr. Williams turned out to be the very same recurring and usual criticism against legal pluralism patterns, i.e. how to deal with the more vulnerable members of a community who are unwilling to undergo a religious system like the Shari'a.

However, these reactions sound astonishing and confusing, especially if we consider that the Archbishop himself clearly highlighted the limits to the recognition of the Shari'a in the British system.

Instead, detractors focused on the alleged support Dr. Williams gave to the idea that the application of Shari'a in Britain is unavoidable. The Archbishop responded to these reactions by stating that it was not his intention to create parallel jurisdictions or bestow on communities the complete management of problems regarding the public and private lives of individuals but, moreover, he intended to argue in theoretical and generic terms the possibility of creating *overlapping jurisdictions*. In particular, from a philosophical perspective, Williams' effort was meant to elaborate a strategy to prevent individuals belonging to minority groups being forced to make the *difficult* choice between loyalty to their religious community and loyalty to the state.

Moreover, it is important to note that in England this proposal had already been put forward when Dr. Williams gave his lecture, since the possibility to solve controversies, regarding exclusively civil disputes, in front of non-state arbitration tribunals was considered legally valid according to the 1996 Arbitration Act (see Griffith-Jones 2013; Turner 2011; Ahdar 2010; Trigg 2007). The Act was devised to create a legal setting for individuals, in order to enable alternative dispute resolution modalities, giving executive validity to the decisions of an arbitration tribunal.

Considering this, if two parties decide and jointly agree, without any coercion, to settle a dispute in front of a religious arbitrate, they should be allowed to do so and an English court should implement the decision of the arbitration tribunal, as long as it is consistent with public policy and consequently with the fundamental rights:

> In any event, a court has a general duty to consider that an arbitral award complies with public policy and is in the public interest. [...] The requirements of public policy would also certainly mean that an English court would not enforce any arbitral award that failed to comply with the provisions of Human Rights 1998 and European Convention on Human Rights (ECHR). (see Edge 2013, 122)

This last issue is not a minor detail because it defines the limits of the binding power of an arbitral award; indeed, these limits are conceived to protect those who could be potentially damaged by the arbitration tribunal, enabling them to contest a decision presenting it in front of a state court.

As a consequence, in the last years, more specifically since 2008, some Shari'a courts have started to act as arbitration tribunals, with the indirect support of British authorities. Indeed, after Dr. Williams' lecture, Lord Chief Justice Phillips of Worth Matravers, the first President of the Supreme Court of England and Wales, made a speech on 3 July 2008 in front of the Muslim Centre in East London, where he expressly acknowledged that:

> There is no reason why principles of Shari'a Law, or any other religious code should not be the basis for mediation or other forms of alternative dispute resolution. It must be recognised, however, that any sanctions for a failure to comply with the agreed terms of the mediation would be drawn from the laws of England and Wales. So far as aspects of matrimonial law are concerned, there is a limited precedent for English law to recognise aspects of religious laws, although when it comes to divorce this can only be effected in accordance with the civil law of this country. (see Phillips, 2008)

In other words, in order to be considered legally binding, the decisions of a religious arbitration tribunal need a written agreement between parties in compliance with the following 'crucial standards' (see Reiss 2009, 762): the prohibiting of presenting recourse to state justice courts, the respect of the principles ratified in the Human Rights Act (1998), the safeguard of women's rights and the impossibility that a decision could affect third parties who did not take part in the arbitration. If these requirements were not met, the decision could not be enforced by English courts.

So far, the focus of the discussion has been mostly on Muslim courts of arbitration, but this discipline could easily be exploited by individuals of other religious communities, as the Jewish community in England has already done. Long before the Muslim arbitrations, the Jewish community instituted *Beth Din*, i.e. Rabbinic arbitration tribunals, where civil law litigations regarding divorce cases and financial and patrimonial disputes could be settled.

This last characteristic must be clearly explained because it is certainly a strong point for this pattern of legal pluralism, since it equates all the religious communities. A community – willing to institute a court of arbitration to settle disputes in family law – does not need a prior state recognition of the *status* of religious community; furthermore, it is not necessary to bargain with the state the rules to abide by. Of fundamental importance to the state is that two individuals choose an arbitrator freely, whether he/she be Christian, Muslim, Jew, Hindu, etc. The arbitrator's religious background or the religious origins of the rules applied are irrelevant for the state, whose only concerns are whether the arbitrator has been chosen freely and that individual rights are respected, giving English courts the possibility to check these preconditions.

Obviously, it is important to stress that the difficulty of implementing this proposal is to establish technically and pragmatically how to ensure the protection of the individual freedom of choice – especially for the more vulnerable members, also in light of the fact that the objective of this pattern, based on legal pluralism, is to give individuals the opportunity of being subjected to a legal system in which they can recognise themselves.

However, aside from the practical difficulties regarding the implementation of this proposal, a system based primarily on legal pluralism implies that the state must renounce the myth of law neutrality and the monopoly of the production of law, allowing individuals to appeal to different legal systems in order to resolve disputes. In other words, this pattern entails a questioning of the myth of a neutral political power, deeply bound to the neutralist secularist concept that law must be fairly equidistant from the different comprehensive doctrines.

As a consequence, in relation to the presence of religious minorities in multicultural democracies, this proposal promotes another vision of secularism. Such a vision claims that state power should abstain from controlling some areas of individuals' lives, especially those areas where cultural and religious references are more evident, allowing each individual to manage them freely *also* in different ways.

Indeed, the contact between individuals belonging to different religions has strengthened the awareness of the *particularity* of the secular language as created by Western culture and has stressed the fundamental role played by a specific religion, Christianity. The Christian religion has been influential in shaping the Western political, cultural and juridical system that we know as secular, and the set of values through which we understand reality.

In this sense, the deepening of other religious experiences and other cultural boundaries helps, essentially, to downsize the importance of the Western secularist language and secondly, while disclosing its continuity with Christian anthropological and cultural background, to emphasise the difference in treatment between secular and/or Christian majority groups and non-Christian minority groups, caused by the belief that Western political and legal systems are actually and neutrally secular.

This becomes increasingly compelling if we consider that cultural and religious minorities who settled in Western democratic states are actually excluded from the main access conduit to the institutions and, hence, they cannot have their subjectivity expressed in political and legal decisions. In this sense, multiculturalism has permanently destabilised two premises that democratic states are based upon: on the one hand, the actual opportunity for everyone to take part in the determination of the contents of the laws and, on the other, the possibility for individuals to identify themselves in these laws.

It is for these precise reasons that scholars and academics are being called upon to generate original solutions in order to find new ways of integration, also considering the possibility of questioning some of the most fundamental traits of contemporary democratic states or, if necessary, the whole system.

References

Ahdar, Rex, and Aroney, Nicholas (ed.) 2010. *Shari'a in the West*. Oxford/New York: Oxford University Press.

Benhabib, Seyla. 2002. *The Claims of Culture: Equality and Diversity in the Global Era*. Princeton: Princeton University Press.

Crowder, George. 2013. *Theories of Multiculturalism: An Introduction*. Malden (MA): Polity Press.

Edge, Ian. 2013. Islamic finance, alternative dispute resolution and family law: developments towards legal pluralism? In *Islam and English Law. Rights, Responsibilities and the Place of Shari'a*, edited by Griffith-Jones Robin, 116–143. Cambridge: Cambridge University Press.

Galeotti, Anna E. 1999. *Multiculturalismo*. Napoli: Liguori Editore.

Griffith-Jones, Robin (ed.). 2013. *Islam and English Law. Rights, Responsibilities and the Place of Shari'a*. Cambridge: Cambridge University Press.

Gutmann, Amy. 1994. *Multiculturalism: Examining the Politics of Recognition*. Princeton: Princeton University Press.

Habermas, Jürgen. 2006. Religion in the Public Sphere. *European Journal of Philosophy* 14:1: 1–25.

Kukhatas, Chandran. 2003. *The Liberal Archipelago: A Theory of Diversity and Freedom*. Oxford: Oxford University Press.

Kymlicka, Will. 1995. *Multicultural Citizenship*. Oxford: Oxford University Press.

Modood, Tariq. 2007. *Multiculturalism*. Malden (MA): Polity Press.

Monceri, Flavia. 2008. *Ordini costruiti. Multiculturalismo, complessità, istituzioni*. Soveria Mannelli: Rubbettino.

Mullhalle, Stephen, and Swift, Adam. 1992. *Liberals and Communitarians*. Oxford: Blackwell.

Murphy, Michael. 2012. *Multiculturalism. A Critical Introduction*. London and New York: Routledge.

Okin, Susan M. 1999. *Is Multiculturalism Bad for Women?* Princeton: Princeton University Press.

Parekh, Bhikhu. 2000. *Rethinking Multiculturalism. Cultural Diversity and Political Theory*. Basingstoke and London: Palgrave MacMillan.

Phillips, Nicholas. 2008. *Equality Before the Law. Speech by Lord Phillips, Lord Chief Justice East London Muslim Centre*. [http://www.judiciary.gov.uk, accessed on 20 September 2014].

Rawls, John. 1993. *Political liberalism*. New York: Columbia University Press.

Rawls, John. 1997. The Idea of Public Reason Revisited. *The University of Chicago Law Review* 64:3: 765–807.

Raz, Joseph. 1998. Multiculturalism. *Ratio Juris* 11:3: 193–205.

Reiss, Maria. 2009. The Materialization of Legal Pluralism in Britain: Why Shari'a Courts Should Be Non-Binding. *Arizona Journal of International & Comparative Law* 26:3: 739–778.

Shachar, Ayelet. 2001. *Multicultural Jurisdictions. Cultural Differences and Women's Rights*, Cambridge: Cambridge University Press.

Shachar, Ayelet. 2008. Privatizing Diversity: A Cautionary Tale From Religious Arbitration in Family Law. *Theoretical Inquiries in Law* 9: 573–607.

Shah, Prakash. 2005. *Legal Pluralism in Conflict. Coping With Cultural Diversity In Law*. London: Glass House Press.

Trigg, Roger. 2007. *Religion in Public Life: Must Faith be Privatized?* Oxford: Oxford University Press.

Turner, Bryan S., and Zengin Arslan, Berna. 2011. Shari'a and legal pluralism in the West. *European Journal of Social Theory* 14:2: 139–159.

Walzer, Michael. 1997. *On Toleration*. New Haven: Yale University Press.

Williams, Rowan. 2010. Civil and Religious Law in England: a Religious Perspective. In *Shari'a in the West*, edited by Ahdar, Rex, and Aroney, Nicholas, 293–303. Oxford-New York: Oxford University Press.

Part VI
State and Crisis

Axelle Reiter

States of Crisis and Crises of the State: Redefining the Limits of National Sovereignty and State Powers in Times of Emergency

1. Introduction

The contemporary evolution of the notions of state and legitimate state powers is the result of a double process of internationalisation of sovereignty and normalisation of exceptional situations.

On one hand, the adoption of universal norms has revolutionised the notion of sovereignty at the international level. The Charter of the United Nations endorses a complete shift in paradigm, from the traditional Westphalian to a universalistic conception of international law. The regime it introduces relies on the existence of an international community, beyond and above the state. It did not merely create one more legal order but established novel institutions and conferred a supranational constitutional status to basic international norms and principles.[1] Fundamentally, the Charter constitutes a radical switch of perspective in international relations, going from a state-centric to a truly cosmopolitan world order, and passing from unconstrained national sovereignty to a new international sovereignty. Following its adoption, the international legal order has become independent from states' sovereign powers. Even though it was originally established by the expression of states' assent, it progressively developed an 'objective' existence of its own. In view of this, the Charter is effectively analogous to an *actual* social contract (see Dupuy 2003, 204, 220–221, 412).

On the other hand, since September 11, governments have implemented counter-terrorism laws and policies, born from reinterpreting domestic and international norms, including the law of armed conflict and the balance between

1 Article 103 of the Charter foresees that, 'in the event of a conflict between the obligations of the members of the United Nations under the present Charter and their obligations under any other international agreement, their obligations under the present Charter shall prevail'. This disposition consecrates the prevalence of states' duties under the Charter over their other international obligations and creates a hierarchy among international norms. The distinctly 'public order' nature of the subsequent prioritisation of the fundamental principles of the Charter, including the protection of individual freedoms and entitlements, permits to relate them to the concept of *ius cogens*.

human rights and national security.[2] This second shift in paradigm is grounded in the idea that the uniqueness of contemporary terrorism, the ensuing perils, and the responses of numerous national authorities justify a thorough transformation of the global system. This more general trend chiefly affects the interpretation of the legal principle of gravity or exceptionality of the circumstances that generates states of emergency.[3] Similarly, attacks are mounted against the existence of core human rights, which cannot be suspended even in the direst situations.[4]

The following sections analyse in turn these two revolutionary processes. The last section puts forward that the contradictory premises of these conflicting phenomena cannot be reconciled in a coherent legal or theoretical framework. It concludes that there is no place for a balancing between legal rights and consequentialist considerations; law itself is the balance.

---

2 While in the past many countries adopted anti-terrorist legislation to fight domestic separatist movements and control emergency situations, the internationalisation of terrorism and states' responses to the perils it creates is a contemporary phenomenon.

3 Article 15 § 1 of the European Convention on Human Rights, Article 4 § 1 of the International Covenant on Civil and Political Rights and Article 27 § 1 of the Inter-American Convention on Human Rights condition the suspension of states' obligations under the relevant human rights instruments to the presence of circumstances of a particularly exceptional gravity. More specifically, recognised derogation motives can be categorised under three main headings: war, hostile occupation, and other public dangers and emergencies that threaten the life of the nation or the independence or the security of the state that invokes them.

4 The derogation clauses inserted in international human rights conventions do not only include requirements relative to the motives of the emergency dispositions. Article 15 § 2 of the European Convention on Human Rights, Article 4 § 2 of the International Covenant on Civil and Political Rights and Article 27 § 2 of the Inter-American Convention on Human Rights list some rights and dispositions that are inalienable in any circumstances, independently of the gravity of the situation. The texts of the three conventions diverge dramatically in relation to the rights whose application may not be suspended, even in an exceptional crisis. Article 15 § 2 of the European Convention only establishes the inalienability of four rights, seen as absolutely indispensable for the protection of individuals in situations of emergency: the right to life, the prohibition of torture and inhuman or degrading treatment or punishment, the proscription of slavery and servitude, and the non-retroactivity of criminal offences and penalties. Article 4 § 2 of the International Covenant on Civil and Political Rights and Article 27 § 2 of the Inter-American Convention on Human Rights entrench other norms beside the fundamental rights already mentioned in Article 15 § 2 of the European Convention. In addition, the three conventions limit the object of the extraordinary measures by banning derogations which do not respect the states parties' other obligations under international law, including more exigent human rights provisions and international humanitarian law.

2. Crisis of the state: sovereignty in the post-Westphalian international legal order

The 1648 Peace of Westphalia, which ended the Thirty Years War, is at the origin of the modern concept of state sovereignty. It gives effect to the principle of territoriality and to the equality of sovereign states that hold absolute unchecked powers and exclusive control over their national territory, independent of their respective size and military strength (see Berlia 1960, 35–42). Under this traditional model, international law was characterised by a strong attachment to bilateralism and reciprocity in interstate relations. Besides, states could only be legally bound to the extent that they had expressly consented to and they were protected against interventions in both their internal and external affairs.

Adopted in 1945, the Charter of the United Nations reflects the contemporary preoccupation to avoid armed conflicts and gross violations of the rights of individuals. The guarantee of international peace and security and the universal protection of human rights constitute the main aims of the United Nations. The UN Charter recognises the emergence of community interests that supersede bilateralism. It entrenches the ideas of international public order and core normative values, shared by all humanity with an aim to protect each and every single human being against instances of aggression and abuse. As the founding text of this organisation, the UN Charter applies immediately and without exceptions or reservations to all its members. This means that it obliges states worldwide to abide by its provisions. The transfer of competences from the domestic to the supranational level and the devolution of traditional state prerogatives to the international community enshrined in the Charter are irreversible; providing legitimacy for a universal legal order and its institutions (see Dupuy 2003, 204, 220–221, 412). Accordingly, the higher rank assigned to the basic principles entrenched in the UN Charter is tied to the notion of *ius cogens*, which grounds the substantive unity of the international system.

A peremptory norm of general international law or a rule of *ius cogens* is defined in Article 53 of the 1969 Vienna Convention on the Law of Treaties as a norm 'accepted and recognised by the international community of states as a whole as a norm from which no derogation is permitted and which can be modified only by a subsequent norm of general international law having the same character'. Article 53 stipulates that 'a treaty is void if, at the time of its conclusion, it conflicts with a peremptory norm of general international law'. Article 64 states that, 'if a new peremptory norm of general international law emerges, any existing treaty which is in conflict with that norm becomes void and terminates'. Peremptory rules are by their legal status placed above the will of states and constitute the core of an emerging concept of international public order. Contrary multilateral agreements or unilateral actions undermine the very foundation of public international law.[5]

International institutions have a mandate to guarantee the respect of the international public order and implement *ius cogens* norms. Whereas it also incorporates other norms, the concept chiefly encompasses the prohibition of aggression and the rules protecting fundamental rights, both in times of peace and of war;[6] which are themselves an expression of the inter-individual application of this principle. In fact, the protection of human rights in the United Nations system is linked to broader issues of peace and security and the core of absolutely inalienable entitlements entrenched in all human rights agreements is composed of precisely those rights most connected to such questions. While this is partly due to the original function and nature of the United Nations as an organisation, it also links individual liberties to a generalised application of the principle of non-aggression, be it among states, communities, private entities or individuals. This

5 I-ACHR, *James Terry Roach and Jay Pinkerton v. United States*, 22 Sept. 1987, No 3/87, §§ 50–54.

6 The peremptory character of the whole body of international human rights treaties and customs has been advanced by a part of the international case law and doctrine, although it has always been an object of controversy. Some authors have contested the very notion of customary international peremptory norms, scepticism stemming from the lack of a clear consensus on the norms benefiting from this status. Yet, this lack of consensus is not enough in itself to cast doubts on the category as a whole. Many decisions of the International Court of Justice affirm the peremptory character of a number of fundamental freedoms and entitlements. For the most part the jurisprudence of the International Court of Justice seems to restrict the scope of *ius cogens* to a limited number of rights and liberties: those considered non-derogable in all human rights instruments; the ban on genocide; the condemnation of crimes against humanity; and the basic principles of humanitarian law, which encompass similar norms, with the adjunction of Article 3 common to the four Geneva Conventions and the rule condemning the killing of prisoners of war. A notable addition to the traditional list of inalienable rights is that of the prohibition of discrimination on the grounds of race, colour, descent and national or ethnic origin. Whereas the major part of the jurisprudence of the International Court of Justice has not done so, some scholars and the dissenting opinion of Judge Tanaka in the African South West Case have suggested that all norms of humanitarian law and the treaties protecting human rights universally ought to be judged as imperative provisions. Along similar lines, the Human Rights Committee underlines the peremptory character of a great number of rights and the Inter-American Commission recognises the *ius cogens* status of all fundamental freedoms and entitlements and the entire American Declaration of the Rights and Duties of Man.

all-encompassing principle of non-aggression legally restricts state sovereignty and constitutes the foundation on which the entire international edifice is built.[7]

Unlike most international rules, human rights norms do not establish reciprocal rights and obligations between states to their mutual benefit, organise a legal frame for their contractual relations, forward their national interests or adjudicate their conflicting claims. On the contrary, human rights conventions are multilateral legal agreements composed of a set of 'absolute', objective or 'self-existent' obligations[8] that states parties unilaterally commit themselves to comply with.[9] They constitute 'integral' treaties, by opposition to 'interdependent' or reciprocal conventions, and the ensuing duties are owed to the entire world rather than the contracting parties. This means that, when they ratify those treaties, members of the international community undertake to respect and guarantee the individual rights they protect, regardless of the actions of other states.

Unlike international human rights law, international humanitarian law is traditionally grounded in reciprocity but three factors strongly mitigate its bilateralism.

---

7 The duties that international human rights law creates for states are not only owed to protected individuals and legal persons. Because they make up a crucial part of the international public order and are defined as superior interests of the international community, they can be sanctioned by the entire international community. The states' duty to respect them exists regardless of the states ratifying the relevant treaties since this duty is derived directly from membership and participation in the international society. Individual rights, then, become mandatory norms in all municipal or transnational legal systems subordinated to international law and the international system guarantees individuals the respect of their rights. It works as a sort of appeal mechanism, at the regional and at the United Nations level – after exhaustion of efficient domestic remedies – when a person claims that her rights have been violated by a public or private actor and that this abuse has not been redressed municipally. This implies a firmly monist attitude towards the reception of international law in national systems and the absolute primacy of international norms over domestic rules. Moreover, it is part of a more general trend, at the supra-national level, which switches the focus of international regulation from states' law to a cosmopolitan law, whose subjects and beneficiaries also include individuals and other private actors.

8 In other words, they are disconnected from the idea of reciprocity that traditionally tainted most international agreements and generate obligations that depend neither legally nor practically on their parallel execution by other states. In contrast, they give rise to autonomously and absolutely binding duties.

9 ICJ, *Reservations to the Convention on the Prevention and Punishment of the Crime of Genocide*, Pleadings, *Reports*, 1951, 387ff; ECHR, *Ireland v. UK*, 18 Jan. 1978, § 239; EComHR, *Austria v. Italy*, 11 Jan. 1961, *Y.E.C.H.R.*, Vol. 4, 138–140; ACHR, *Ivcher Bronstein v. Peru*, 24 Sept. 1999, § 42; *Aguirre Roca et al. v. Peru*, 24 Sept. 1999, § 41.

First, in application of Article 38 of the 1969 Vienna Convention on the Law of Treaties, the customary status of most humanitarian rules now mandates their application to non-signatory states. Secondly, reprisals against the lives and rights of protected persons are prohibited.[10] This seriously waters down the reciprocal character of states undertakings and, here again, binds them to respect humanitarian norms independently of other states' compliance with their legal obligations. Thirdly, the minimum core provisions entrenched in Article 3 common to the four 1949 Geneva Conventions is composed of integral obligations applicable in all types of armed conflicts (see Article 3).

The unique 'integral' nature of human rights and humanitarian treaties justifies some departure from the classical secondary rules of general international law that regulate methods of interpretation, reservations and withdrawal from treaties. This is explicitly recognised in international agreements codifying secondary international norms. In particular, Article 60 § 5 of the 1969 Vienna Convention on the Law of Treaties specifies that a material breach of an integral treaty does not result in its suspension or termination and never justifies mirror abuses against nationals of the infringing state. The duties undertaken are due – by all subjects of international law – to the international community at large and do not cease to exist simply because of one country's failure to comply. The International Court of Justice stressed that these treaties embody a notion of 'common interest'.[11] Human rights obligations are *erga omnes* 'obligations of a state towards the international community as a whole': every state has a legal interest in their protection and can validly claim their respect.[12] As such, they partake to the respect of the rule of law at the international level. Interstate complaints mechanisms are a direct upshot of the *erga omnes* nature of human rights obligations. By definition, they embody the very idea that 'how a government threats its own citizens is no longer its exclusive business, but a matter of legitimate concern for other states' and their individual inhabitants (see Ingram 1994, 12; Sieghart 1985, vii).

Like the International Court of Justice, the International Law Commission consecrates the distinctiveness of peremptory norms in its codification of the

---

10 1949 Geneva Convention I, Article 46; 1949 Geneva Convention II, Article 47; 1949 Geneva Convention III, Article 13; 1949 Geneva Convention IV, Article 33 ; 1954 Hague Convention Cultural Property, Article 4 § 4; 1977 Additional Protocol I, Articles 20, 51 § 6, 52 § 1, 53 (c), 54 § 4, 55 § 2, 56 § 4; 2005 Customary International Humanitarian Law Rules, No's 146–148.

11 ICJ, *Reservations to the Convention on the Prevention and Punishment of the Crime of Genocide*, 28 May 1951.

12 ICJ, *Barcelona Traction Light and Power Company Limited*, 5 Feb. 1970, § 33.

responsibility of states: the 2001 Draft Articles on the Responsibility of States for Internationally Wrongful Acts. Under Article 42 (b) (ii) of the Draft Articles, personally injured parties can invoke liability for the violation of interdependent obligations specifically owed to them. By contrast, the application of Article 48 is not conditioned by a personal lesion of the state that brings it into play. It institutes an *actio popularis* to the benefit of associations of states and the international community. Article 48 § 1 refers to two groups of integral obligations: (a) obligations 'owed to a group of states including that state' which invokes the responsibility of another and (b) obligations 'owed to the international community as a whole'.

Article 48 § 1 (a) protects the interests of regional organisations or of other states' groupings, inasmuch as they differ from the interests of their members. Thereby, Article 48 § 1 (a) allows a sort of a narrow *actio popularis* in relation to the protection of the interests of international organisations and *de facto* gives them a certain form of international legal personality. Article 48 § 1 (b) permits any state to intervene in the event of a breach of *erga omnes* obligations. Every government may ask for the cessation of infractions to these norms[13] and some reparation on behalf of the victim. This constitutes the foundation for a multilateral frame, where the notion of reciprocity is diluted and an authentic *actio popularis* is open to all states, aimed at the protection of the international public order and the restoration of international legality, even in cases where the wronged state is a small powerless country without enough weight on the international scene and which will not challenge a stronger nation in fear of retaliation. Article 48 § 1 (b) of the Draft Articles does not speak of an 'international community of states' but of the 'international community as a whole', extending the scope of the concept to cover non-state actors. Any state can use the *actio popularis* consecrated in Article 48 to oppose and sanction violations of *erga omnes* obligations to the benefit of individuals who are not its own nationals or residents (International Law Commission 2000, 422). This institutionalises a universal system of interstate applications.

The Draft Articles confer the status of *ius cogens* to the prohibition of aggression, the whole set of human rights and non-reciprocal humanitarian rules. The project adopted on second reading in 2001 mixes the notions of *erga omnes* obligations and *ius cogens* in different dispositions and in successive versions of the same provisions. The International Law Commission has interchangeably made use of both expressions during its debates and justifies the resulting confusion by alleging that the obligations arising under these two types of norms largely coincide (see Crawford 2000, 372–374; International Law Commission 2001, 7; Simma

13 ICTY, *Furundžija (Lašva Valley)*, IT-95–17/1-T, *Judgement*, 10 Dec. 1998, § 151.

1989, 825). Accordingly, the norms whose *erga omnes* character is traditionally recognised also benefit from the status of peremptory obligations or *ius cogens*. In addition, Article 50 § 1 of the Draft insulates four types of obligations from the effects of counter-measures: '(a) the obligation to refrain from the threat or use of force as embodied in the Charter of the United Nations; (b) obligations for the protection of fundamental human rights; (c) obligations of a humanitarian character prohibiting reprisals' and '(d) other obligations under peremptory norms of general international law'. It expressly recognises the peremptory character of the first three categories of obligations cited.

In failing to differentiate noticeably between the two concept, the International Court of Justice has paved the way for the International Law Commission.[14] Furthermore, the Court of First Instance of the European Communities recognised that the protection of private property, the entitlement to a fair hearing and the access to an effective judicial remedy are part of the core human rights provisions that benefit from *ius cogens* status, even though it only sanctions arbitrary deprivations of these liberties.[15] This militates for the recognition of a peremptory character to all individual rights. Indeed, the right to individual property is omitted from most human rights treaties and their supervisory organs give lesser ranking in the hierarchy of rights to this entitlement than to most others. Subsequently, rights that traditionally trump property claims in most jurisdictions logically belong to *ius cogens* norms.

Aside from its impact on state sovereignty, the peremptory status of human rights and core humanitarian norms raises the issue of the use of force by the international community in situations of crisis that involve widespread abuses of fundamental rights within a state's national boundaries or the question of the resolution of conflicts between the United nations' two central aims. Article 2 §§ 4 and 7 of the United Nations Charter prohibits the use of armed force in international relations. Article 42 allows the Security Council to organise or authorise military actions when required to uphold or restore international peace and security. Article 51 temporarily consecrates 'the inherent right of individual or collective self-defence if an armed attack occurs against a member of the United Nations, until the Security Council has taken the measures necessary to maintain international peace and security'. Article 52 permits the creation of regional

---

14 ICJ, *Application of the Convention on the Prevention and Punishment of the Crime of Genocide*, 11 July 1996, § 31.

15 CFI, *Ahmed Ali Yusuf and Al Barakaat International Foundation v. Council and Commission*, T-306/01, 21 Sept. 2005, §§ 292–293, 343; *Yassin Abdullah Kadi v. Council and Commission*, T-315/01, 21 Sept. 2005, §§ 241–242, 288.

defence arrangements and agencies and Article 53 § 1 entitles the Security Council to use these regional mechanisms to enforce its resolutions, under its authority and supervision. However, the Charter clearly outlaws regional enforcement actions in other instances. The consecration of the promotion of human rights in Article 56 does not institute a supplementary exception to the blanket ban on the use of unauthorised force. The doctrinal theory calling for 'humanitarian' intervention, to prevent gross violations of human rights, is deprived of customary status in the absence of consistent state practice and *opinio iuris* to this effect (see Francioni 2000, 117–118). Moreover, the prohibition of aggression benefits from the same peremptory status as the protection of individual rights. It is similarly situated on top of the normative hierarchy and cannot be overruled by other *ius cogens* rules.

The interdiction to evade *ius cogens*, through a bilateral or multilateral treaty binding the sole parties to this agreement, constitutes its superiority over *ius dispositivum*. As underlined by several judges of the European Court of Human Rights, 'the basic characteristic of a *ius cogens* rule is that, as a source of law in the now vertical international legal system, it overrides any other rule which does not have the same status'. Hence, 'in the event of a conflict between a *ius cogens* rule and any other rule of international law, the former prevails', with the result that 'the conflicting rule is null and void, or, in any event, does not produce legal effects which are in contradiction with the content of the peremptory rule'.[16] Peremptory norms create a normative hierarchy and function as a Hartian rule of recognition for the international legal system (see Reiter 2012). They are legally removed from the scope of state sovereignty and they curtail its legitimate scope. Essentially, they constitute the foundation and the keystone of a transfer of the ultimate sovereignty to the international community, to the detriment of the powers and competences of its member states. This leads to a new 'bounded' conception of sovereignty.

The organs of the Council of Europe have expressly recognised the supremacy of *ius cogens* in relation to international human rights law[17] and defended that the European Convention on Human Rights is 'a constitutional instrument of European public order'.[18] The system of interstate complaints under Article 33 of the European Convention is considered as a remedy against a breach of Europe's

16 ECHR, *Al-Adsani v. UK*, 21 Nov. 2001, L. CAFLISCH *et al.*, Joint Dissenting Opinion, §§ 1 and 3.

17 ECHR, *Al-Adsani v. UK*, 21 Nov. 2001, §§ 60–61.

18 ECHR, *Open Door and Dublin Well Woman v. Ireland*, 29 Oct. 1992, §§ 68–69; *Loizidou v. Turkey*, 23 Mar. 1995, §§ 75, 93; *Matthews v. UK*, 18 Feb. 1999, § 49; *Banković et al. v. Belgium et al.*, 12 Dec. 2001, § 80; EComHR, *Chrysostomos, Loizidou et al. v. Turkey*, 4 Mar. 1991, *Y.E.C.H.R.*, Vol. 34, 52.

public order. The same applies to the optional systems of interstate requests under Article 41 of the International Covenant on Civil and Political Rights and Article 45 of the Inter-American Convention.[19] This reinforces the logical primacy of supranational human rights norms over contradictory rules which are part of the national legal order, even though domestic authorities are usually charged with the enforcement of those international dispositions (see Rigaux 2000, 1198–1199). Subsequently, domestic norms and decisions that ostensibly infringe fundamental rights are not only unjust but also legally invalid.[20] In this perspective, the development of international human rights law and the creation of transnational institutions consecrate the evolution 'away from the classic regime of state sovereignty […] toward the firm entrenchment of the liberal regime of international sovereignty' (see Held 2002a, 2; Held 2002b, 94). International human rights law constitutes the personal rights of each and every individual into universal absolute obligations that the international community owes to her because of her humanity.

3. States of crisis: emergency rule and state powers in the 'war' on terror era

The 'war' on terror endangers the entrenched position of human rights in the supranational arena and diminishes the strength of their core principles in helping maintain the international public order. The attacks on the World Trade Center and the Pentagon have provided to the governments worldwide the ideal excuse for an all-encompassing legal and political revisionism. Terrorism and the necessity to protect democracy against its enemies are invoked to advocate a thorough transformation of the global system (see Ignatieff 2004; Wedgwood 2004, 114, 117). A total revolution of public international law is taken for granted and the annihilation of the current international regime is even prophesised.[21]

Most international organs have resisted the downgrading of human rights standards in the fight against terrorism. Instead of opposing liberty and security, they emphasise that compliance with human rights and an efficient anti-terrorist policy

---

19 ACHR, *Effects of Reservations on the Entry into Force of the American Convention*, 1982, §§ 29–30.

20 ECHR, *Streletz, Kessler and Krenz v. FRG*, 22 Mar. 2001, § 87.

21 In this respect, it is often asserted that the control of terrorism calls for a new interpretation of domestic and international norms, a new management of globalisation, a new approach to international relations, a new formulation of the laws of armed conflicts, a new handling of human rights, a new balance between security and liberty, and so on; in a nutshell, a new paradigm for a new century.

are 'complementary and mutually reinforcing' objectives; which must be pursued concomitantly (UN General Assembly, Resolution 60/825, 27 Apr. 2006, 5, 118; Scheinin 2010b, 8, 12–13). Unhappily, state officials often forget to reflect on the probable outcomes of endorsing illiberal tactics and rarely resist the mirage of mirroring the abuses committed by their enemies, at the price of losing all credibility. Not unlike an Orwellian nightmare, the current counter-terrorism discourse legitimises war on the claim that it will bring peace, promotes slavery and tyranny because they might protect freedom, and encourages ignorance and censorship since they give strength to the prevailing official position. The American government has also chosen a fourth motto to describe its new creepy voyeuristic regime: 'knowledge is power',[22] the modern equivalent to 'Big Brother is watching you'.

In this context, it has been suggested that a new 'war-on-terror law paradigm' should be applied in times of stress falling short of real emergencies. It would mix elements of the laws of war, criminal law and regular police powers. Additionally, it would evolve permanently so as to adapt itself to the ever changing realities of a self-styled endless 'war' on terror. The author of this devious proposition even advocates the reconfiguration of extraordinary measures along the lines of an everlasting phenomenon (see Rosenfeld 2008, 392–394). This completely ignores the conditions that international human rights law imposes on states for the invocation of exceptional circumstances.[23] How a situation of lesser gravity than traditionally required for states of war or emergency, *voire* of mere tension, can justify further departures from the usual legal regime than actual threats to the existence and integrity of the country is puzzling. Besides, states of emergency adopted as part of the legendary 'war' on terror are a clear example of *sine die* rule of exception, in contravention with states obligations under the International Covenant on Civil and Political Rights.[24] Indeed, the Human Rights Committee

---

22 The Pentagon's program to develop a Total or Terrorism Information Awareness (TIA) system, which annihilates the very notion of privacy, adopted the Latin version of this aphorism, *scientia est potentia*, as a motto. See the official site of DARPA, http://www.darpa.mil.

23 1950 ECvHR, Article 15; 1966 ICCPR, Article 4; 1969 I-ACvHR, Article 27.

24 In addition to limiting the derogative measures 'to the extent strictly required by the exigencies of the situation', the Inter-American Convention on Human Rights expressly calls for their application to be carefully restricted to the duration of the emergency, by stipulating that these measures are allowed only 'for the period of time strictly required by the exigencies of the situation'. In contrast, the texts of the European Convention and the International Covenant do not include any such explicit limitation of the extraordinary powers to the duration of an exceptional situation. This being said, the European organs and the Human Rights Committee apply the principle of proportionality and

states in its general comment on Article 4 of the Covenant that measures adopted under this disposition 'are of an exceptional and temporary nature and may only last as long as the life of the nation concerned is threatened'.[25]

Although the rhetoric of war is dangerous since it implies that there will be innocent casualties of indiscriminate destruction, it presents the significant advantage of triggering the application of the laws of war.[26] Yet, too often, governments do not comply with either set of international prescriptions. The use of the neologisms 'unlawful enemy combatant' and 'alien unprivileged enemy belligerent', totally foreign to the laws of war, was most likely motivated by the willingness to create a legal black hole (see Maxwell and Watts 2007; Scheinin 2010a, 208). Governments confronted with terrorism or insurgency ought to try individuals involved in these subversive activities in accordance with international human rights standards or detain them in the same conditions as those granted to prisoners of war. Even if they were not recognised the status of prisoners of war, they remain 'protected persons' under the scope of the Geneva Conventions and are entitled to the respect of core humanitarian principles (ICRC 1987, 869–870).[27] The Council of Europe has called upon member states to refrain from any derogation to the European Convention in their fight against terrorism (Assembly, Resolution 1271, 24 Jan. 2002, 9, 12 *alinea* 5) and the European Court of Human Rights condemned an emergency declaration that granted extended arrest and detention powers to the British government.[28]

---

the theory of the absolute necessity of the measures to their temporal extent. The control exercised over the duration of the measures has, therefore, to be considered similar in the three conventions.

25 HR Committee, *General Comment No 5 (13) on Derogation of Rights (Article 4)*, 28 July 1981, § 3; HR Committee, *General Comment No 29 on States of Emergency (Article 4)*, 24 July 2001, § 2.

26 The 1949 Geneva Conventions and their 1977 Additional Protocols require that their provisions be respected in armed conflicts and failure to do so engages states' responsibility under international law. Accordingly, the numerous legal black holes created under the 'war' on terror do not constitute an exception to that rule but a serious breach of international norms.

27 1949 Geneva Convention III, Articles 4–5; 1949 Geneva Convention IV, Article 5; 1977 Additional Protocol I, Articles 45 § 3, 75; 1977 Additional Protocol II, Article 6; ICJ, *Corfu Channel*, 9 Apr. 1949, 22; ICJ, *Military and Paramilitary Activities in and against Nicaragua*, 27 June 1986, 112; ICTY, *Delalić et al. (Čelebići Camp)*, IT-96-21-T, *Judgement*, 16 Nov. 1998, § 271; ECHR, *Kononov v. Latvia*, 17 May 2010, §§ 203–204; I-ACHR, *Detainees in Guantanamo Bay, Cuba*, 13 Mar. 2002.

28 ECHR, *A et al. v. UK*, req. No 3455/05, 19 Feb. 2009.

The anti-terrorist assault on human rights and on the prevalence of public international law takes its roots in the contention that, in times of emergency, a new balance needs to be struck between liberty and security, which grants people more security and less liberty. The ensuing attacks on core individual rights have systemic effects: they corrupt the entire structure of the polity and taint the complete state apparatus with irregularity and blood, leaving the door open to abuses by functionaries acting secretly and without any control. The whole country then risks becoming a police state and an abomination like torture 'one of the normal items on the menu of practical consideration'. If the use of torture by state officials is validated, it follows that everything seems to be permitted under the colour of order or necessity and the rule of law is reduced to a question of utilitarian arithmetic; collapsing the divide between state power and unmitigated terror, law and savagery (see Waldron 2005, 1718–1739).

Regrettably, the denigration of public international law and instantaneous creation of exceptional customs have led to condone targeted killings and the erosion of the ban on torture. Many suspects have been detained *incommunicado* in self-styled 'classified locations' or 'rendered' to other countries in order to be interrogated and tortured by the local authorities. In this framework, the traditional rights discourse is exploited for clearly opposite ends. The recognition of states' positive obligations under human rights treaties is distorted into an alleged duty of public officials to torture suspected terrorists, so that the collective and positive right to security of the whole population obtains in hypothetical 'ticking bomb' scenarios (see Gunther 2005, 379–391; Kumm 2007, 160–162). The European Court of Human Rights judges that, since the ban on torture and inhuman or degrading treatment cannot be suspended during states of emergency, 'the prohibition on ill-treatment of a person in order to extract information from him applies irrespective of the reasons for which the authorities wish to extract a statement, be it to save a person's life or to further criminal investigations'.[29] Indeed, 'the philosophical basis underpinning [its] absolute nature' rules out 'any exceptions or justifying factors or balancing of interests, irrespective of the conduct of the person concerned and the nature of the offence at issue'.[30] The ban on torture is *the* 'legal archetype', on which the rule of law rests (see Waldron 2005, 1718–1739).[31] In consequence, commitment to the rule of law requires considering horrific

29 ECHR, *Gäfgen v. FRG*, 30 June 2008, § 69.

30 ECHR, *Gäfgen v. FRG*, 1 June 2010, § 107.

31 HR Committee, *General Comment No 24 (52) on Reservations*, 2 Nov. 1994, § 10.

abuses like torture as always beyond the pale, effectively investigating allegations of ill-treatment or rendition for torture, and punishing the culprits.[32]

The notion of terrorism has been over-stretched to punish self-styled offences of a type perfectly epitomised by protests against the war, civil disobedience or hacking. In effect, 'overly broad definitions of terrorism' often lead to the 'deliberate misuse of the term' (see Scheinin 2010b, 26). The 'war' on terror and 'security *versus* liberty' paradigms have been accompanied by an arsenal of surveillance, misinformation and silencing measures. The European Court of Human Rights condemns the misuse of the state secret privilege, in order to impede 'the search for the truth' and foster impunity,[33] and the systematic and indefinite retention of fingerprints, cellular samples and DNA profiles of non-convicted suspects.[34] In addition, the Court judges that anti-terrorist stop and search measures must respect the rule of law and provide some 'protection against arbitrary interferences by public authorities'.[35] By contrast, it endorses systematic attacks on freedom of expression in the name of the fight against incitement to terrorism.[36] A critical appraisal of the potential effects of this decision motivated the inclusion in the United Nations best practices regarding incitement to terrorism of a reference to actions that generate 'an objective danger of a terrorist offence being committed' (see Scheinin 2010b, 30–32).

The normalisation of rules of exception – that is, the application of these rules in normal circumstances rather than in genuine states of emergency and their subsequent banalisation – is grounded in the construction of a collective right to security that state authorities ought to guarantee to their citizens. The question is assumed to be a matter of cost-benefit analysis and all members of society are presumed to benefit from the trade-off, as long as they are not guilty. However, the weighting process generates problems even from a purely instrumental perspective. Internal security is largely tributary to states overseas' activities and foreign policy. The only adequate avenue open to counter terrorism and effectively bring about peace and security is not to target its symptoms but its causes; above all, poverty, discriminations and human rights abuses (see Emerson 2012, 31–32; Scheinin 2007a, 80, 82; Scheinin 2007b, 64, 69–71; Scheinin 2010b, 8).

States resorting to terror when trying to curb insurgent terrorism offer on a golden plate to their opponents exactly what they are looking for, including a total

---

32 ECHR, *El-Masri v. Macedonia*, 13 Dec. 2012, §§ 192–193.

33 Ibid., §§ 191–193.

34 ECHR, *S and Marper v. UK*, 4 Dec. 2008, §§ 105–126.

35 ECHR, *Gillan and Quinton v. UK*, 12 Jan. 2010, §§ 76–87.

36 ECHR, *Leroy v. France*, 2 Oct. 2008, §§ 27, 36–48.

discrediting of the states' authority and a shift of part of the responsibility for the terrorist attacks. Using the same means and the same apocalyptic discourse of good *versus* evil as terrorists confronts governments involved in anti-terrorism campaigns with the risks of mimetism and the likelihood to become terrorist themselves. Governments involved in grave human rights violations destroy themselves the prospects of a free and democratic alternative to brute violence, initiate a vicious circle of escalating ripostes and reprisals, and inescapably undermine any claim to legitimacy of the established system. Apart from the fact that the actual empirical link between the two sides of the equation appears at best contentious, trading individual rights for public security plainly misses the point that the struggle against terrorism is also a fight for democracy and the rule of law. The opposite path leads to a regime of governmental terror, not unlike that which insurgent terrorists are hoping to set up. Basic rights must be respected when fighting terrorism and security cannot be guaranteed through their sacrifice, precisely because this 'would hand the terrorists a victory beyond their dreams' (UN Secretary General 2002). In a nutshell, freedom cannot be abolished in the name of security, even if only not to play the terrorists' game. Furthermore, 'diminishing liberty might also diminish security against the state, even as it enhances security against terrorism' (see Waldron 2003, 194–195, 205–208); paradoxically, making people ultimately less safe than they were in the first place.

There is also a much more fundamental reason to sharply criticise the opposition between security and liberty, and its presentation as a matter of necessary trade-offs between the two concepts: it deprives an ultimate victory over terrorism of any conceivable value. In the by now famous words of Thomas Jefferson, 'a society that will trade a little liberty for a little order will lose both and deserves neither' (Letter to James Madison). Such a society is inherently based on violence and enslavement, not unlike a state of endemic terrorism, and does not possess any rightful privilege to fight over destabilising efforts. More dramatically put, 'whether or not a society is justified in taking steps to preserve itself must depend both on what sort of society it is and what the steps to be taken are'. Where society is largely oppressive and cruel, the ruling authorities are not justified in preserving its existence, since its continuation constitutes *per se* a wrong. Besides, not all available means are acceptable to protect even a desirable society from disintegration (see Hart 1963, 19). Some methods are simply intolerable and their use is sufficient to qualify a society as brutal and its institutions as illegitimate. This is the reason why international norms regulating states of emergency are indexing the suspension of fundamental freedoms and entitlements in the most extreme situations to the respect of strict conditions relative to the aim, motives and object of the derogations.

4. Clashes between the rule of exception and the internationalisation of sovereignty

The defenders of the 'war' on terror and 'security *versus* liberty' paradigms totally ignore international law and put forward efficiency or other policy considerations, instead of relying on sound legal argumentation. This position must be criticised because, 'in a society that values adherence to the rule of law, the most decisive arguments are those that can claim to derive from the law itself'. Indeed, 'one cannot simply re-engineer a judicial system as one goes along simply because that would make policy sense' but 'something more distinctly legal is needed to justify that shaft', unless one wishes to dismiss the law altogether (see Mégret 2003, 335, 340). Carl Schmitt focuses on the notion of exception as the purest representation of the political, where the 'sovereign is he who decides on the exception' and 'it is precisely the exception that makes relevant the subject of sovereignty, that is, the whole question of sovereignty'. Subsequently, the exception becomes normalcy, takes the place of the general rule and defines it. This leads to a permanent state of emergency, the suspension of the entire legal order and unlimited authority. As a result, 'the state remains, whereas law recedes'. Legitimacy is exclusively grounded in unconstrained sovereignty and the rule of law is abolished (see Schmitt 1922, 5–6, 12). Steering clear of an apology of tyranny and inhumanity, under the mask of legality, commands to respect the rule of law rather than the rule of exception.

Adhesion to the rule of law implies the submission of the state to the law (see Dupuy 2006, 243). Sovereignty becomes rule-based. Rules precede sovereignty and circumscribe its limits. Public actions need to be hemmed in the formal framework provided by a legal order and cannot be allowed to straight outside of it for merely prudential motives. The concept of law or norm expresses a high degree of formalism, because of its rule-based composition (see Schauer 1991, 77–111, 137–145). Moreover, the notion of rights is even more resistant to consequentialism. Whereas there is always a possibility to find another way to resolve the problem of security, 'rights would be worthless – and the idea of a right incomprehensible – unless respecting rights meant taking some risks' sometimes (see Dworkin 2005, 95). There is no place 'for a balancing between human rights and security, as the proper balance can and must be found within human rights law itself'. Indeed, 'law is the balance, not a weight to be measured' (see Scheinin 2010b, 12). Finally, the peremptory nature of human rights means that their violation contravenes the international public order. It explodes the boundaries of national sovereignty in the post-Westphalian legal order and engages the international responsibility of the state.

To conclude, the consecration and normalisation of states of crisis endangers individual rights, the societal structures of affected countries and the international legal order, by entrenching inside the law a practice of illegality likely to outgrow its original anti-terrorist purpose and contaminate the whole handling of public matters. The simple fact that terrorism might strike anywhere and at any time cannot legitimise the implementation of extraordinary regimes. The endorsement of the contrary assumption is conducive to extend states of emergency to the world's limits, making the exception the norm in a Schmittian fashion. The judicial and doctrinal paradigm shift from human rights protection to mere human rights tolerance, whenever they conflict with security interests, irremediably clashes with the internationalisation of sovereignty that grounds the contemporary international law system. An effective response to the abuses witnessed passes by a stricter adherence to the rule of law and to states international obligations than is generally put forward, including respect for the integrity and prevalence of core individual rights, at the heart of the international conception of normativity.

References

Berlia, Georges. 1960. Remarques sur la paix de Westphalie. In *Mélanges Basdevant*, 35–42. Paris: Pedone.

Buergenthal, Thomas. 1968. Proceedings against Greece under the European Convention of Human Rights. *American Journal of International Law* 2: 441–450.

Crawford, James 2000. *Third Report on the Responsibility of States*. UN Doc. A/CN.4/507/Add.4.

Dupuy, Pierre-Marie. 2003. *L'unité de l'ordre juridique international*. Leiden: Nijhoff.

Dupuy, Pierre-Marie. 2006. *Droit international public*. 8th ed. Paris: Dalloz.

Dworkin, Ronald 2005. Terror and the Attack on Civil Liberties. In *The Philosophical Challenge of September 11*, edited by Joseph Margolis, Armen T. Marsoobian and Tom Rockmore, 81–95. Oxford: Blackwell.

Emerson, Ben. 2012. *Framework Principles for Securing the Human Rights of Victims of Terrorism*. UN Doc. A/HRC/20/14, 4 June 2012.

Francioni, Francesco 2000. Of War, Humanity and Justice. *Max Planck Yearbook of United Nations Law*, 107–126.

Gunther, Klaus. 2005. World Citizens between Freedom and Security. *Constellations* 12: 379–391.

Hart, Herbert L. A. 1963. *Law, Liberty and Morality*. Oxford: Oxford University Press.

Held, David. 2002a. Laws of States, Laws of Peoples: Three Models of Sovereignty. *Legal Theory* 8: 1–44.

Held, David. 2002b. Violence, Law, and Justice in a Global Age. In *Understanding September 11*, edited by Craig J. Calhoun, Paul Price and Ashley S. Timmer, 92–105. New York: New Press.

ICRC. 1987. *Commentary on the Additional Protocols of 8 June 1977 to the Geneva Conventions of 12 August 1949*. Geneva: Nijhoff.

Ignatieff, Michael. 2004. *The Lesser Evil*. Edinburgh: Edinburgh University Press.

Ingram, Attracta. 1994. *A Political Theory of Rights*. Oxford: Oxford University Press.

International Law Commission. 2000. *Report on the Work of its 52nd Session*. UN Doc. A/55/10.

International Law Commission. 2001. *Report on the Work of its 53rd Session*. UN Doc. A/56/10.

Kumm, Mattias. 2007. Political Liberalism and the Structure of Rights. In *Law, Rights, and Discourse*, edited by George Pavlakos, 131–166. Oxford: Hart.

Maxwell, Mark D. M., and Watts, Sean M. 2007. 'Unlawful Enemy Combatant': Status, Theory of Culpability, or Neither? *Journal of International Criminal Justice* 5: 19–25.

Mégret, Frédéric. 2003. Justice in Times of Violence. *European Journal of International Law* 14: 327–345.

Reiter, Axelle. 2012. Hedgehogs, Foxes and Hart's Rule of Recognition: The Concept of Law in the post-Westphalian International Legal Order. In *Jurisprudence and Political Philosophy in the 21st Century. Reassessing Legacies.* Central and Eastern European Forum for Legal, Political, and Social Theory Yearbook. Vol. 2, edited by Miodrag Jovanović and Bojan Spaić, 88–100. Frankfurt am Main et al: Peter Lang GmbH.

Rigaux, François. 2000. Logique et droits de l'homme. In *Protection des droits de l'homme: la perspective européenne: mélanges à la mémoire de Rolv Ryssdal*, edited by Paul Mahoney, Franz Matscher, Herbert Petzold and Luzius Wildhaber, 1197–1211. Koln: Heymanns.

Rosenfeld, Michel. 2008. Judicial Balancing in Times of Stress. In *Counterterrorism*, edited by Andrea Bianchi and Alexis Keller, 357–394. Oxford: Hart.

Schauer, Frederick. 1991. *Playing by the Rules*. Oxford: Clarendon.

Scheinin, Martin. 2007a. *Report of the Special Rapporteur on the Promotion and Protection of Human Rights and Fundamental Freedoms While Countering Terrorism*. UN Doc. A/HRC/4/26, 29 Jan. 2007.

Scheinin, Martin. 2007b. *Report of the Special Rapporteur on the Promotion and Protection of Human Rights and Fundamental Freedoms While Countering Terrorism.* UN Doc. A/HRC/6/17, 21 Nov. 2007.

Scheinin, Martin. 2010a. *Communications to and from Governments*, UN Doc. A/HRC/16/51/Add.1, 14 Feb. 2010, § 208.

Scheinin, Martin. 2010b. *Ten Areas of Best Practices in Countering Terrorism.* UN Doc. A/HRC/16/51, 22 Dec. 2010.

Schmitt, Carl. 1985 [1922]. *Political Theology*, translated by George Schwab. Cambridge (Mass.): MIT Press.

Sieghart, Paul. 1985. *The Lawful Rights of Mankind: An Introduction to the International Legal Code of Human Rights.* Oxford: Oxford University Press.

Simma, Bruno. 1989. Bilateralism and Community Interest in the Law of State Responsibility. In *International Law at a Time of Perplexity: Essays in Honour of Shabtai Rosenne*, edited by Yoram Dinstein and Mala Tabory, 821–844. Dordrecht: Martinus Nijhoff.

UN Secretary General, *Human Rights Must Not Be Sacrificed to Counter-Terrorism.* 12 Apr. 2002, SG/SM/8196, HM/CN/989.

Waldron, Jeremy. 2003. Security and Liberty: The Image of Balance. *Journal of Political Philosophy* 11: 191–210.

Waldron, Jeremy. 2005. Torture and Positive Law: Jurisprudence for the White House. *Columbia Law Review* 105: 1681–1750.

Wedgwood, Ruth. 2004. Countering Catastrophic Terrorism. In *Enforcing International Law Norms against Terrorism*, edited by Andrea Bianchi and Yasmin Naqvi, 103–117. Oxford: Hart.

Robin Caballero

Peacebuilding and Recognition of States: Failures of the International Territorial Administrations in Bosnia and Herzegovina and Kosovo

1. Introduction

During the elections in Kosovo on the 3rd of November 2013, almost fifteen years after the deployment of the *United Nations Interim Administration Mission In Kosovo* (UNMIK), incidents took place, people were attacked and ballot boxes in many polling stations were destroyed by masked individuals. The low participation rate by Kosovo's Serbian community (less than 13%) underlines the failure of the International Territorial Administration (ITA) to build legitimate institutions in Kosovo. Even if the relationship between Kosovo's authorities and Belgrade's government appears to have improved, the Serbian government does not seem ready to recognise Kosovo as an independent state. Kosovo's Serbian community is reluctant to comply with Kosovo's institutions and finds it difficult to integrate. The riots and demonstrations in Bosnia and Herzegovina, during which protesters set fire to many official buildings in February and March 2014, almost 20 years after the Dayton Agreement, clearly demonstrate that disputes in the country have yet to be resolved. These examples highlight how the problem of peacebuilding still exists in the Balkans.

Although the current situation of both countries is very different, they have much in common. First, Kosovo, as well as Bosnia and Herzegovina, originate from the dissolution of the former Yugoslavia and thus share a common history. Second, their creation was the result of two violent conflicts. Third, they have to confront the issue of several nationalities cohabiting in the same country. Finally, International Territorial Administrations are present in both countries to help stabilise the situation and build viable institutions. The Kosovar situation influences Bosnia and Herzegovina and *vice-versa* (Bieber and Keil 2011, 74). Why is it that the issues in the other states originating from the dissolution of the former Yugoslavia (Slovenia, Croatia, Macedonia and Montenegro) were resolved quickly, and yet no solution has been found in the case of Kosovo and Bosnia and Herzegovina?

The ITAs have accomplished many positive achievements, particularly that of introducing peace after many violent domestic conflicts. The failures cannot solely be attributed to third party states and their representatives, which have faced much resistance from both criminal organisations and parallel institutions established during the conflicts. The concept of peacebuilding and its application in the Balkans has been widely and thoroughly analysed by many authors. The multi-ethnic aspect of the two states is often put forward as an important reason for failure (Belloni 2013, 282–283; Wilde Ralph 2008, 451). However, they often forget to insist on the impact of the policies led in the neighbouring countries, particularly important in the cases analysed here. In particular, the influence of the State recognition policy at the time of the dissolution of the former Yugoslavia and its effects on the peacebuilding missions in the region have often been occulted. This article will focus on the development of the concept of peacebuilding in the last decade (section 2), analyse the lack of a coordinated policy at the time of the peace negotiations and the declarations of independence (section 3) as well as explain the lack of democracy and legitimacy of the institutions in Kosovo and Bosnia and Herzegovina and the negative perception of the institutions by certain segments of the population (section 4). Effectively, the failures in both countries challenge the concept of peacebuilding under international law as well as its efficiency.

2. Definition of peacebuilding

According to the Max Planck Encyclopedia of International Law,

> the concept of (post-conflict) peacebuilding fills a commonly perceived gap between peacekeeping and the situation after an armed conflict. It aims at assisting war-torn States and societies to avoid a relapse into armed conflict by creating the conditions necessary for a sustainable peace. Peacebuilding supports medium- and long-term processes of comprehensive post-conflict strategies. It combines mechanisms of peacekeeping with elements of State- and nation-building, humanitarian action, transitional justice, and reconciliation [...]. The key issue is supporting national authorities to develop country-specific peacebuilding strategies in core peacebuilding sectors, such as security sector reform ('SSR') and the rule of law. (Marauhn and Simon 2013)

The theory of peacebuilding can thus be defined as the construction or the re-construction by foreign actors of the governing institutions of a new, a weak or post-war State. Peacebuilding is thus closely linked to the concept of failed States and implies a gradual intervention by external actors, such as international peacekeeping missions.

The evolution of the theory of peacebuilding in the last decade, particularly in English literature, can be seen as an answer to the criticism of humanitarian intervention and the '*droit d'ingérence*', sometimes qualified as a new form of imperialism (Chandler, 2012). Whilst at the end of the Cold War, the discourse was focused on the individual as a reason for humanitarian intervention, the concept of peacebuilding now often focuses on its corollary, state-building, and hence on the State, its sovereignty and its responsibility to protect its citizens. Whereas humanitarian intervention usually insists on the necessity to limit the sovereignty of States, state-building tends more towards the requirement for a strong State guaranteeing that human rights are upheld through democratic institutions.

3. The recognition of Kosovo and Bosnia and Herzegovina

At the time of the peace agreements, the question of the future status of the entities was still not resolved, and limited the international territorial administrations in their state-building actions (section 3.1.). The lack of coherence of the policy of recognition by the international community also prevented finding a consensus between the different parties in both countries (section 3.2.).

3.1 The issue of the future status of the entities at the time of the peace agreements

Since 1992, the conflict in Bosnia and Herzegovina has been perceived by the international community to be essentially ethnic. Due to this perception and to the one-state approach, the Dayton Agreement was based on the division of power between the three most important ethnic groups in order to impeach the domination of one group over the others. This distribution of power among ethnic groups has enhanced the power of local institutions to the detriment of central institutions. As Tansey (2009, 15) wrote,

> [w]hile the parties all agreed to remain within a sovereign Bosnian state, neither the Croat nor Serb forces gave up their separatist political orientations, and in order for them to accept a united Bosnia, its Constitutional Framework had to reflect their positions.

Indeed, the partition of Bosnia and Herzegovina was made between the Serb federation called Republika Srpska on the one side, and the Bosnian-Croat associated with the Bosniaks on the other. But at the time of the peace agreement, the Bosnian-Serb leaders, in particular, did not resign themselves to the creation of a future Serbian independent state within the actual borders of Republika Srpska. Facing the refusal of the international community to recognise Republika Srpska as an independent state, they only accepted this agreement as provisory. Thus, even if Bosnia and Herzegovina had officially been mentioned in the Dayton Agreement as an independent state existing within the borders of the former Socialist Republic of Bosnia and Herzegovina, the agreement was signed without any consensus on the details of the future status of the Bosnian State and on the degree to which both federated entities should remain autonomous from each other. However, contrary to Kosovo, the Dayton Agreement had the merit of fixing a clear framework for the ITA present in Bosnia and Herzegovina. Thus the ITA in Bosnia and Herzegovina could work within a clearly defined framework with the aim of building the institution of a normal state.

In Kosovo, the international community faced a different problem than the one in Bosnia and Herzegovina because of the undetermined status of the whole entity at the time of the Resolution 1244. Hence, Kosovo not being a recognised State at that time raised the questions of the context of intervention and its limits in facing the sovereignty of Serbia. As Zaum (2007, 141) states, '[t]his uncertainty underlines the importance of sovereignty as an organizing principle of political authority'. Thus the UN authorities present in the country had to face the problem of an open-ended undefined mandate. Further, it sustained the opposition between the Serbian and the Kosovo-Albanian community for years. The Kosovo-Albanians proclaimed the independence of Kosovo in February 2008, while the Serbs still wanted to stay within Serbia. The riots of 2013 and the continuing ethnic conflict are thus, *inter alia*, a direct consequence of the undetermined status of the entities at the time of the peace agreements and of the deployment of the international territorial administration, as well as of the incoherent recognition policy.

3.2 The lack of coherence in the policy of recognition

3.2.1 The inconsistencies with the former practice

Other than the undetermined status at the time of the peace agreements and the value of previous cases, one of the most important problems for the peacebuilding missions in Kosovo and Bosnia and Herzegovina has come to light through the chaotic recognition policy. On the one hand, there is a will to maintain the unity of Bosnia and to refuse the recognition of Republika Srpska and thus discourage the secession trend. But on the other hand, the support given to the violent secession of Kosovo from Serbia is contradictory with the non-recognition policy led in Bosnia. This led to the legitimisation of violence as a way to secede and has further complicated the state-building missions in both countries (Stillhoff Sörensen 2013, 278).

In the early 1990s, during the dismemberment of Yugoslavia, the so-called Badinter Commission declared Yugoslavia in dissolution, whilst at the same time reaffirming the principle of inviolability of the international borders of a State. The Commission made a statement in favour of the conservation of the borders of the former Republics as the international borders of future States which would emerge from this dissolution, in compliance with the *uti possidetis* principle. The principle of inviolability of frontiers affirmed in 1975 in the Helsinki Final Act was then also used as an argument to deny the recognition to Republika Srpska Krajina in Croatia (International Conference on Yugoslavia, Arbitration Commission, Opinion No. 4, 1500). Republika Srpska Bosne i Hercegovine was also denied a right to secession, in coherence with the opinion previously adopted concerning the Krajina (International Conference on Yugoslavia, Arbitration Commission, Opinion No. 5, 1503). However, despite Kosovo not having the status of a Republic in the former federated Republic of Yugoslavia and in contradiction with this principle, over 110 states have recognised Kosovo since the unilateral declaration of independence in February 2008. Thus, Kosovo was granted the legitimacy denied to Republika Srpska in Bosnia and Herzegovina and in Croatia all this time, thus constituting a breach of the inviolability of the international borders of Serbia and contradicting the principle enforced by the Badinter Commission.

Moreover, during the war in Yugoslavia, an international territorial administration entitled the United Nations Transitional Administration for Eastern Slavonia, Baranja and Western Sirium (UNTAES) was deployed in Eastern Slavonia, in the so-called Republika Srpska Krajina controlled by the Serbs. However, the Badinter Commission denied any right to Republika Srpska Krajina to secede from Croatia, according to the principles mentioned above. Thus, the goals of the UNTAES were merely to insure the rule of law, i.e. of human rights, and to implement peace after a conflict. The ITA had to progressively transfer the power to the central Croatian administration and logically, the former territory of Republika Srpska Krajina was 'reintegrated' under Croatian sovereignty (Zimmermann and Stahn, 2001, 433). Although, the powers of UNTAES were very limited, its two-year mandate did not include any mission of state-building, serving only as precedent for the Serbs who expected Kosovo to remain a part of Serbia as Republika Srpska Krajina and Republika Srpska Bosne i Hercegovine after the deployments of the UNTAES and the United Nations Mission in Bosnia and Herzegovina (UNMIBH). So why could Kosovo, with no Republic status in former Yugoslavia, secede and how come it was immediately recognised by many States? The decision to recognise Kosovo as a State by validating its secession was in total contradiction with the solutions put forward during the dissolution of the former Yugoslavia.

The events in Kosovo had a strong influence on Serbian Bosnian policy makers, who did not understand why the international community was ready to accord Kosovo what was being refused to them. This incoherence further complicated the task of the International Territorial Administration in Bosnia and Herzegovina. Moreover, it created frustration and mistrust among the Serbian population in

Bosnia and Herzegovina and Kosovo. One good example is the year 2005, when the legislative assembly of Republika Srpska accepted the creation of a unified Bosnian army, which can be regarded as a path to the centralisation of the Bosnian state. Four years later, after the declaration of independence by the provisional institutions of Kosovo in February 2008 and the immediate recognition by most western States, the same assembly requested the return of their rights transferred to the central government of Bosnia. Furthermore, almost two years after the declaration of independence of Kosovo, the assembly of Republika Srpska passed a law allowing the organisation of a referendum of independence in Republika Srpska on 10 February 2010 (see Légaré 2011, 392). The recognition policy led in Kosovo had a direct influence on the peacebuilding mission in Bosnia and Herzegovina, preventing the integration and the progressive centralisation of the powers. It also caused the Serbian community to decide to move back after the recognition of Kosovo and to dream of their own independent state once again.

3.2.2 The discord on the status of Kosovo

'Kosovo is the most controversial case of state-building in contemporary Europe and the question of recognition continues to divide the EU as well as UN member states' (Stillhoff Sörensen 2013, 269). Indeed, the international community remains divided regarding the case of Kosovo. In January 2015, 110 states recognised Kosovo as a state while the rest still consider it as a part of Serbia. Although most EU member states recognise Kosovo as a state, Spain, as well as Slovakia, Romania and Greece six years after the declaration of independence on 17 February 2008 still refuse to recognise the State of Kosovo. These countries share a common trait. They face independence issues on their own territory and fear that the recognition of Kosovo will create a precedent. As a matter of fact, Republika Srpska understood this precedent and has begun to demand the same independence. The recognition of the other former Yugoslav States, i.e., Croatia, Slovenia and Macedonia, has been coordinated and coherent. Germany was the first EU state to recognise Croatia and Slovenia. The EU's failure to develop a coherent recognition policy towards Kosovo has stirred the Serbian Bosnians' independence claims, causing difficulties in the ITA mission in Bosnia.

The example of Kosovo makes apparent how much the questions of legal sovereignty and recognition can influence and limit the powers and capacities of an ITA. As long as the status of Kosovo is not officially established, the mission cannot fulfil its aims of peacebuilding, particularly because of the impossibility of transferring full political authority to Kosovo's institutions, even if they already possess considerable administrative power. The Kosovar economy still depends on international aid, on the market created by the international presence, on the remittances from the diaspora and on the black market (ibid., 277). The only real solution to Kosovar institutions being able to exert their power is either full recognition by the international community and by Serbia or the opposite, complete refusal.

The lack of a coherent and coordinated policy of recognition has directly caused political tensions between the different ethnic groups, provoking a desire to secede. The risk of a new split is still very much prevalent and is hampering any possible reconciliation or development of sustainable institutions and social programs (Zaum 2007, 127; Stillhoff Sörensen 2013, 269 and 273). This also has a direct repercussion on the authority of the head of International Territorial Administrations in both countries.

4. Recognition policy consequences and the undetermined authority of the representatives at the head of the international missions

The peacebuilding mission is being implemented by an International Territorial Administration, which can be defined as

> [...] situations where governmental functions in a specific territory are exercised not by the territorial State, but by an entity mandated to do so under international law, i.e. an international organization, a single State, or a group of States under an international mandate. The instances of ITA are very diverse, making any uniform legal assessment impossible and calling for a differentiated analysis. In many, though not all cases, ITAs are installed after the end of an armed conflict in order to contribute to post-conflict peacebuilding. In other instances, ITA is used to decolonize a territory. The common feature of all ITAs is, however, that the territory concerned is internationalized either fully or to a certain degree, meaning that the territorial sovereignty of the territorial State is limited in favour of another State, a group of States, or an international organization and that decisions of the external entity are directly applicable in the legal order of the territory concerned (Internationalization). (Benzing, 2013)

In Bosnia and Herzegovina and Kosovo, the implementation of peace agreements has been entrusted to representatives who are responsible for the coordination of the different organisations present, the stabilisation of the country and the building of democratic institutions. However, due to the uncertainty of the future status of the two states, the representatives of the United Nations in both countries face resistance in the process of stabilising the country through centralisation. The local populations in Bosnia and Herzegovina (section 4.1.) and Kosovo (section 4.2.) perceive them as authoritative.

4.1 The OHR in Bosnia and Herzegovina

The status of the Office of the High Representative (OHR) in Bosnia and Herzegovina was defined in Article 5 of Annex 10 of the Dayton Agreement. Its status derives from the Peace implementation council (PIC), an *ad hoc* institution composed of fifty-five governmental and international organisations not mentioned in the Dayton Agreement. The High Representative in Bosnia and Herzegovina originally did not have much power, which is related to the absence of a consensus about the future status of the state, but also due to the lack of a structure to implement the decisions made (Légaré 2011, 384). In 1997, after observing that the goals for implementing the return of the displaced populations had failed, the powers of the high representative were expanded thanks to the so-call 'Bonn *system*'. A new election law for Bosnia was discussed in the context of the PIC in Madrid in 1998, which defined the goals to follow in the declaration resulting from the summit. The PIC decided to particularly encourage the multi-ethnic character of the new Bosnian state and to support non-ethnic based parties and coalitions. This has been interpreted as the limitation of the nationalist parties' influence by Carlos Westendorp, the High Representative from 1997 to 1999. The '*system of Bonn*' thus led to a '*de facto* protectorate' (Belloni 2013, 283; see also Tansey 2009, 188).

The decision to extend the powers of the OHR is directly linked to the ambitions of the Serbian nationalists, who felt forced to accept the Dayton Agreement and, encouraged by the uncertain status of the federated entities, were still willing to create an independent state of Republika Srpska. After 1998, the High Representative decided on several occasions to remove many civil servants, including some elected by the population (see Tansey 2009, 161–162). Those examples reflect the authoritative role of the OHR in Bosnia, which imposed and still imposes its policy and decisions even against local legitimate actions. 'This goes against the popular will insofar as it was meaningfully exercised in the vote that brought the official in question to office in the first place' (Wilde 2008, 451). Thus, from the beginning, the peacebuilding mission has been perceived as an instrument of foreign domination by the local population. As Roland Paris (2002, 653–654) states,

> [t]o the extent that these standards reflect the ideological predilections of the most powerful states in the world – the core of the international system – peacebuilding is not merely a tool of conflict management, but a new phase in the ongoing and evolving relationship between the core and the periphery of the international system, with the core continuing to define the standards of acceptable behaviour and international peacebuilding agencies serving as 'transmissions belts' that convey these standards to the periphery.

However during the mandate of Paddy Ashdown, the High Representative in Bosnia between 2002 and 2006, the practice of interventions by his office in domestic policy decreased considerably. In June 2006, the PIC even announced its plans for the withdrawal of the Office of the High Representative by mid-2007. However, given the results of the 2006 elections and the success of nationalist parties, the decision was made to retain the OHR and a new High Representative, Miroslav Lajčák was appointed. In October 2007, the High Representative changed the decision-making procedure in the Council of Ministers in order to facilitate the process for the latter.

The lack of accountability of the OHR, as well as the necessity to limit and control its acts, have been underlined through some decisions by various jurisdictions, such as the Constitutional Court of Bosnia and Herzegovina since 2000 and the European Court of Human Rights. In its Decision of 3 November 2000 concerning the Law on the State Border Service (Case No. 9/00), the Constitutional Court affirmed its power to control all acts affecting the Constitution, regardless of the author and thus established its control over the conformity of any act emitted by the High Representative. In the case *Milorad Bilbija et al.* (Case No. AP-953/05) concerning decisions of removals of official representatives by the High Representative, the Court noticed that 'there is no effective legal remedy available within the existing legal system of Bosnia and Herzegovina against individual decisions of the High Representative', and concluded that it violated Article 13 of the European Convention for the Protection of Human Rights and Freedoms. However, in its decision *Berić and others v. Bosnia and Herzegovina* (Case 36357/04, Decision of 16 October 2007), the European Court of Human Rights (ECtHR) declined its power *ratione materiae*, considering that the High Representative acted in virtue of his mandate and attributed his decisions to the United Nations. Moreover, the decisions of the Constitutional Court concerning the Law on the State Border Service and *Milorad Bilbija* remain fruitless because the High Representative refuses to apply them. And later, in the case of *Sejdić and Finci v. Bosnia and Herzegovina* (Applications nos. 27996/06 and 34836/06) the ECtHR stated that the constitution of Bosnia and Herzegovina was in 'violation of Article 14 of the Convention taken in conjunction with Article 3 of Protocol No. 1 as regards the applicants' ineligibility to stand for election to the House of Peoples of Bosnia and Herzegovina'. In this case, members of the Jewish and the Romany communities sued because they were not eligible. The reason for this was that they do not belong to any of the three official eligible groups (Croats, Muslims and Serbs). Because of the authoritative attitude of the OHR in Bosnia and a constitution based on the existence of official different ethnic groups, it can be concluded that the goal of a democratic state has still not been achieved in Bosnia. The uncertain status at the time of the Dayton Agreement partially obliged the OHR to adopt an authoritative policy concerning the reluctance of the nationalists. The main office in charge of implementing democratic values acts outside of the basic democratic principles (Oellers-Frahm 2005, 210–211). The protagonist for the democratic transition in Bosnia has been ambiguously acting from outside the democratic context for almost 20 years and has limited state-building by assuming too much responsibility in the course of the democratic transition at the expense of the local actors (Tansey 2009, 201).

However, despite the authoritative attitude of the OHR, the different entities combined with the local population have progressively accepted the centralisation of the powers, with the Bosnian-Serbs nationalists abandoning their dream of an independent Republika Srpska. The homogenous attitude toward Serbian nationalists in Croatia and Bosnia and Herzegovina as well as the systematic application of the principle of *uti possidetis* has entirely discouraged this idea of secession. The recognition of Kosovo woke up their ambitions and the OHR had to face the revival of resistance by many nationalists, which prevented any advances in the democratisation and the centralisation. This absence of a central authority in the international territorial administration of Bosnia and Herzegovina has generally been considered as one of its weaknesses (see Zaum Dominik 2007, 88ff). Hence, the democratic development in Bosnia and Herzegovina is directly linked to the situation in its neighbouring country Kosovo and the latter's recognition as a state.

4.2 The SRSG in Kosovo

In Kosovo, the ITA was based on the Security Council Resolution 1244. Two days after the Resolution had been passed, the first report by the UN Secretary General on Kosovo was published, already underlining the necessity of granting extensive powers to the international territorial administration. The second report published one month later, on 12 July 1999, included the necessity for the international territorial administration to have an executive as well as a legislative authority, which was confirmed by the first regulation issued by the UNMIK in Kosovo on 25 July 1999 in which the UNMIK defined its own authority with the Special Representative of the Secretary General (SRSG) at its head (Knoll 2008, 188; Zaum 2007, 133–134). These powers even include the '*compétence de la compétence*': the SRSG has the ability to interpret the extent of his own powers. This has been underlined by the Regulation of the Executive Branch of the Provisional Institutions of Self-Government in Kosovo of 13 September 2001 (SRSG UNMIK/REG/2001/19), which stated that the SRSG 'shall have the final authority to interpret the scope and any other parameters of the executive responsibilities of the Provisional Institutions of Self-Government set out in the present regulation'. The representative is hence not submitted to any system of checks and balances, which is in total opposition with the basic democratic principles it has to implement. As Ralph (2008, 456) stated:

> Fundamentally, if trusteeship itself is a flawed concept, for example, because democracy that is 'imposed' will not take root, then it is hardly a surprise that those involved in it come up against formidable 'practical' challenges. If the policies being promoted in the projects reflect, in part, objectives that have little to do with the interests of the local population, the possibility that such policies fail to resonate locally forms part of the enterprise itself – success or failure will not depend exclusively on how well international administrators do their job on the ground.

These extensive powers seemed to be necessary in the context of the withdrawal of the Serbian administration from Kosovo as well as the problems previously faced in Bosnia and Herzegovina. Thus, in Kosovo the UNMIK has direct authority over the territory and the population, whereas in Bosnia and Herzegovina the OHR still exercises and shares the power jointly with the local actors. However, despite its broad powers, the UNMIK has established the Kosovo Transitional Council to try to include local actors and representatives in the decision-making process. Furthermore, the SRSG had to dismantle the parallel structures established by the LDK (Lidhja Demokratike e Kosovës – Democratic League of Kosovo) and the UCK (Ushtria Çlirimtare e Kosovës – Kosovo Liberation Army) during the nineties and include local leaders thanks to the 'Agreement on a Kosovo–UNMIK Joint Interim Administrative Structure' signed on 15 December 1999. However, the UNMIK and the SRSG Bernard Kouchner quickly began to notice the problems created by its unaccountability and its isolation from the local population. The immunity of the ITA, established by UNMIK Regulation No. 2000/47, soon turned into impunity, although the submission of the actions of the UNMIK and the SRSG to human rights standards has been confirmed by Regulation 2000/38 of 30 June 2000. The policies run by the UNMIK have even been criticised by the UN itself.

The lack of legitimacy of the SRSG through elections and the concentration of powers in its hands have been widely criticised and have contributed to its unpopularity in the local society, which has lead to boycotts by parts of the population (De Vrieze 2008, 123). This was highlighted during the influential riots of 2005 and once again by the weak participation of the Serb community in the November 2013 elections. Similarly to the situation in Bosnia and Herzegovina, the total immunity of UNMIK's agents has once again contributed to its bad perception by the local population. Eventually, it excludes the local population from any decision-making process, hence providing a terrible example of the ideals of democracy, despite the fact that it aims to build a state respectful of human rights. As Knoll (2008, 393) noticed, '[…] a state-building mission that started out with unlimited powers to meet extraordinary circumstances may indeed end up as an uncomfortable caricature of a utilitarian despot'.

Thus, due to the undetermined status of the country, directly linked to the recognition policy led, the ITA in Kosovo faces many problems. Effectively, the Kosovar Albanians and the Kosovar Serbs have yet to agree on the institutions built after 1999. The former aimed at state institutions while the latter want to refrain from the autonomy of the institutions and stay a part of Serbia. The declaration of independence by the provisional institutions of Kosovo in 2008 has increased the opposition by the local Serbian population to the UNMIK.

The consequent confused recognition policy has given false hopes to both sides, preventing the SRSG from finding a consensus and implementing democratic institutions that would be accepted by all the populations.

5. Conclusion

The precedent of Kosovo's recognition has weakened international law and is nowadays frequently evoked with respect to all cases of secession, such as Abkhazia, South Ossetia and the current crisis in Ukraine. The central government of Bosnia Herzegovina has understood the risks the recognition of Kosovo would create and thus has still not recognised Kosovo as a state.

With regard to Bosnia and Herzegovina, it would have been better to stay coherent and to follow the principles applied during the dissolution of the former Yugoslavia, especially the principle of *uti possidetis*. The coherence in the cases of Republika Srpska Krajina and Bosnia discouraged over time the inclination of the nationalists. The ITA in Bosnia and Herzegovina as well as it policy of centralisation and democratisation were increasingly accepted by the population. However, the recognition of the independent state of Kosovo by more than half of the international community increased the contestation, ruining the progress achieved in Bosnia and Herzegovina. The failures of the ITAs in Bosnia and Herzegovina and Kosovo can hence be attributed to the incoherent policy of recognition towards Kosovo, which serves as a precedent for many independent movements and prevents the ITA from implementing its missions. Indeed, Bosnia has suffered times of political crisis and spent 16 months without government after the elections of 3 October 2010 before a coalition could be constituted. However, the governmental coalition split in 2013 and the president of the federation Živko Budimir had to resign following accusations of corruption.

These failures weaken international law and the international order insofar as they are perceived as the imposition of the will of powerful states on the rest of the international community, despite the basic democratic values they pretend to implement.

Even if the abuse and human rights violations committed by the International Territorial Administrations could have been avoided in the presence of an incoherent policy of recognition of states, we cannot ignore its decisive influence on the attitude of the ITAs and their relations with the local populations. As long as the recognition of states and the peacebuilding missions are submitted to the personal interests of third party states and as long as the recognition policy changes from one case to another, the conflicts will not be resolved.

Acknowledgements

I would like to thank the organisers of the Central and Eastern European Forum of Young Legal, Political and Social Theorists and in particular to Luka Burazin and the University of Zagreb for their warm welcome. I also thank Mia Schlichtling, Andrew Ryan and Anasuya Raj for their help and corrections.

References

Belloni, Robert. 2013. Bosnia: Building states without societies? NGOs and civil society. In *The Routledge Handbook of International Statebuilding*, edited by David Chandler and Timothy D. Sisk, 281–292. London: Routledge.

Benzing, Markus. 2013. International Administration of Territories. *Max Planck Encyclopedia of International Law*. Oxford: Oxford University Press.

Bieber, Florian, and Keil, Soeren. 2011. The Bosnian Crisis and the Independence of Kosovo. In *Kosovo: independence, status, perspectives: adjusting regional policies of ethnicity and borders*, edited by Hylber Hysa and Dušan Janjić, 69–83. Ravenna: A. Longo Editore.

Chandler, David. 2012. Comment le state-building affaiblit les Etats. *Alternatives Sud, (Re-) construire les États, nouvelle frontière de* l'ingérence, 23–36. Paris: Centre Tricontinental and Editions Syllepse.

De Brabandere, Eric, 2009. *Post-conflict Administrations in International Law. International Territorial Administration, Transitional Authority and Foreign Occupation in Theory and Practice.* Leiden: Martinus Nijhoff Publishers.

De Vrieze, Franklin. 2008. Building parliamentary democracy in Kosovo. In *Security and Human Rights*, no. 2, edited by Armin von Bogdandy and Rudiger Wolfrum, 121–126. Leiden: Brill.

Friedrich, Jürgen. 2005. UNMIK in Kosovo: Struggling with Uncertainty. *Max Planck Yearbook of United Nations Law* 9: 225–293.

Légaré, Kathia. 2011. Le haut représentant, de despote éclairé à repoussoir. Les stratégies locales et la politique de l'intervention internationale en Bosnie-Herzégovine. *Études internationales* 42/3: 377–397.

Marauhn, Thilo, and Simon, Sven. 2013. Peacebuilding. *Max Planck Encyclopedia of International Law.* Oxford: Oxford University Press.

Oellers-Frahm, Karin, 2005. Restructuring Bosnia-Herzegovina: A Model with Pit-Falls. *Max Planck Yearbook of United Nations Law* 9: 179–224.

Paris, Roland. 2002. International peacebuilding and the 'Mission Civilisatrice'. *Review of International Studies* 28: 637–656.

Stahn, Carsten. 2008. *The law and practice of international territorial administration: Versailles to Iraq and beyond.* Cambridge: Cambridge University Press.

Stillhoff Sörensen, Jen. 2013. Intervention and statebuilding in Kosovo. *The Routledge Handbook of International Statebuilding*, edited by David Chandler and Timothy D. Sisk, 269–280. New York and London: Routledge.

Tansey, Oisin. 2009. *Regime-Building: Democratization and International Administration.* Oxford: Oxford University Press.

Wilde, Ralph. 2008. *International Territorial Administration: How Trusteeship and the Civilizing Mission never went away.* Oxford: Oxford University Press.

Zaum, Dominik. 2007. *The Sovereignty Paradox: The Norms and Politics of International Statebuilding.* Oxford: Oxford University Press.

Zimmermann, Andreas, and Stahn, Carsten. 2001. Yugoslav Territory, United Nations Trusteeship or Sovereign State? Reflections on the Current and Future Legal Status of Kosovo. *Nordic Journal of International Law* 70: 423–460.

Court rulings

Constitutional Court of Bosnia and Herzegovina Decision of 3 November 2000, *Official Gazette of Bosnia and Herzegovina*, cases No. 2/97, 16/99 and 20/99.

Constitutional Court of Bosnia and Herzegovina, Milorad Bilbija *et al*, case No. AP-953/05, 8 July 2006, *Official Gazette of Bosnia and Herzegovina,* No. 60/05.

European Court of Human Rights, Berić and Others v. Bosnia and Herzegovina, Decision 16.10.2007, Section IV, 36357/04, *Information Note on the Court's case-law*, No. 101.

Legislation

United Nations Security Resolutions UNSC S/2004/932.

United Nations Interim Administration Mission in Kosovo (UNMIK) Regulation No. 2000/47 of 18 August 2000 on the Status, privileges and immunities of KFOR and UNMIK and their personnel in Kosovo, UNMIK/REG/2000/47.

International Conference on Yugoslavia, Arbitration Commission, 1992. Opinion No. 4 of 11 January 1992, ILM 31.

International Conference on Yugoslavia, Arbitration Commission 1992. Opinion No. 5 of 11 January 1992, ILM 31.

Central and Eastern European Forum for Legal, Political, and Social Theory Yearbook

Edited by Jürgen Busch / Péter Cserne / Michael Hein /
Miklós Könczöl / Miodrag Jovanović / Marta Soniewicka

Vol. 1 Péter Cserne / Miklós Könczöl (eds.): Legal and Political Theory in the Post-National Age. Selected papers presented at the Second Central and Eastern European Forum for Legal, Political and Social Theorists (Budapest, 21–22 May 2010). 2011.

Vol. 2 Miodrag A. Jovanović / Bojan Spaić (eds.): Jurisprudence and Political Philosophy in the 21st Century. Reassessing Legacies. 2012.

Vol. 3 Péter Cserne / Miklós Könczöl / Marta Soniewicka (eds.): The Rule of Law and the Challenges to Jurisprudence. Selected papers presented at the Fourth Central and Eastern European Forum for Legal, Political and Social Theorists, Celje, 23–24 March 2012. 2014.

Vol. 4 Antonia Geisler / Michael Hein / Siri Hummel (eds.): Law, Politics, and the Constitution. New Perspectives from Legal and Political Theory. 2014.

Vol. 5 Luka Burazin / Đorđe Gardašević / Alessio Sardo (eds.): Law and State. Classical Paradigms and Novel Proposals. 2015.

www.peterlang.com

www.ingramcontent.com/pod-product-compliance
Ingram Content Group UK Ltd.
Pitfield, Milton Keynes, MK11 3LW, UK
UKHW021011120926
8556IPUK00039B/1001

9 783631 666920